IMAGES
of America

INGRAM

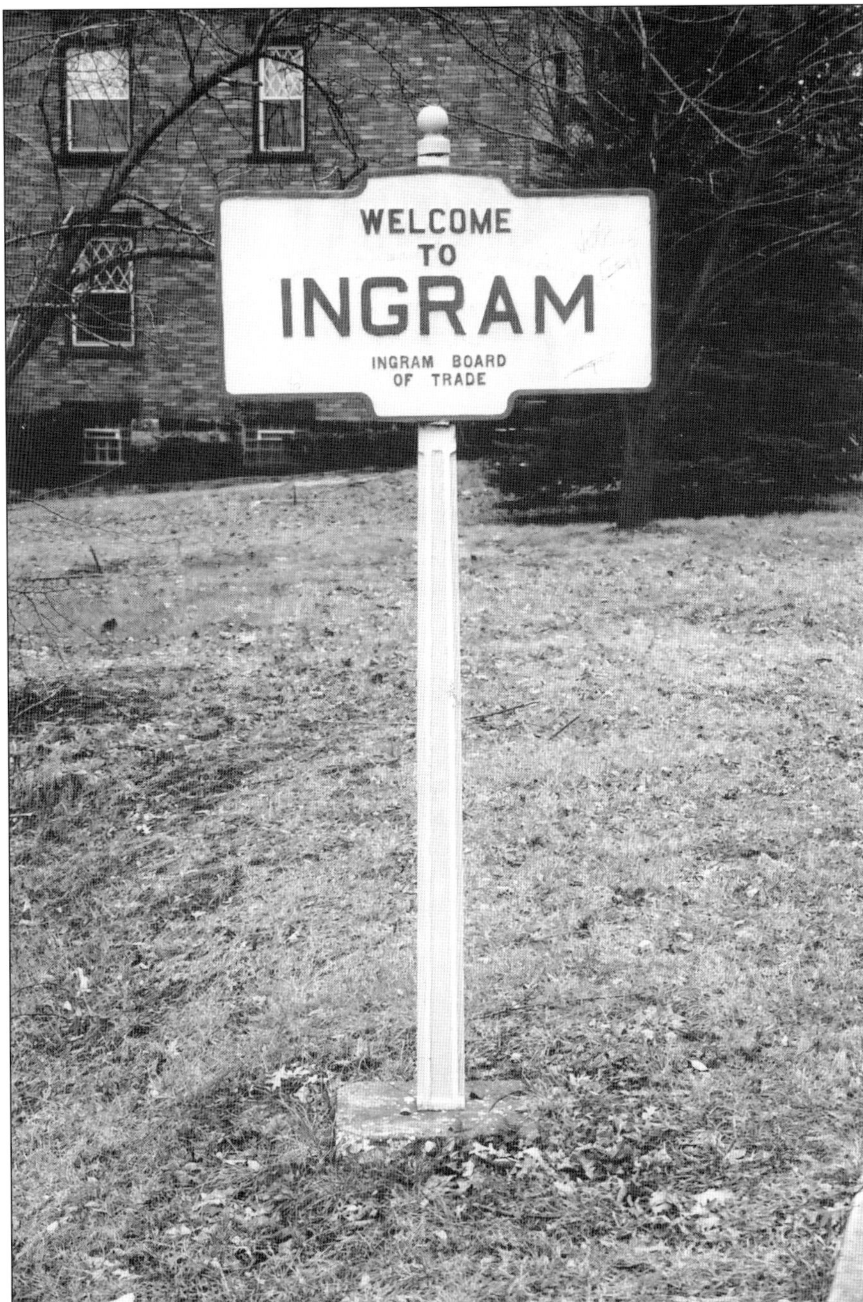

For more than half a century, this sign, at the intersection of Union Avenue, Cross and Center Streets, has been greeting visitors as they enter Ingram Borough. Two other signs were installed at the intersections of Windgap Road, Center and Berry Streets, and at the entrance to Ingram, on Ingram Avenue. These signs are made of cast iron and were commissioned by the Ingram Board of Trade. They were refurbished as an Eagle Scout project.

On the cover: Please see page 97. (Courtesy of the Ingram Volunteer Fire Department.)

IMAGES
of America

INGRAM

Ingram Historical Society

ARCADIA
PUBLISHING

ISBN 978-0-7385-4993-4

Published by Arcadia Publishing
Charleston SC, Chicago IL, Portsmouth NH, San Francisco CA

Printed in the United States of America

Library of Congress Catalog Card Number: 2006939685

For all general information contact Arcadia Publishing at:
Telephone 843-853-2070
Fax 843-853-0044
E-mail sales@arcadiapublishing.com
For customer service and orders:
Toll-Free 1-888-313-2665

Visit us on the Internet at www.arcadiapublishing.com

Dedicated to all those who gave their lives for our country and our borough. From soldiers who left this town to defend the United States, to the first railroad workers who died in the completion of a permanent connection to the outside world. To the victims and rescue workers of the 1968 gas explosion, and to the departed members who started the Ingram Historical Society. Without all of these people, there would be no history to write about, and no one to write it.

Contents

Acknowledgments 6

Introduction 7

1. Early History 9
2. Transportation 19
3. Houses 33
4. Churches and Schools 49
5. Businesses and Stores 63
6. The 1968 Gas Explosion 81
7. Borough Government 93
8. Community Life 105

ACKNOWLEDGMENTS

The Ingram Historical Society would like to acknowledge all those who contributed to this book. First, all the members, past and present, of the group, especially those who showed up at every meeting to work on the book. Also those members and friends of members that have donated the pictures in the past that made this book possible. Since 1994, the main goal of this organization has been to produce a book on the town's history. The long evenings, Saturdays, and working at home have paid off with a finished product.

Also the various departments of the Borough of Ingram, including the Ingram Borough Council, the Ingram Civic Club, the borough building secretaries, the Ingram Police Department, the Ingram Volunteer Fire Department, and the Ingram Department of Public Works need to be thanked.

A debt of gratitude is also owed the private parties that have contributed to this book and to the society's collection of historical documents and photographs. Some of whom are Gil Pietrzak of the Carnegie Library of Pittsburgh, the Montour School District and the Montour High School Library, Jennifer Brawdy, Patrick Knight, the Church of the Ascension, Richard L. Bowker and Edward H. Lybarger of the Pennsylvania Trolley Museum, Tom and Chris Griffith, Jim and Judy Adams, Bob Crockett, Kinsley Draper and the Historic Rockford Plantation Foundation, Claire Rex, John Sacco, Judy Jessep, and all of the residents who granted permission for their photographs to be used.

INTRODUCTION

The following is a poem by an unknown author that adorns a beautiful mural in Ingram's borough building. Looking at this collection of pictures, and reading this beautiful poem, one can quickly get an idea of just what kind of town they are standing in.

There's a little town called Ingram,
Just across the city line,
Where the air is clean and wholesome,
And the people mighty fine.
It nests in Chartiers Valley, a
Beauty spot that thrills.
And a picture of great splendor,
When the sun sets o'er its hills.

Its people are the happy kind,
That make a place worthwhile.
Who welcome you among them,
With a handshake and a smile.
Its up to date in all its needs,
Its streets are paved and clean.
And the pretty lawns and shade trees,
Make it's beauty more sincere.

There are churches where to worship.
And a school of highest grade;
Stores and shops to serve your want,
And a hustling Board of Trade.
While the place is fine to live in,
We will also here explain.
Its convenient to the city both
By trolley and by train.

The area in which Ingram now sits was first settled in 1752 as Chartiers. As with most towns, Ingram started to flourish with the addition of a railroad. In 1865, the Pittsburgh and

Steubenville Railroad completed its line connecting the cities of its name. The railroad became the "Panhandle Division" of the Pennsylvania Railroad, and carried at one time 98 trains a day, making it one of the busiest lines west. By 1902, the area was incorporated as a borough, and people with jobs in the city were finding housing available in this land where, "the air is pure only a few miles from Pittsburgh, on the Panhandle."

As the town began to populate, it became evident that community togetherness and pride were two standards thought highly of in this town. Churches and schools popped up along with stores. Soon, Ingram was a thriving town. Unfortunately, in January of 1968, a broken natural gas line caused a large building, part of Ingram's business district, to blow up. Many people were injured, some killed in the explosion, but the town stuck together even more, all coming together to help in search and rescue, comfort and cleanup.

In the 1980s, the railroad that had helped in the forming of this town was removed and left abandoned for a decade, until the Port Authority of Allegheny County reopened the right-of-way. A dedicated highway for buses and emergency vehicles was built on the old railroad grade. Ingram has seen many changes through its over 100 years of incorporation. Presented in this book are several of the things that have changed in this community-based borough.

One

EARLY HISTORY

1876 - Atlas of the Cities of Pittsburgh, Allegheny, and Adjoining Boroughs: Plate 45 (Chartiers)

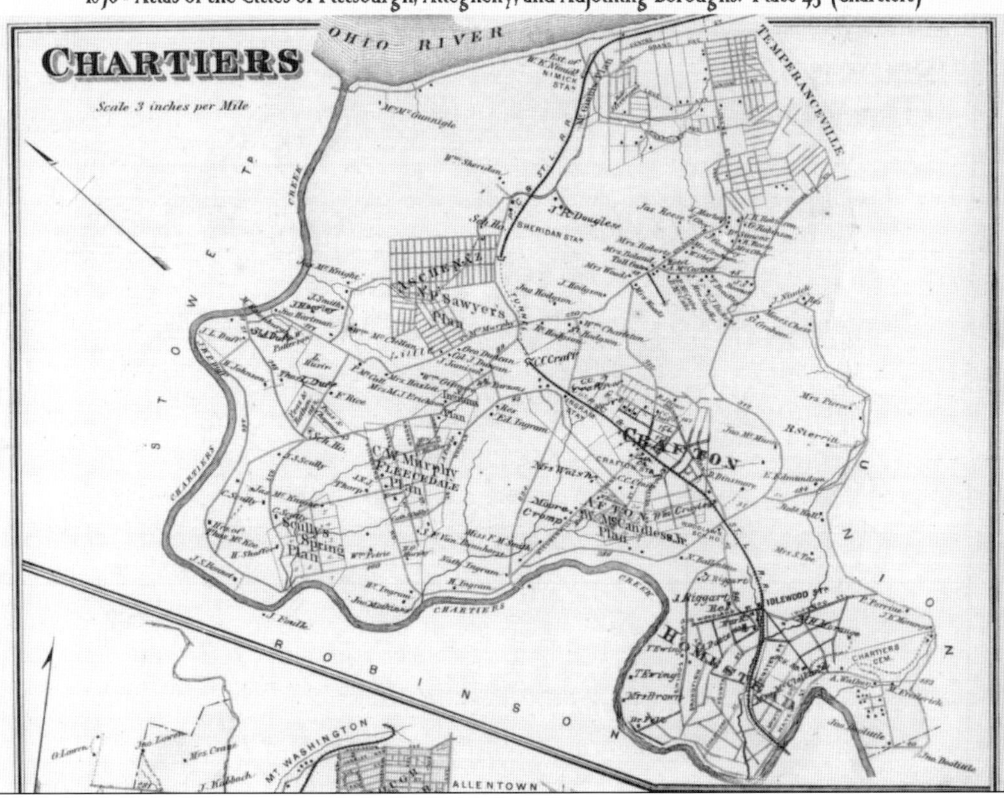

This map, dating from 1876, shows the Ingram area when it was a part of Chartiers Township. Many of the present day street names had their origins from early landowners shown on this map. Ingram Avenue, Hodgson Avenue, and Charleton Street are all named after prominent individuals who were instrumental in the early development of the area. It would be another 26 years before Ingram was incorporated as a borough.

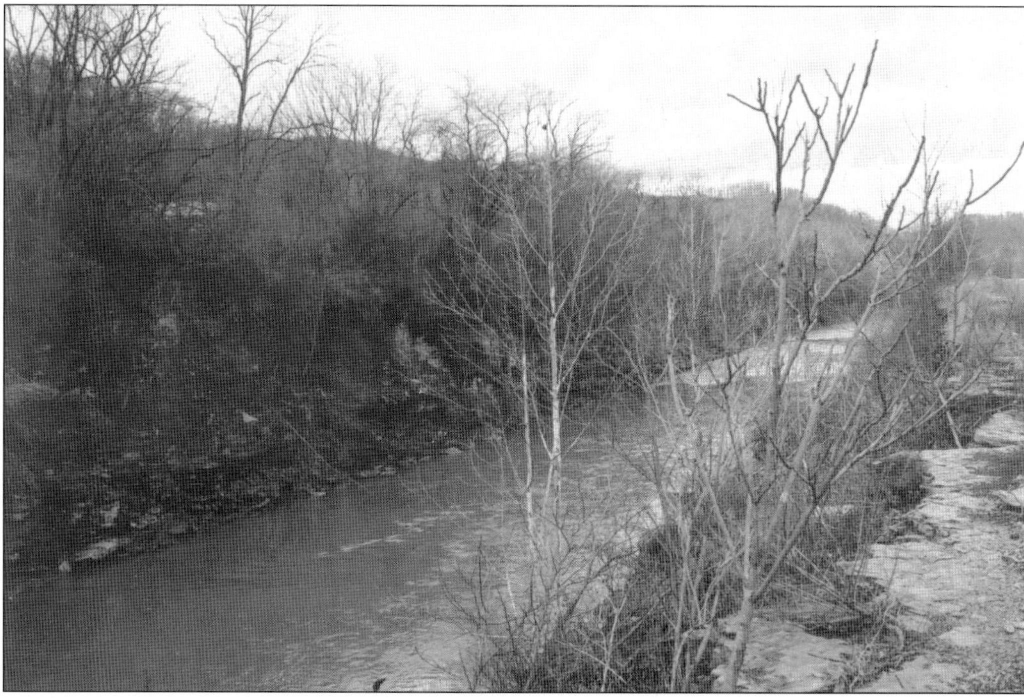

This photographic journey of Ingram begins at Chartiers Creek, which is located 0.2 miles west of the present borough line. The creek was named after Peter Chartiers, a licensed British trader of both French and Shawnee blood. He came to this area from Lancaster County and built a trading post along the creek. The surrounding valley was abundant with deer and small game for the Delaware and Seneca tribes. Due to frequent flooding, the soil was also rich for growing crops.

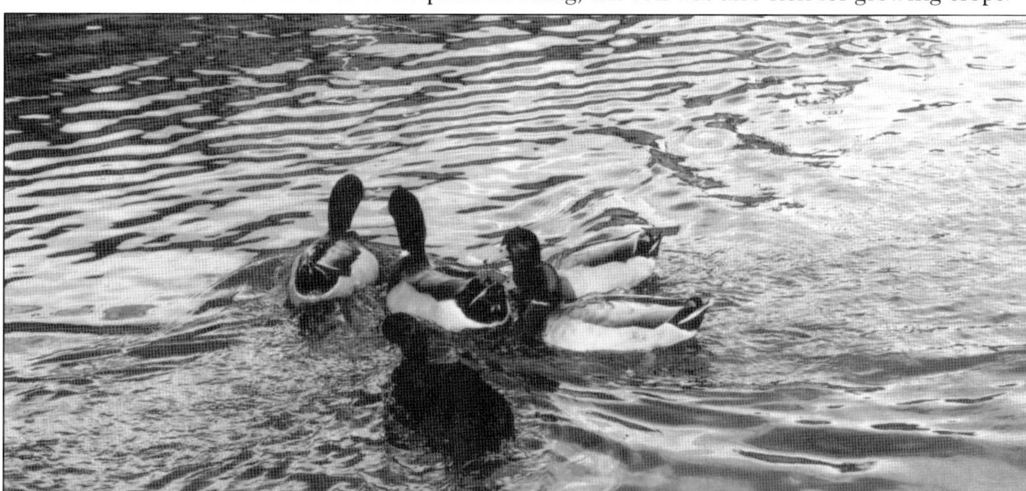

Although Chartiers Creek and its surrounding landscape continue to be a haven for wildlife, its serene beauty should not be underestimated. Throughout its long history, rabid flooding has always been a reality. The most recent episode occurred on the afternoon of September 17, 2004, when Hurricane Ivan dumped nine inches of rain on western Pennsylvania. While the creek has never posed a threat to Ingram, many surrounding communities along its path have been victims of its devastating fury.

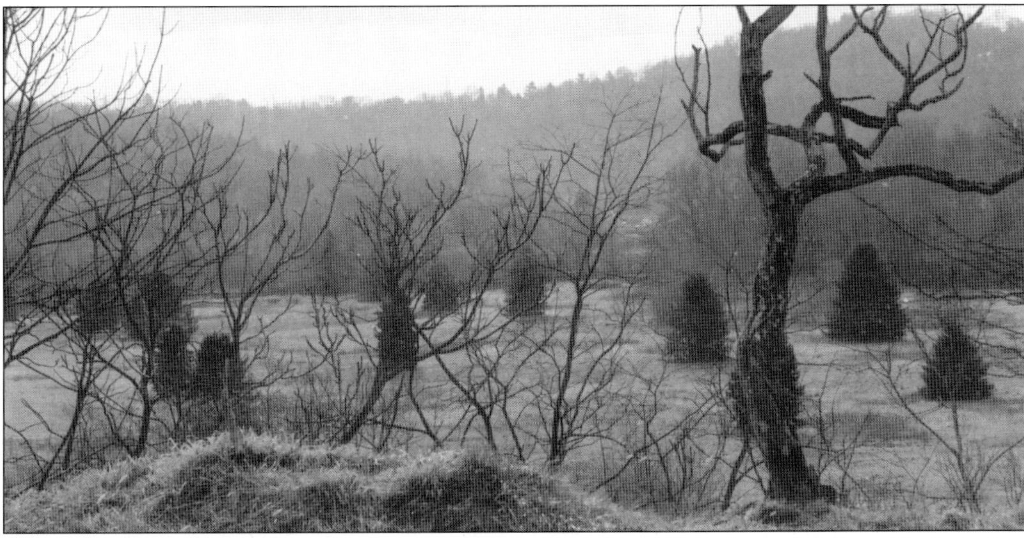

This birds-eye view of the Chartiers Creek valley was taken from Crafton Boulevard in neighboring Crafton Borough. It was from this vantage point that the Seneca observed the abundance of wildlife as well as approaching enemies, who were traveling the area by foot or canoe. The Seneca tribe was one of six Iroquois Nations migrating from the New York area. Others included the Cayuga, Mohawk, Oneida, and Tuscarora. Early British settlers and land speculators were displacing Native Americans and taking their hunting ground for development. An early settlement was built upon this hilltop, which Seneca chief Corn Planter named Killemun.

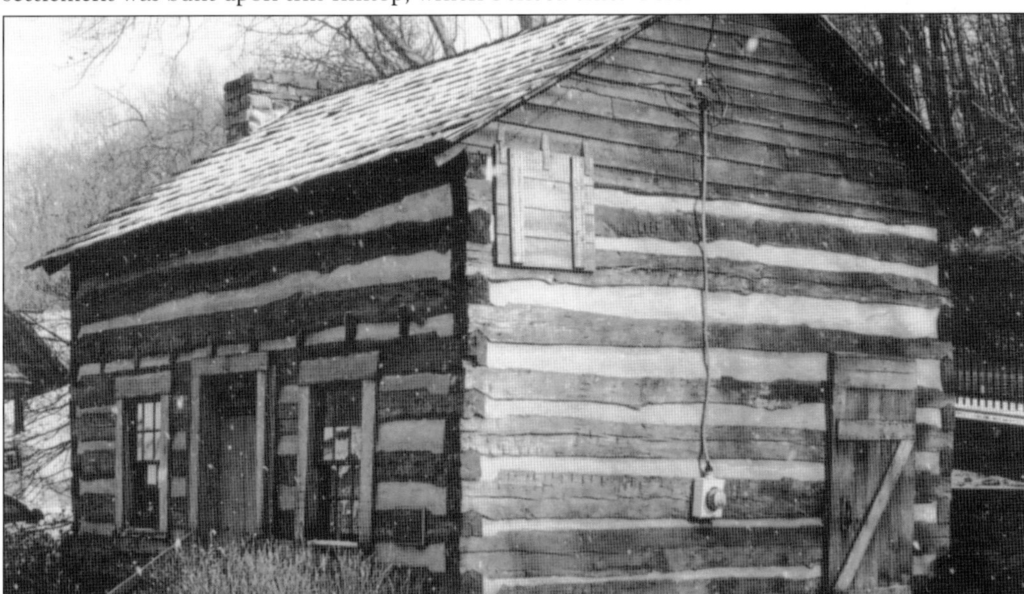

Early settlers to this area built log homes near Chartiers Creek because of its pure water supply. By the late 1920s, the last of these cabins had quietly crumbled away due to age and years of neglect. This recent photograph shows the beautifully restored Dickson Log House, which was built around 1797, in Ben Avon Borough. It provides an excellent example of the homes, once present throughout the Chartiers Creek valley. Ben Avon is located approximately eight miles away, on the opposite side of the Ohio River from Ingram.

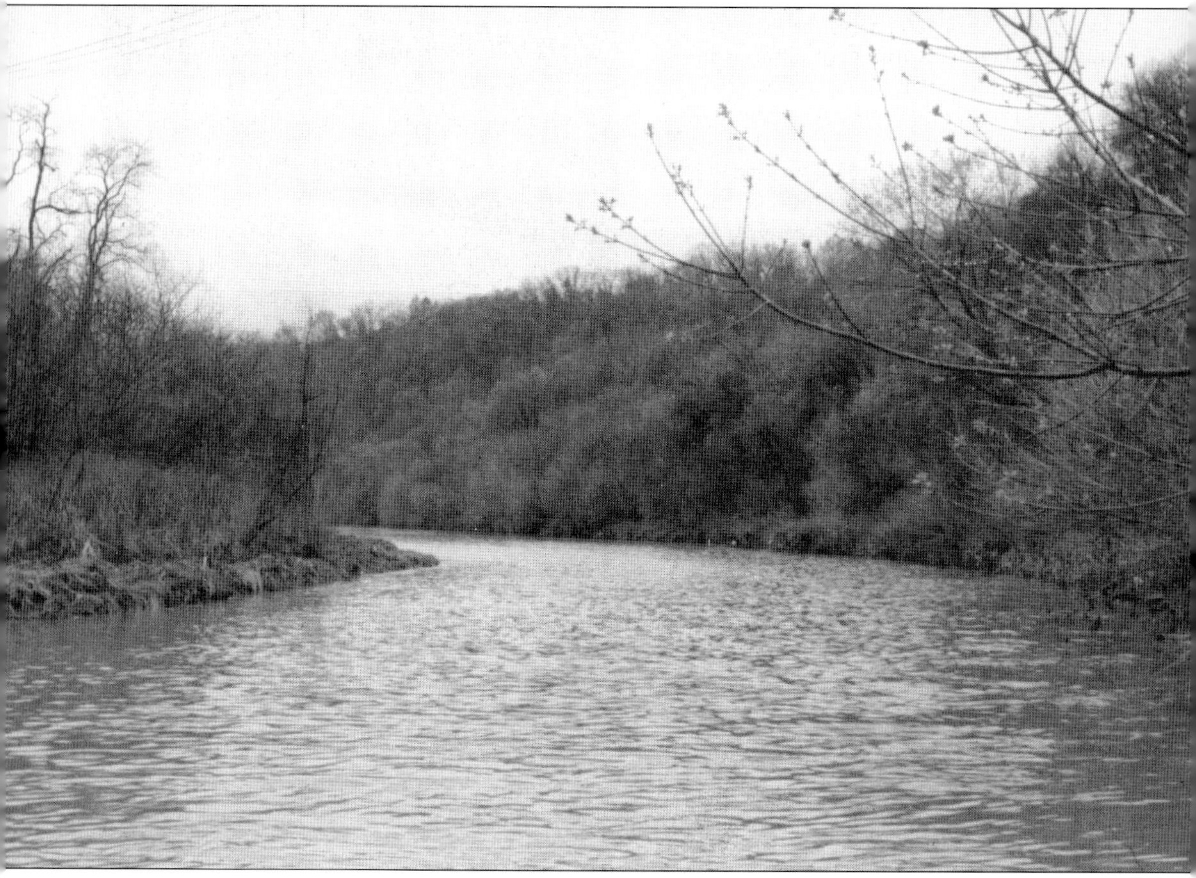

Because of Native American disturbances in the 1780s, most settlers in the Chartiers Creek area traveled to Fort Pitt at night for safety. The Stoops family, probably too tired to make the journey, had decided to spend the night in their cabin. On this unfortunate night about a half dozen Wyandot warriors attacked their cabin and captured Jennie Stoops and her son, William. Mr. Stoops had been able to crawl out a window and run to the fort for help. Samuel Brady, a famous American Indian scout, who was in the area on assignment from Col. Daniel Brodhead, happened upon the group and was able to rescue Jennie. There are two versions of the fate of her son. In one version, he was rescued with his mother; while in another he remained captive for a number of years. It is known that in his adult years he settled in Lawrence County where his mother had been rescued.

Edward Hand started life in Ireland and ended as a Pennsylvania gentleman farmer and physician. During the American Revolution, Hand accepted a commission in the Continental Army. Upon promotion to brigadier general, Hand was ordered to western Pennsylvania as commander of Fort Pitt. His assignment was to protect the colonists against the British and Native Americans. While in western Pennsylvania, Hand patented a tract of land on which he built a hospital for his workers and soldiers. For 69 years, the hospital was the only medical facility west of the Alleghenies. Ingram is situated on that part of Hand's patent known as Mount Pleasant Tract. (Courtesy of Kinsley Draper, Historic Rock Ford Foundation.)

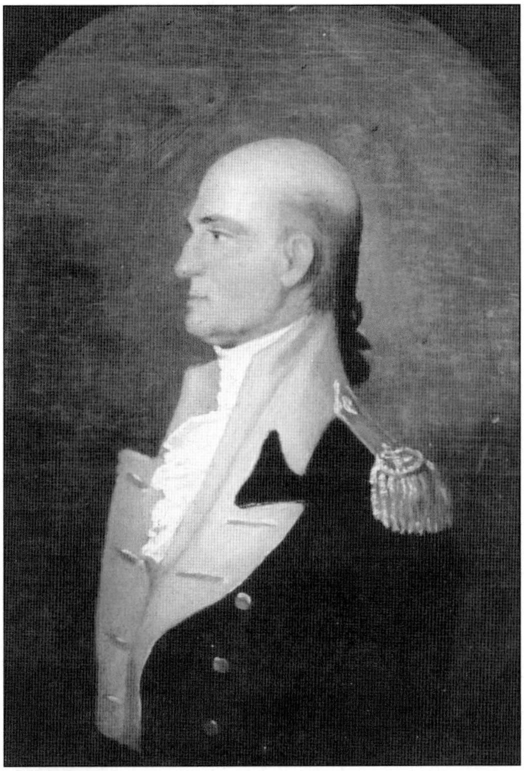

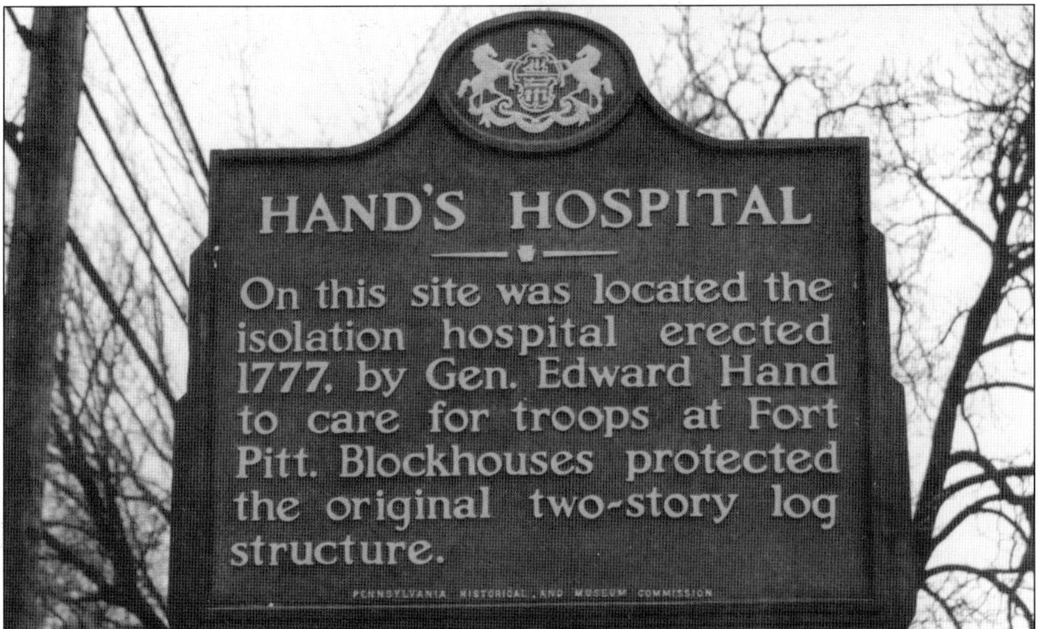

Hand purchased 1,423 acres of surrounding land and founded the first Federal Hospital in 1777. Hand was a surgeon who served at the British occupied Fort Pitt, near the three rivers in Pittsburgh (Allegheny, Monongahela, and Ohio Rivers). Although a marker was placed on West Steuben Street, many speculate the exact location near Chartiers Creek.

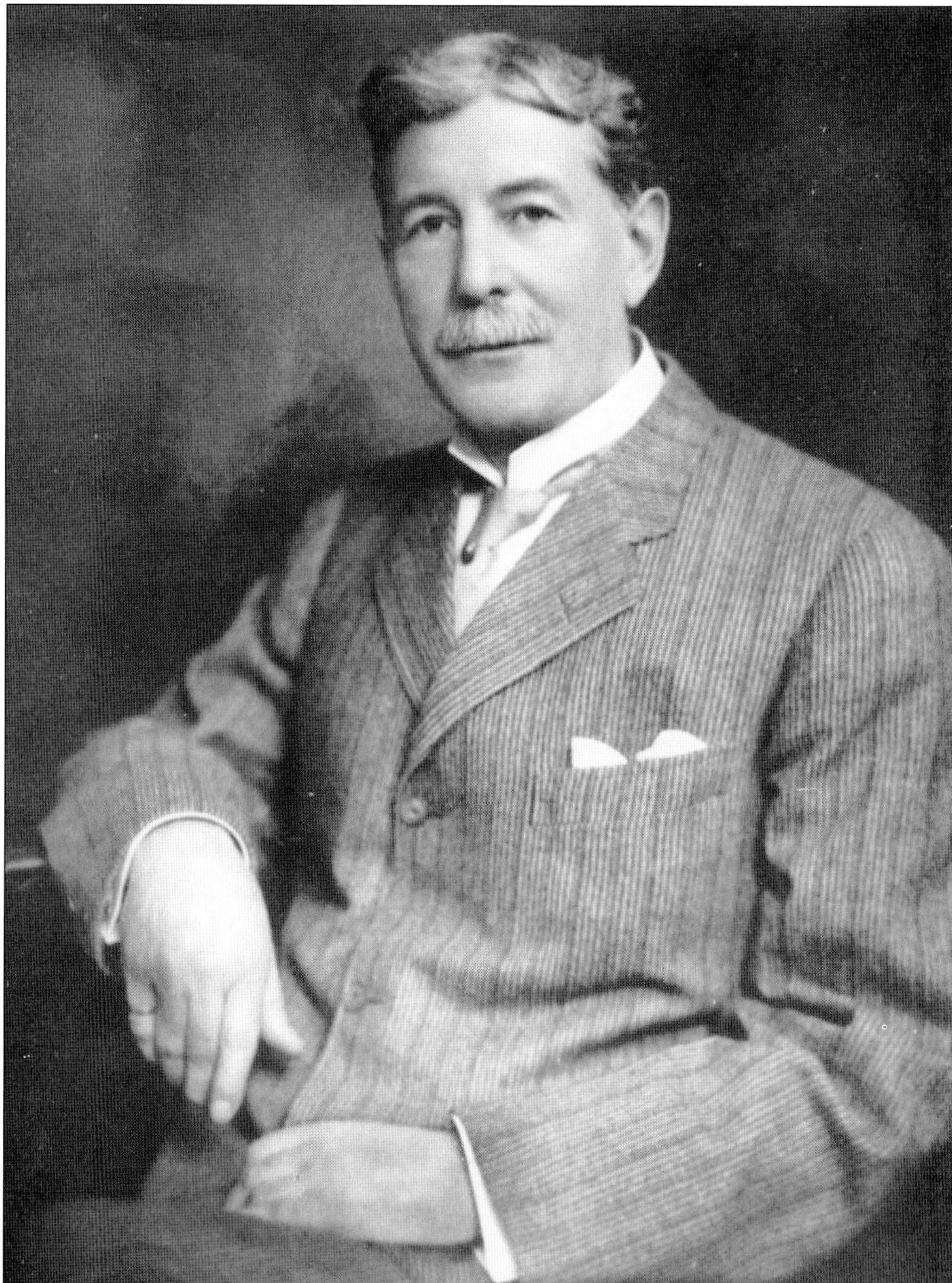

Thomas Arthurs Ingram was born July 1854 in Chartiers Township, Allegheny County. In 1880, he opened for sale the land his grandfather had purchased in Chartiers Township. During his lifetime he worked for the Lake Erie Railroad and the South Penn Oil Company. In 1876, he married Nannie Force and later divorced in 1913. He then married Helen Killeen. Thomas Ingram died May 15, 1928, at his home in Ingram.

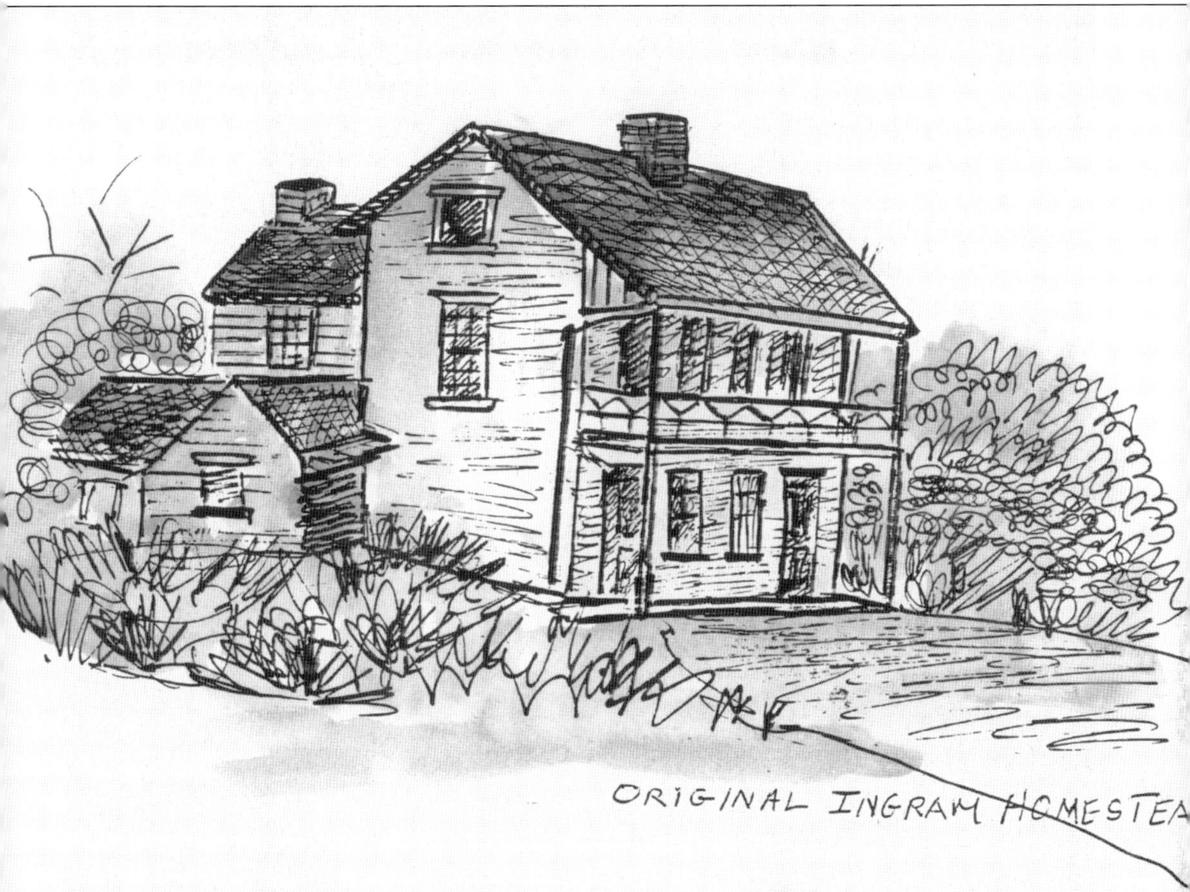

In the year 1823, Edward Ingram and his son Thomas purchased several hundred acres of land in Chartiers Valley from Nathanial Burt of Philadelphia. Edward built his home along what is now Windgap Road. Not much is known about this house as it was never photographed. The only information that can be gathered about it is from a description written by the Ingram family. Shown here is a sketch of the home. Later, Thomas would build a house on what became West Prospect Avenue, where he could survey his land. (Drawing by Jonathan Upstill.)

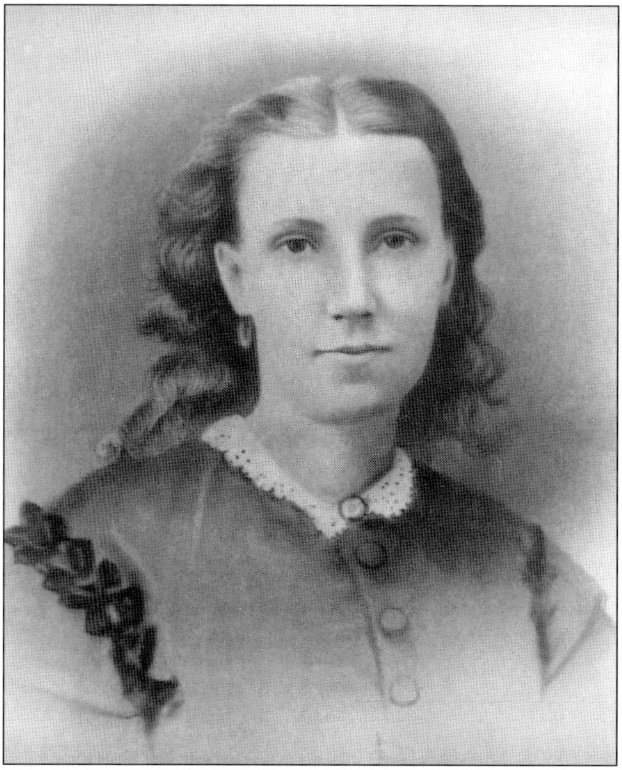

Nannie Force was born in March 1856, in Pittsburgh. She married Thomas A. Ingram on April 24, 1876. Nannie and Thomas had a stormy relationship, and she left him on several occasions, alleging cruelty. In 1910, she permanently left Thomas, and they were divorced around 1913. Nannie passed away in 1939.

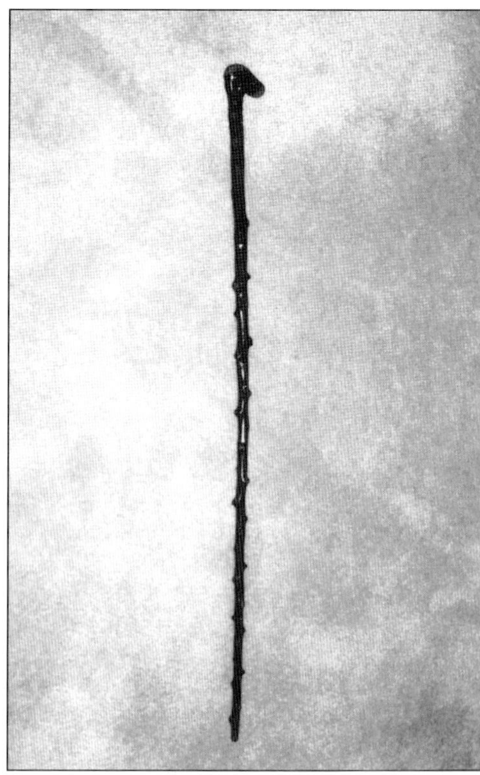

Thomas's Irish Blackhorn walking stick dates back to the late 19th century. Its origin is the Blackhorn tree, which grows all over Ireland with folklore dating back to St. Patrick. After cutting the stick, it is seasoned for two to three years. It is steamed, straightened, sanded, and polished. The spacing and regularity of the characteristic thorns, along with the weight, balance, taper, size, and shapeliness add to the value of the walking stick. Although only one or two sticks in every 1,000 are nearly perfect, many Blackhorns become presentation pieces.

David Johnson Rex was born in Jefferson County, Ohio, at the Rex farm on January 7, 1851. He was the son of John and Rachel Scott Rex. In 1872, David settled in Pittsburgh. He met and married Harriet Elizabeth Reed, daughter of Samuel and Eleanor Reed, in November 1881. David and his family moved to Ingram. On August 2, 1902, Ingram became a borough and David was elected the first burgess. David lived in the community for 65 years and was a respected civic leader, pillar of his church, and business leader. He owned extensive real estate in Ingram, including the Rex Building. David and his wife had nine children and over 35 grandchildren and great-grandchildren. David died in his home in Ingram on September 6, 1946.

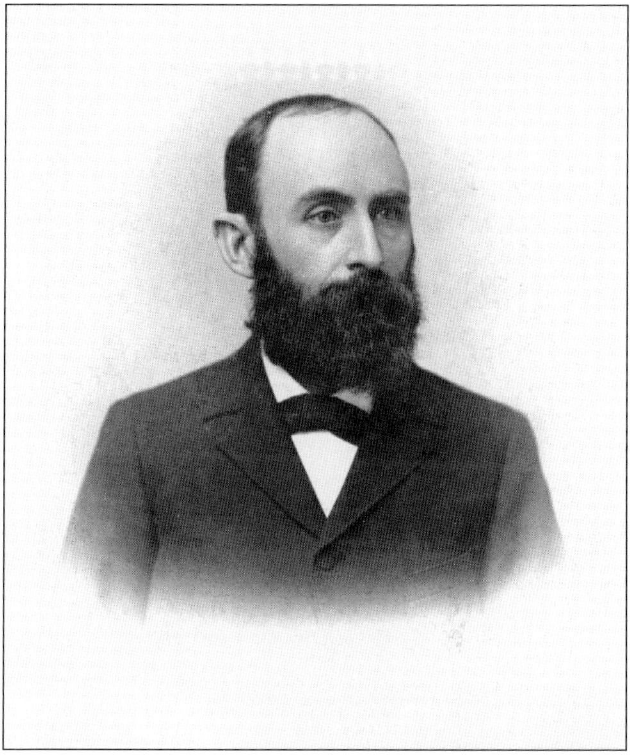

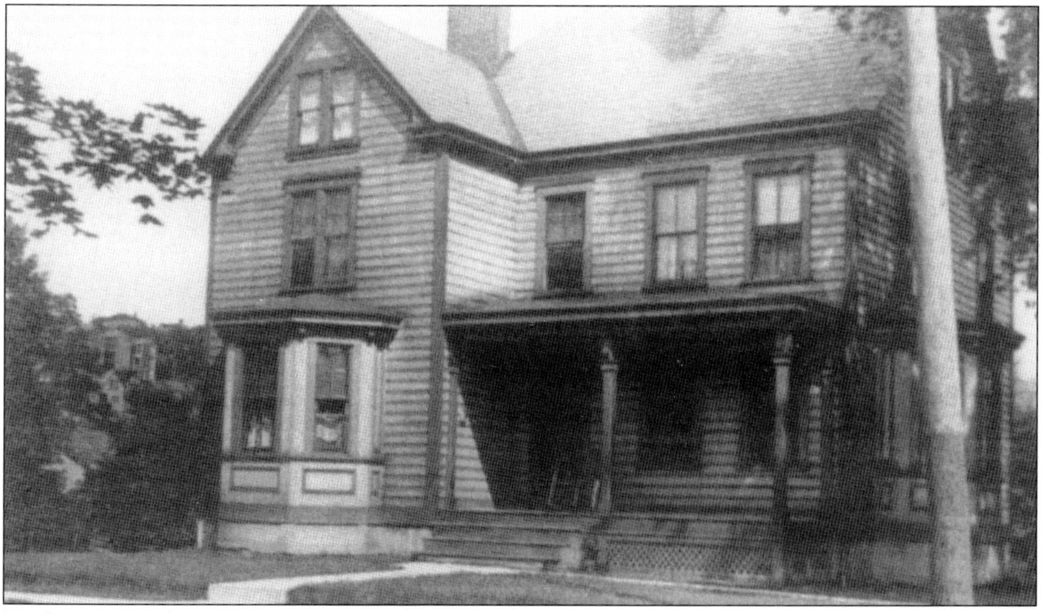

In the 1880s, there were roughly 20 original families that settled in Ingram, including the Rex family. The property was purchased to have a place where David could pasture the horses used for the lumber wagons of D. J. Rex's business, the Crafton Lumber Company. The family also grew a large garden in the back, which David cultivated until he was in his 90s, supplying his children and their families with abundant produce. The Rex home was located at 24 Mainsgate Street and the family resided there for over 65 years until the death of the patriarch, David Rex.

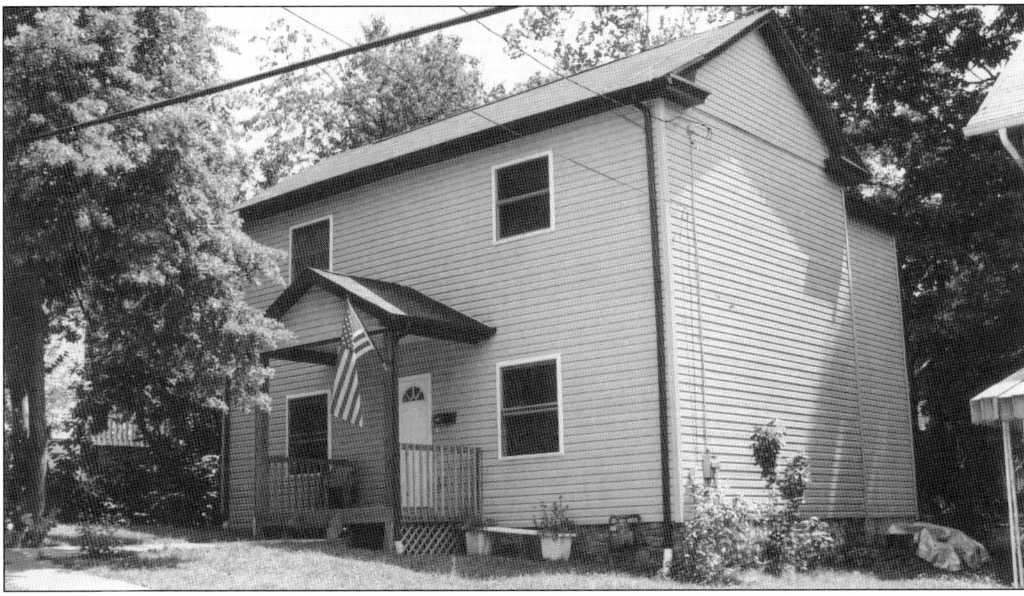

Mary Miller Corey was born to John and Sarah Miller in 1879 as one of nine children. The family resided at 40 Hodgson Avenue (Ingram) before moving to Steuben Street in nearby Elliott. Ingram Historical Society member Lillian Wehner Hoffman (the niece of Mary Miller Corey) recalls family stories of sitting on the large front porch, which was later removed during remodeling. Mary's brother Albert was the last family member to occupy this house before his passing in 1963.

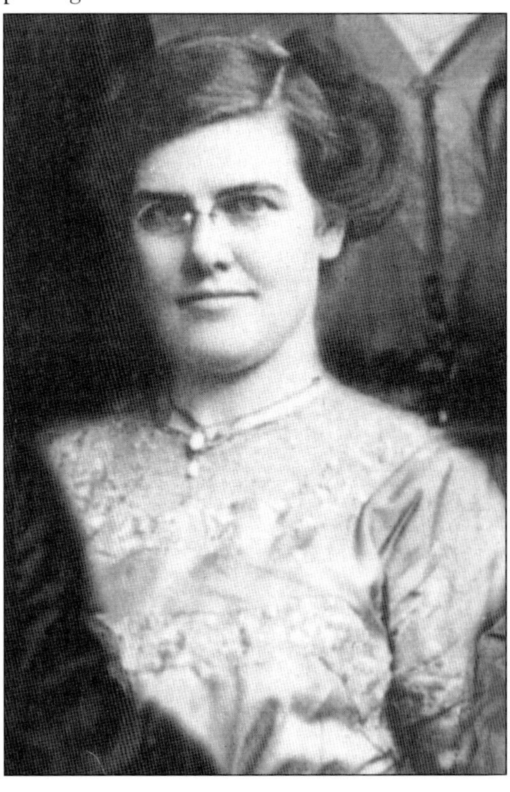

Mary was a grade school teacher at Westlake School in Elliott. She later fell in love and married Percy Corey, a successful businessman who worked for the Idio-Burma Petroleum Company. While living abroad, she became a friend of Mrs. J. Frank Karnes, who was from Pittsburgh. After becoming pregnant, Mary chose to return to Pittsburgh to have her baby. Mary and Karnes both decided to return to the states aboard the new R.M.S. *Titanic*. Tragically they both perished when the steamer struck an iceberg at 11:40 p.m. on April 12, 1912.

Two

TRANSPORTATION

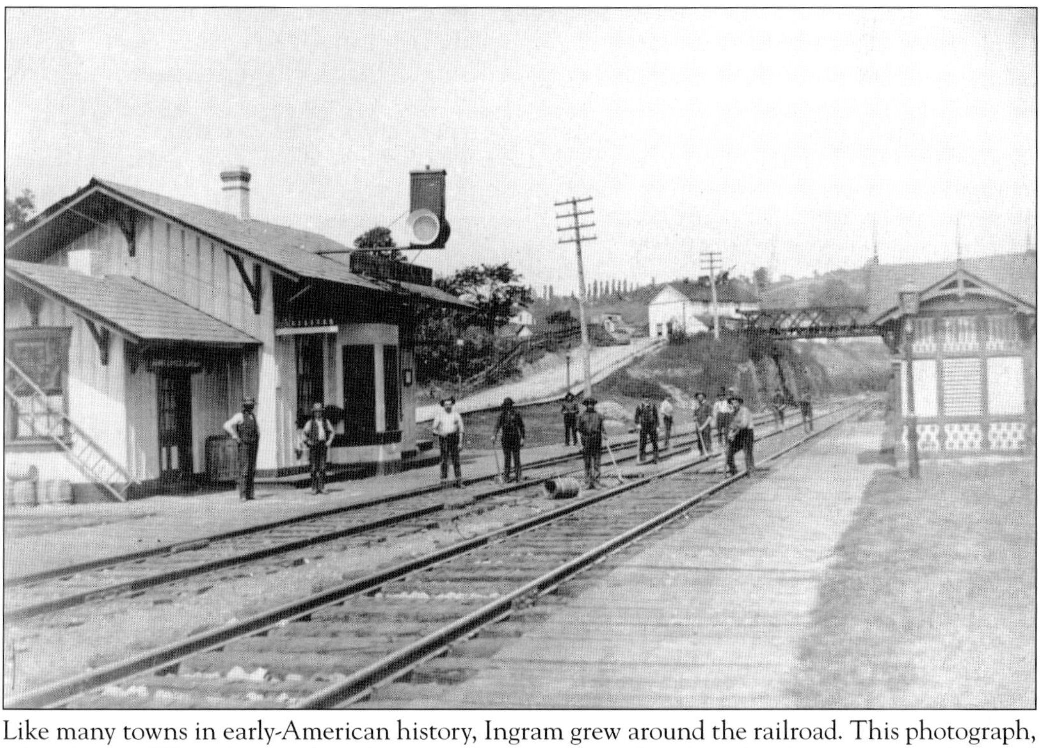

Like many towns in early-American history, Ingram grew around the railroad. This photograph, taken in the 1890s, depicts the original station and the railroad tracks viewed eastward, toward Pittsburgh. The wooden building not only served as a train depot, but also as a town meeting place, where telegraphs were received. Note the lack of houses in the background, as Ingram was mostly farms serving the neighboring bustling city of Pittsburgh. The workmen on the track are gandy dancers employed by the Pittsburgh and Steubenville Railroad, probably stabilizing the track by using picks to push dirt and ballast under the ties. These tracks were soon to be upgraded to the high standards of the Pennsylvania Railroad when it took over the line. (Courtesy of John Sacco.)

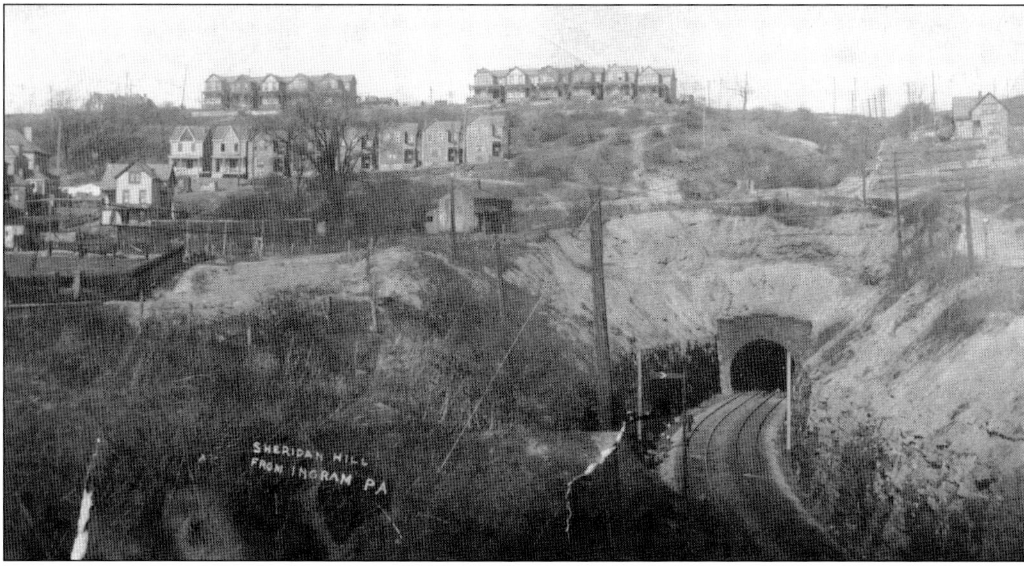

In 1851, the Pittsburgh and Steubenville Railroad began the excavation of a 2,100-foot-long, 70-foot-deep tunnel. It took nearly 800 workers to dig the tunnel, and because of the lack of safety regulations of the day, many workers were injured or killed. Due to these unsafe conditions, the first name for tunnel No. 2 on the line became "the dismal cave." Delayed by financial issues, construction halted in 1856, but with a grant, was resumed six years later. By the time it was completed in 1865, it had to be almost entirely repaired because of construction defects. The single track tunnel was expanded to double track by 1871. This picture represents the tunnel in its phase as a double track tunnel, one of the first railroad tunnels in the United States.

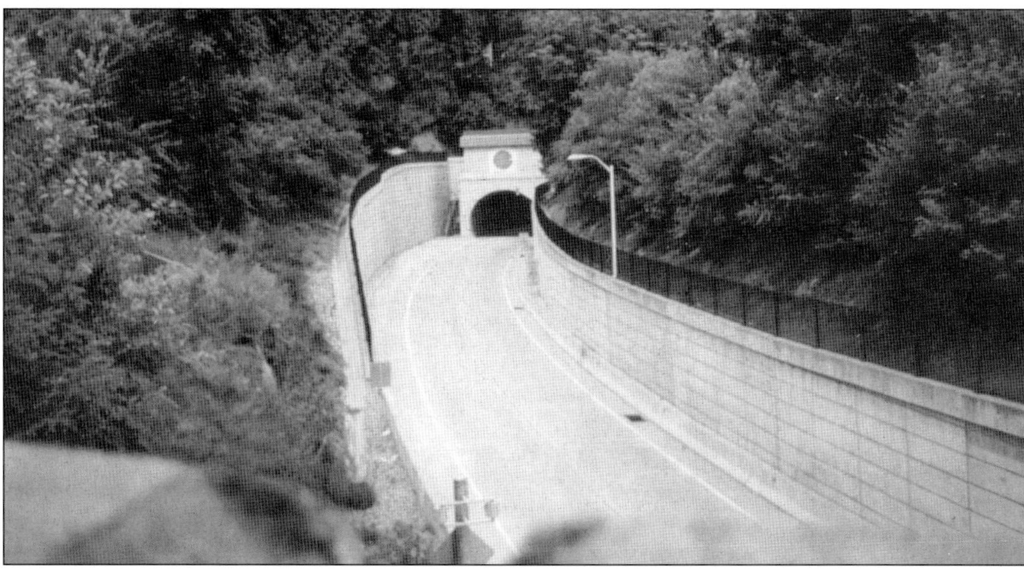

In the early 1900s, tunnel No. 2 began to be called the Berry Street tunnel, named after the street that crosses over it. The tunnel was "gauntlet" tracked around this time, which meant two tracks would share the space of one. This lead to the movement of wider and taller trains, but also more chances for derailments. The tunnel served the railroad well until 1984 when Conrail bricked up both entrances. In 1995, it was rebuilt, and now serves as a vital part of the Port Authority Transits West Busway.

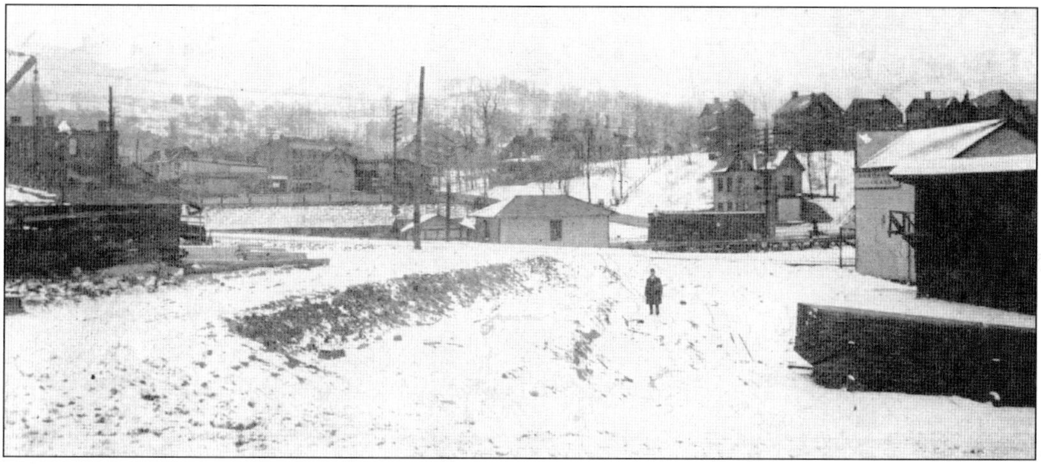

Taken from the future location of Craig Way, inside the yard of Martin and Miller Lumber Company, this photograph gives a good survey of the early railroad structures in Ingram. From left to right are the top of the westbound waiting room/shelter, freight station, a boxcar on the team track, and in the background, a house owned by the railroad to house employees. Note the garage-type door, most likely for track maintenance equipment. Out of the picture are the interlocking tower and the westbound station. An interesting note is that the house owned by the railroad is still standing today.

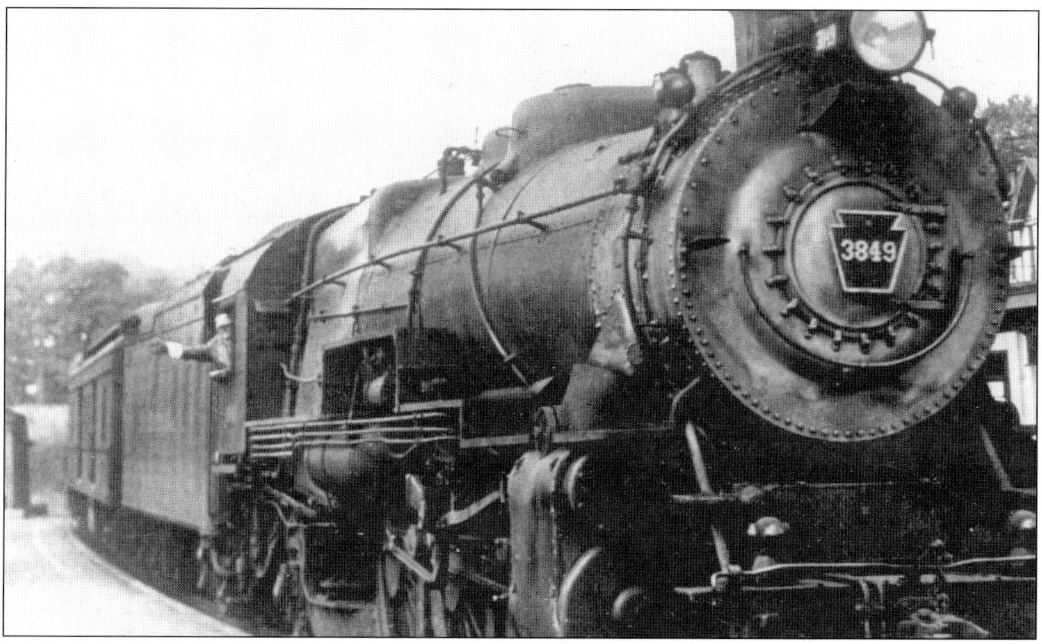

Pennsylvania Railroad K4 Pacific Type No. 3849 has just passed through the borough on its journey from New York to St. Louis. This engine was built at the Pennsylvania Railroad Juniata car shops in Altoona. Between 1914 and 1957, these 234-ton locomotives pulled many of the Pennsy's luxury passenger trains. The locomotive was known to reach speeds of up to 90 miles per hour on good track. Following World War II, most railroads began phasing out steam power in favor of diesel engines. In November 1957, the K4 made its final trip. Longtime Ingram residents recall the wailing steam whistles and trail of smoke as the mighty K4s passed through town. Ingram resident Robert Chisnell, seen piloting this behemoth, had spent 41 years on the Pennsylvania Railroad as an engineer.

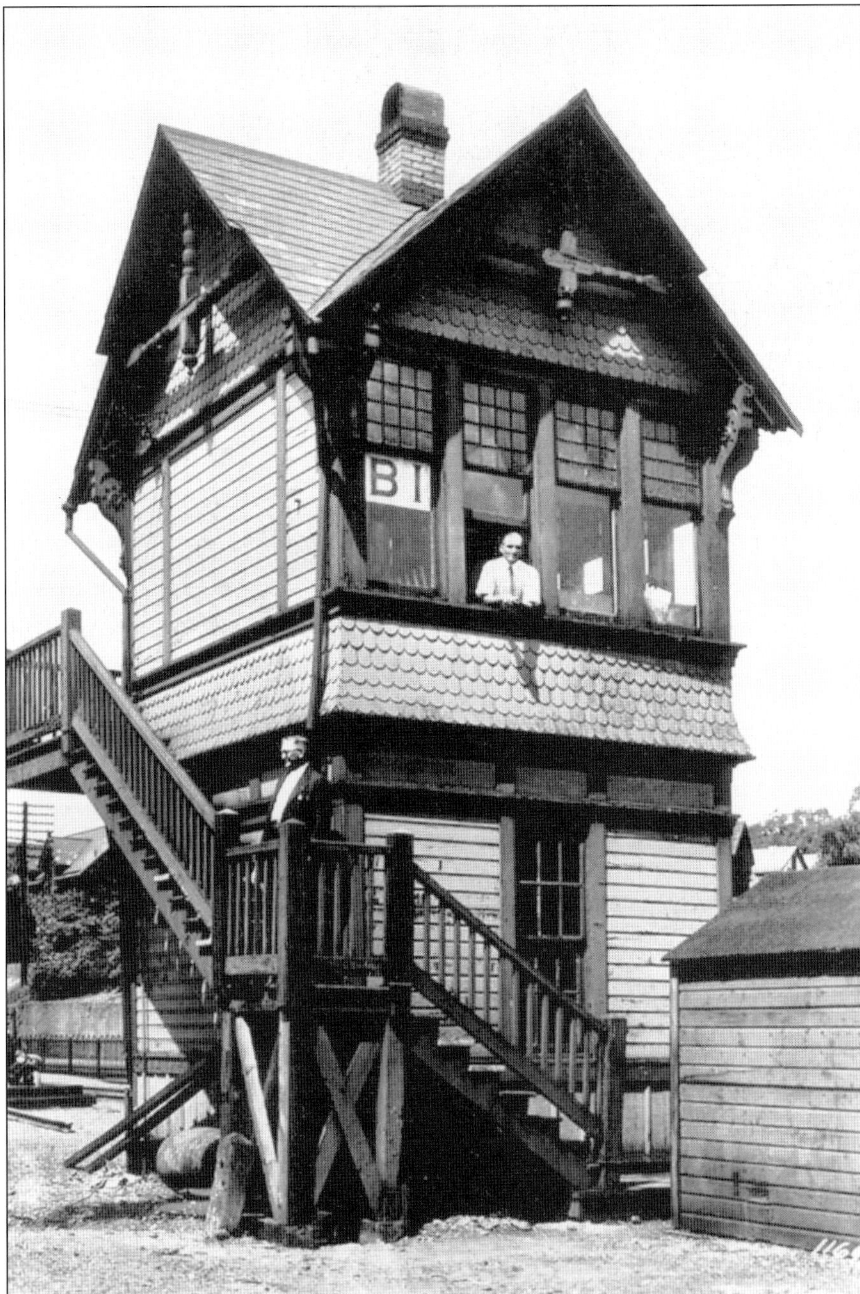

The busy mainline that ran through Ingram handled many passenger and freight trains daily. The former *Spirit of St. Louis*, and the *Penn-Texas Limited* bound for the golden southwest, were a few of the many passenger trains. The busy interlocking tower controlled the movement of trains with signals, track switches, and written instructions. Morse code was used by the operator/telegrapher to communicate with other towers along the line and connect Ingram residents with the outside world before telephones were common. The interlocking towers all had "call" letters and Ingram's was BI. Note the operator leaning out the window and the station in the background. (Courtesy of the Carnegie Library of Pittsburgh.)

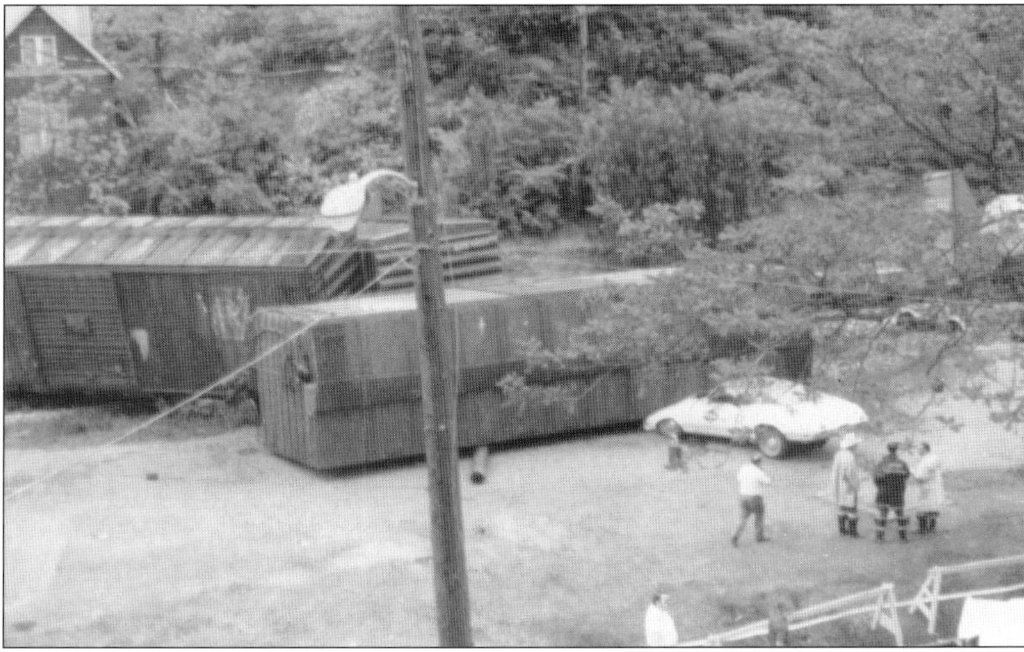

In 1975, a train car, which was part of a long freight passing through Ingram, suffered a broken axle. The axle caused the car to jump the tracks, which in turn caused the rest of the train to slam into the front cars. Some of the cars fell over onto the right-of-way and the parking lot of the old station. Besides a vehicle parked near the tracks being damaged in the incident, there were no injuries or fatalities. Although freight equipment and track conditions would get better when Conrail absorbed the bankrupt Penn Central, Ingram would only see the early years of this service. The Panhandle was put out of service between West End Pittsburgh and Carnegie in 1981 and later removed in 1984. Note the Ingram sign placed by the Penn Central railroad. (Courtesy of John Sacco.)

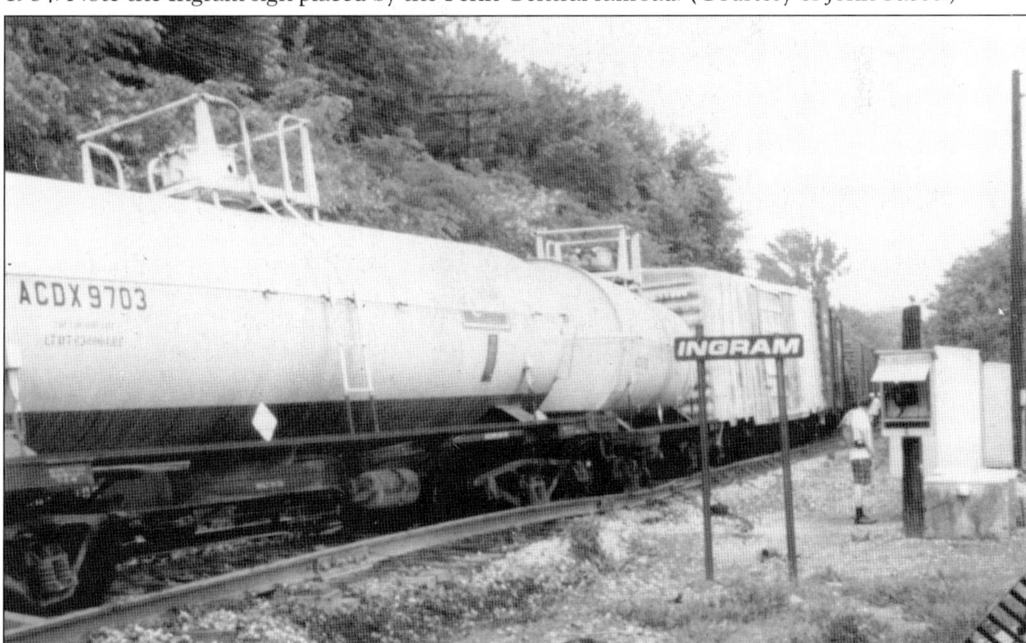

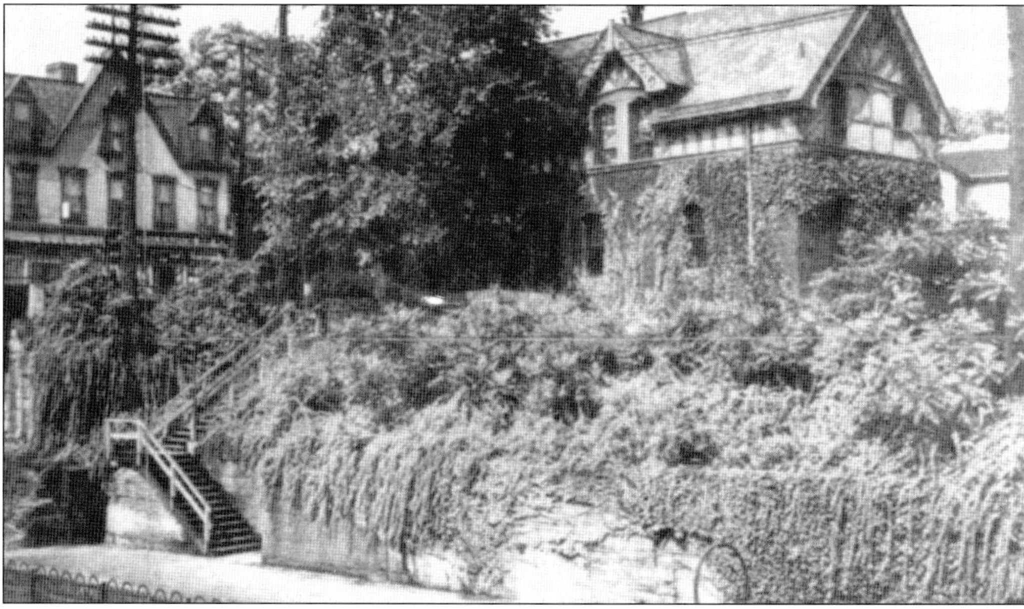

From the vantage point of Ingram Avenue, Ingram Station is one of the few remaining landmarks of the Pennsylvania Railroad. The first floor of the building is red brick and the second is in Tudor fashion. The picture shows the stairs leading down to the tracks that commuters and travelers would see on their way to the trains. Note in the background is Marx's Dairy Store, another popular gathering place for Ingramites.

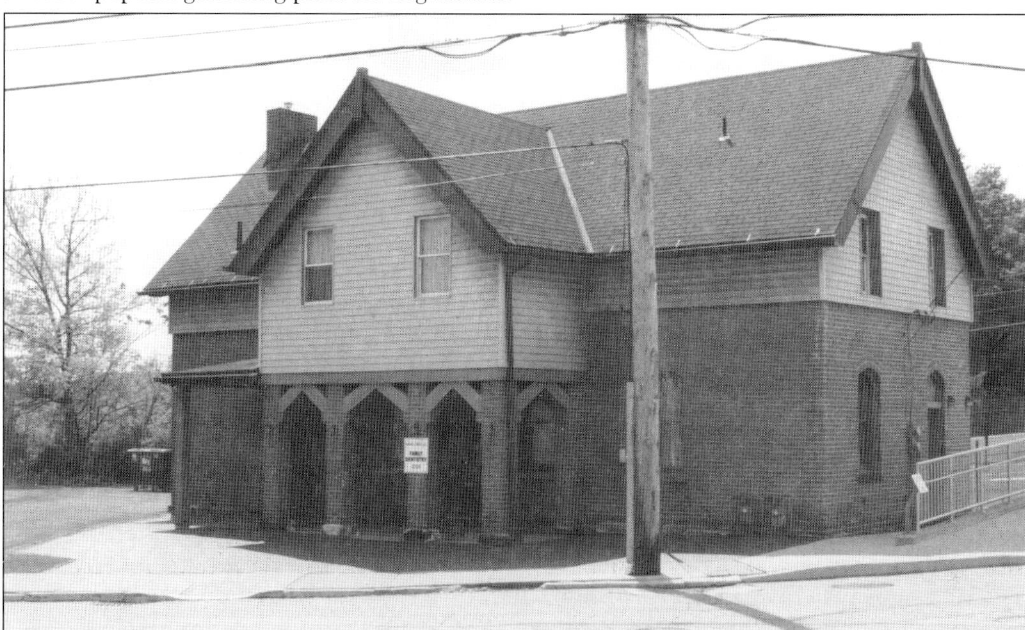

Ingram's ex–Pennsylvania Railroad station at 2725 Center Street currently houses the Family Dentistry of Nicole Podatrt, D.M.P. Underneath the siding is beautiful Tudor paneling painted in the same color scheme that was standard to all Pennsylvania Railroad stations. Commuter train service ended on November 27, 1964, and the station, a gathering point for many borough residents, was closed.

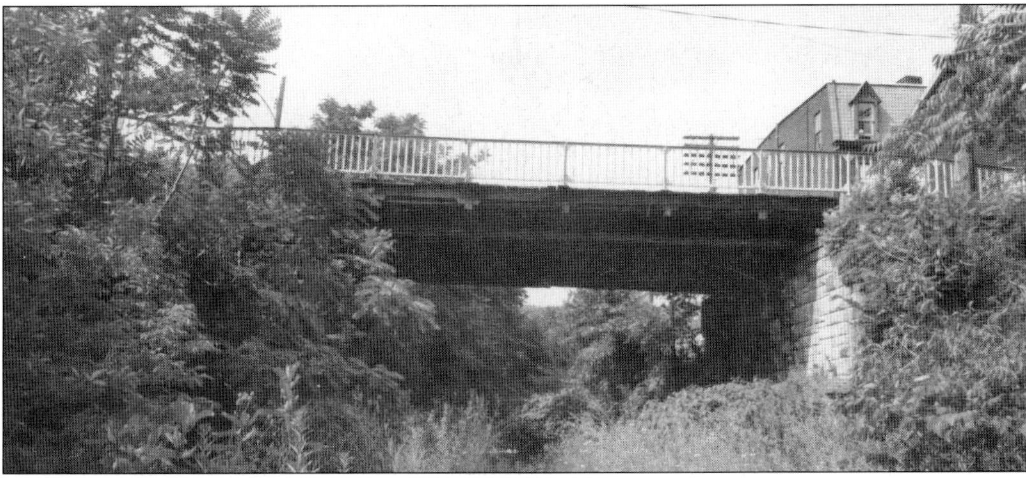

In October 1979, Amtrak's *National Limited* between Kansas City and New York became the last passenger train to operate over the former Pennsylvania Railroad's Panhandle Division. Conrail continued to operate freight through Ingram until the main line went out of service in 1981. At that point, the line was used as storage tracks for aging cars that were surplus under the 1976 merger that created Conrail. When Conrail dispatched a train to pick up the remaining stored cars, the last train rumbled out of Ingram, ending 118 years of fast, dependable service. Not long after Wagner tower in Carnegie closed, the Interstate Commerce Committee granted Conrail permission to remove the tracks. Although the track was heavily ballasted, the right-of-way grew over quickly, mimicking a lush valley more than a high-speed train corridor.

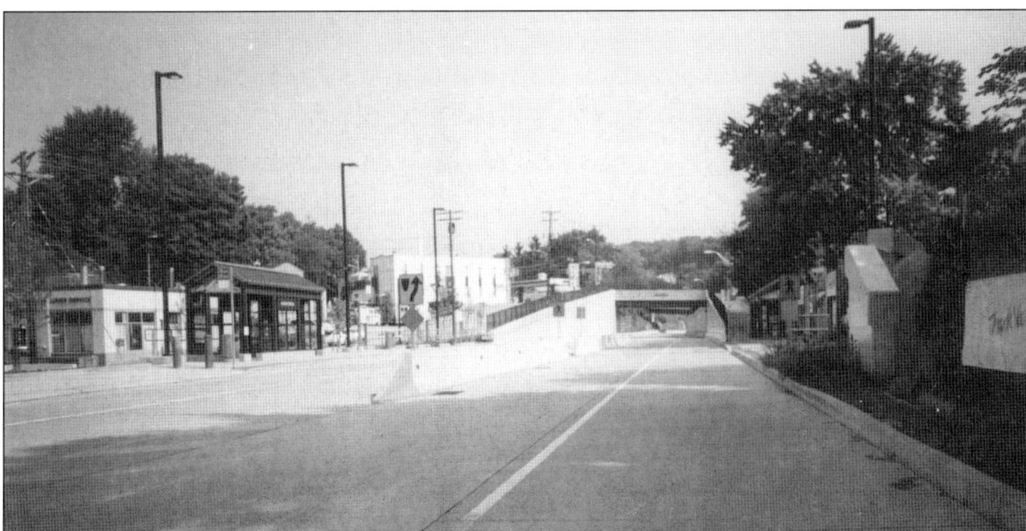

It was not until 1995 that the Port Authority of Allegheny County received approval to convert the old railroad right-of-way into the West Busway (a private roadway used only by buses and emergency vehicles). Work began in earnest during the early part of 1996 and continued over the course of four and a half years. On September 9, 2000, the West Busway opened with great fanfare. Giveaways, free rides, and a concert, performed by surf and hot rod legends Jan and Dean were held at the Carnegie Station. Once again, commuters are walking to the Ingram station for a 10 minute bus ride to Pittsburgh.

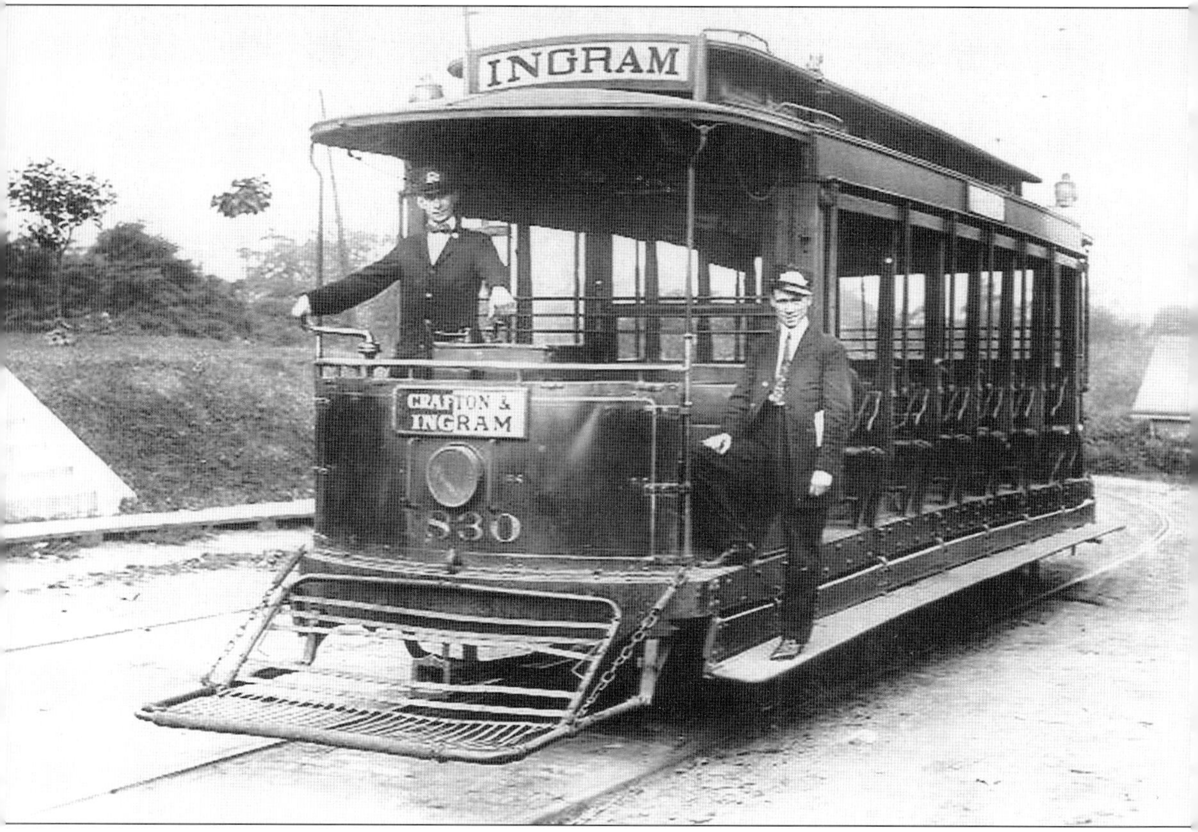

Open car No. 1830 is seen on the Crafton–Ingram line around the beginning of the 20th century. Open cars were very popular during the summer months, long before the advent of air conditioning. Church groups and schools often chartered these cars for summer picnics as well. A streetcar loop and waiting shelter were built near Oakwood park, just off the Carnegie line on Crafton Boulevard. Local residents often walked to the park, however, to save the nickel car fare. Open cars were built for two-man operation and operated throughout the country. The motorman was responsible for operating the car, while conductor collected and recorded fares. (Courtesy of the Carnegie Library of Pittsburgh.)

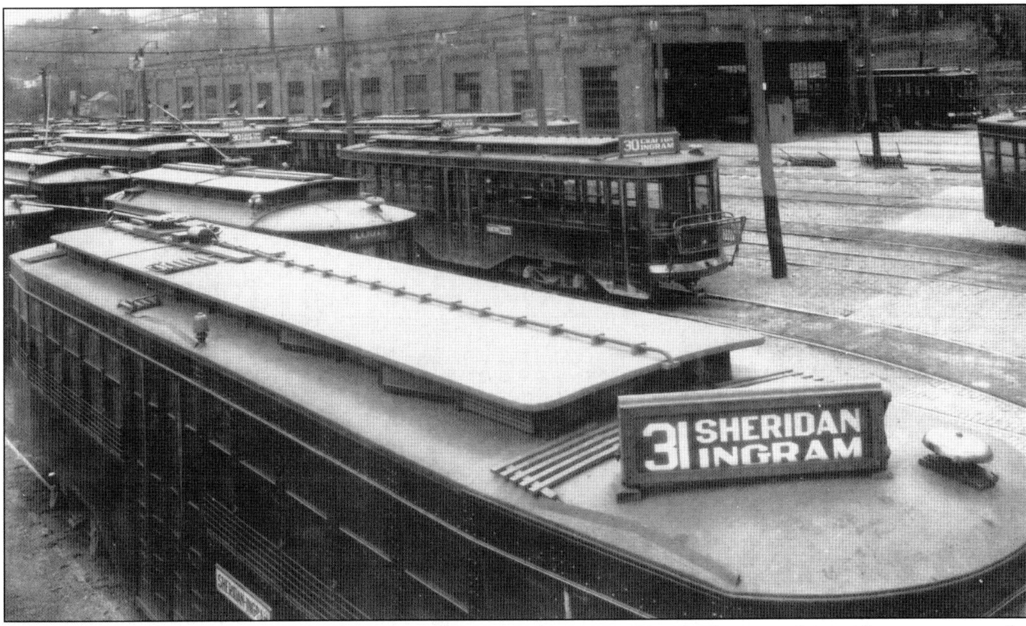

This photograph, dated May 11, 1924, shows a lineup of high-floor and low-floor cars at the Ingram Car Barn. These cars were phased out for the new streamliners known as Presidents Conference Committee (PCC) cars. (Courtesy of the Pennsylvania Trolley Museum.)

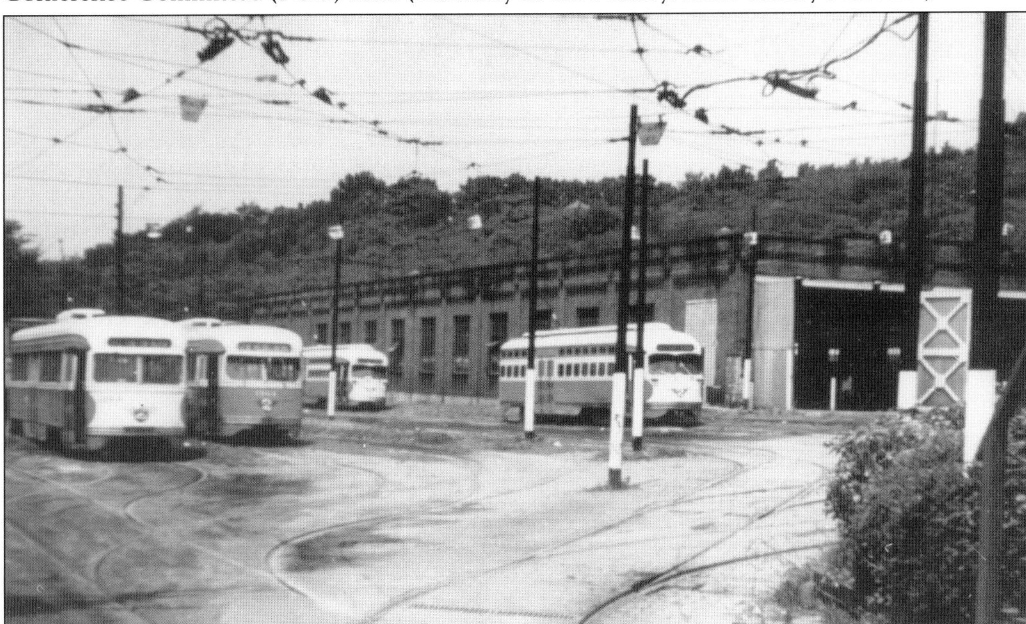

Late in the life of Pittsburgh Railways trolley service, the Ingram Car Barn housed mostly streamlined PCC cars. These cars were built by the St. Louis Car Company between 1936 and 1949. By the summer of 1957, all West End routes were operated out of Ingram. This included routes 25-Island Avenue, 26-West Park, 27-Carnegie, 28-Heidelberg, 30-Crafton-Ingram, and 34/31-Elliot-Sheraden. Two years latter, on June 20, 1959, trolley service was abandoned in the West End, with the closing of the Point Bridge in Pittsburgh.

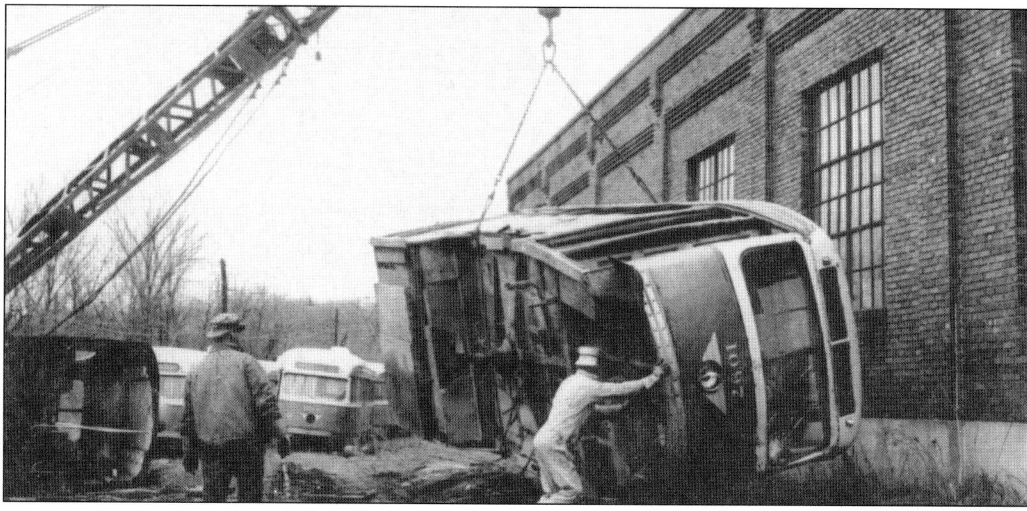

During the final week of West End trolley operation, newer PCC cars were transferred from Ingram to other carbarns throughout the Pittsburgh Railways system. At the same time, 30 older PCC cars in the 1000 through 1100 series were brought to Ingram, awaiting final approval from the Public Utilities Commission to abandon trolley service. These cars never operated again once they came to the Ingram and were scrapped on the site between March and April 1961. One exception was car No. 1138, which was purchased for the Arden Trolley Museum by member Dick Bowker for $250 scrap value. This car was transported via flatbed truck from Ingram to the trolley museum on April 5, 1961. It has the distinction of being the first trolley to operate at the museum in December 1962. (Courtesy of the Pennsylvania Trolley Museum.)

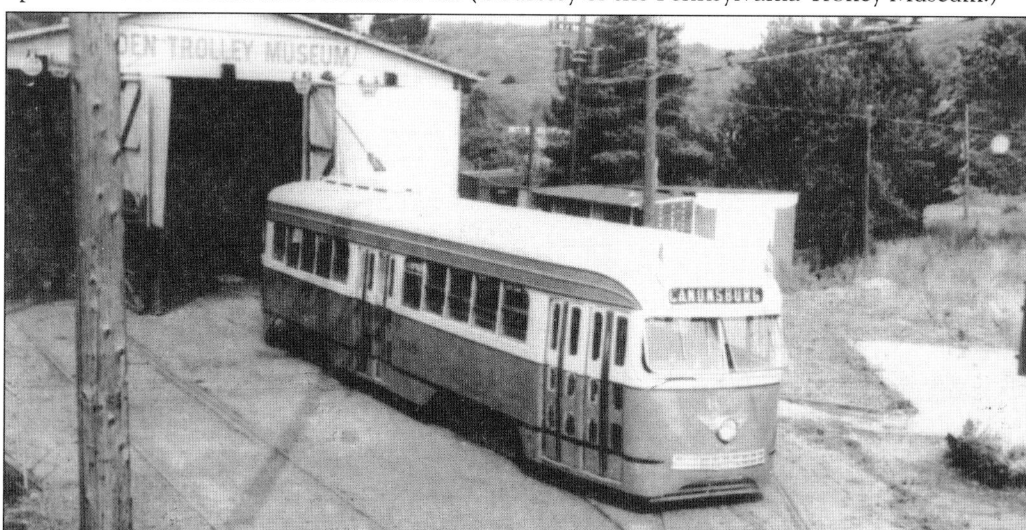

This photograph shows PCC car No. 1138 after arriving at Arden Trolley Museum (now Pennsylvania Trolley Museum). Although No. 1138 eventually ended up in Ingram, it was originally assigned to Craft Avenue Car Barn in the Oakland section of Pittsburgh. This car entered service in November 1937 and operated over many of Pittsburgh Railways East End routes. Today No. 1138 has been beautifully restored and can be seen at the Pennsylvania Trolley Museum in Washington. The museum's collection includes 48 different types of streetcars built between 1893 and 1988. Visitors can enjoy a ride on several of these cars and learn of the role that trolleys had in shaping America's history. (Courtesy of the Pennsylvania Trolley Museum.)

After the scrapping process concluded, Ingram Car Barn was abandoned. This mid-1960s scene captures the empty interior of the building, which contained four tracks, and a storage capacity of 20 cars. As unlikely as it seemed, people would be worshiping here by the end of the decade. (Courtesy of the Ascention Church.)

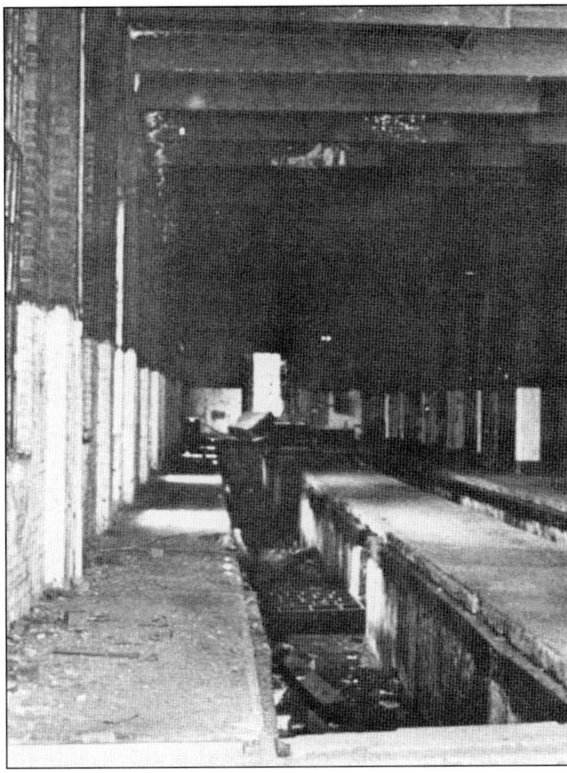

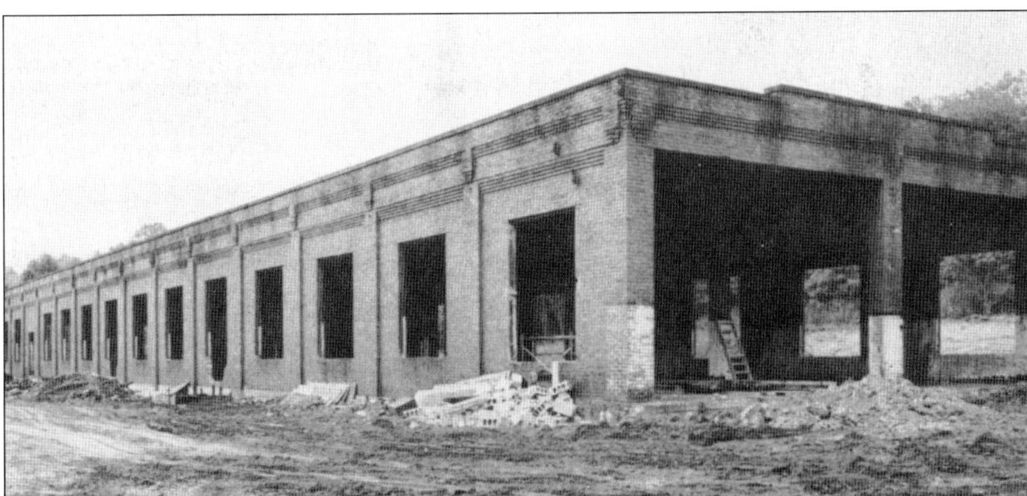

The former Ingram carbarn is shown during the transition period. After the building was completely gutted, service pits were filled in and yard tracks removed. Work began on bricking up the garage door openings and portions of the window areas. The finished church would be painted white and adorned with modern appointments. One of Ascension Churches treasures are its beautiful stained glass windows. (Courtesy of the Ascention Church.)

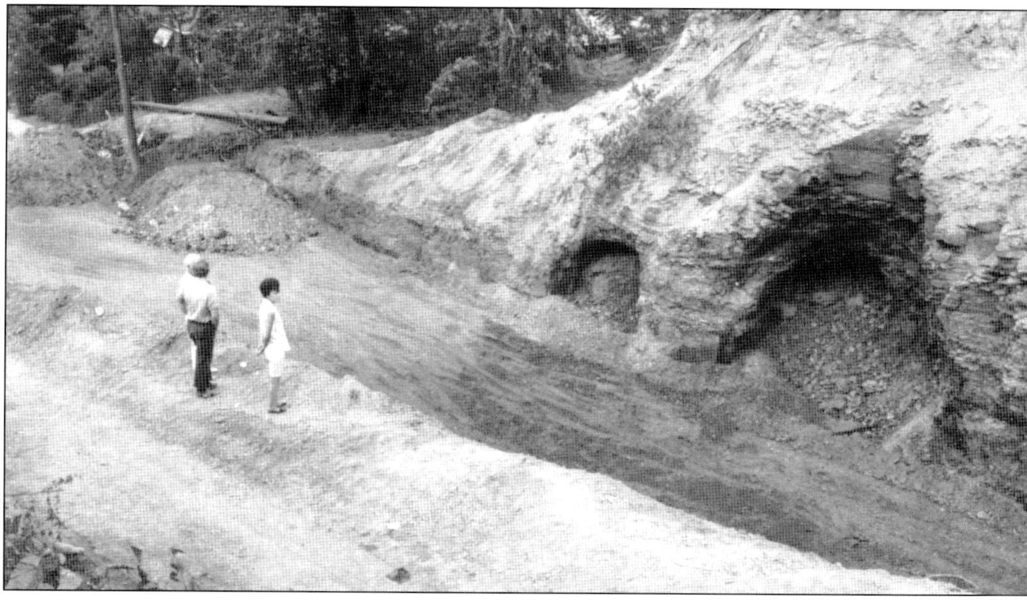

Middletown Road is Ingram's eastern boundary with the city of Pittsburgh. In the process of upgrading the road in 1971, two abandoned underground bituminous coal mine tunnels were uncovered. The mines, part of the Pittsburgh Coal Seam, were located only in upper Ingram's southeastern corner of Middletown Road and Hodgson Avenue and were active in the 1870s. Remaining coal was strip mined on the city side of Middletown Road after the underground mines were abandoned. The mines were exposed and later collapsed, providing a brief view of Ingram's only coal source. The road was rebuilt into a modern concrete thoroughfare. Also note in the lower photograph, the new Ingram Volunteer Fire Department company firehouse being constructed on the hill. Built partly by the public works department and volunteers, this fire hall would replace the old garage used until this time. In this photograph, the windows have yet to be installed.

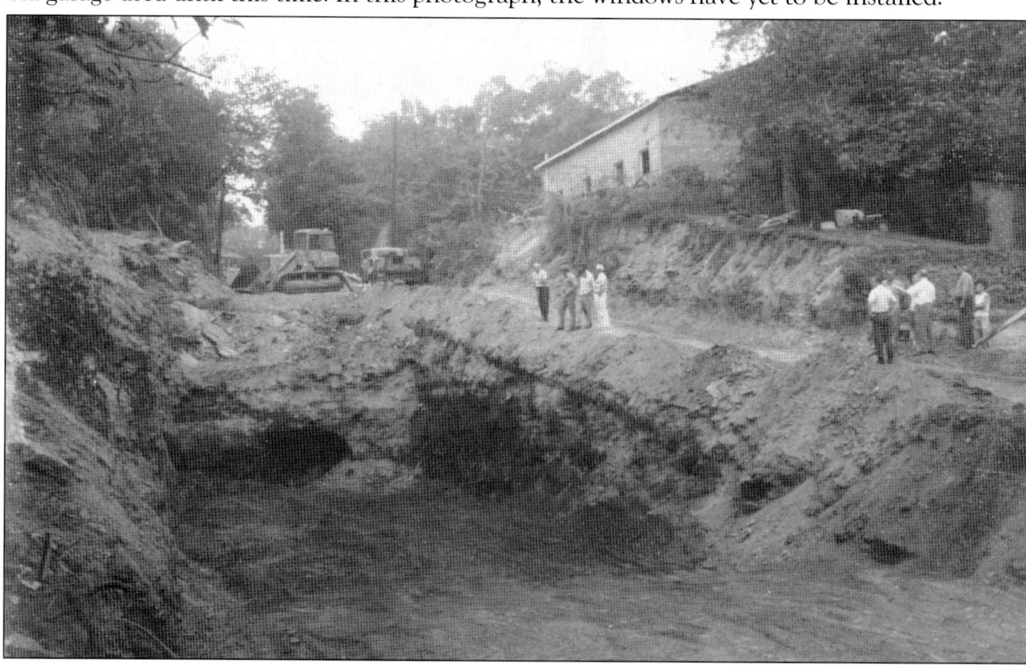

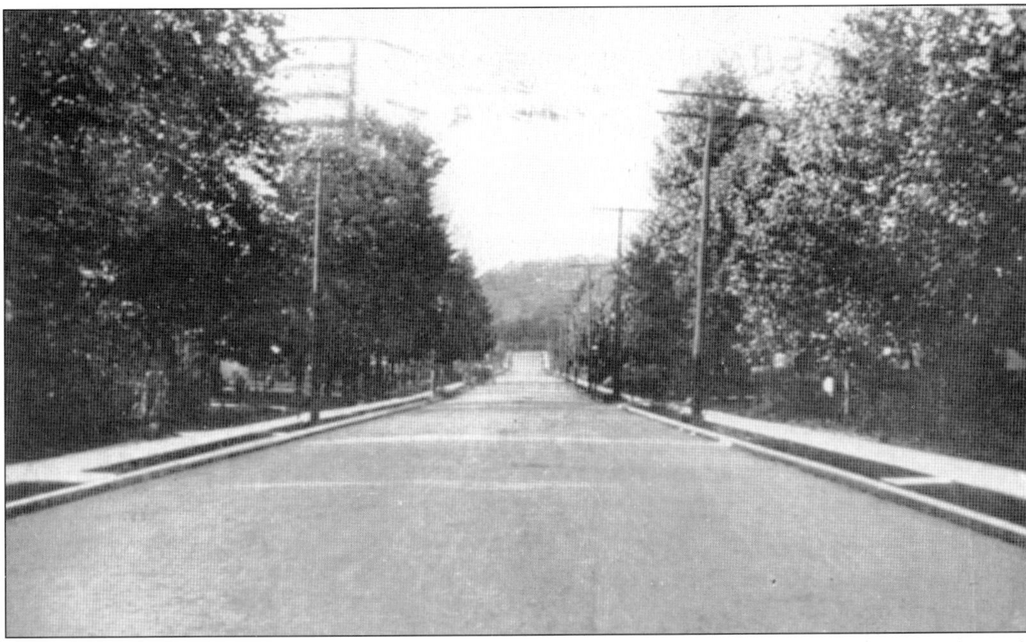

Looking north on Linden Avenue reveals the new brick paving, manicured lawns, and neatly pruned trees. Later the name of the street would be changed to Linshaw Avenue, an important name in the Spanish American War.

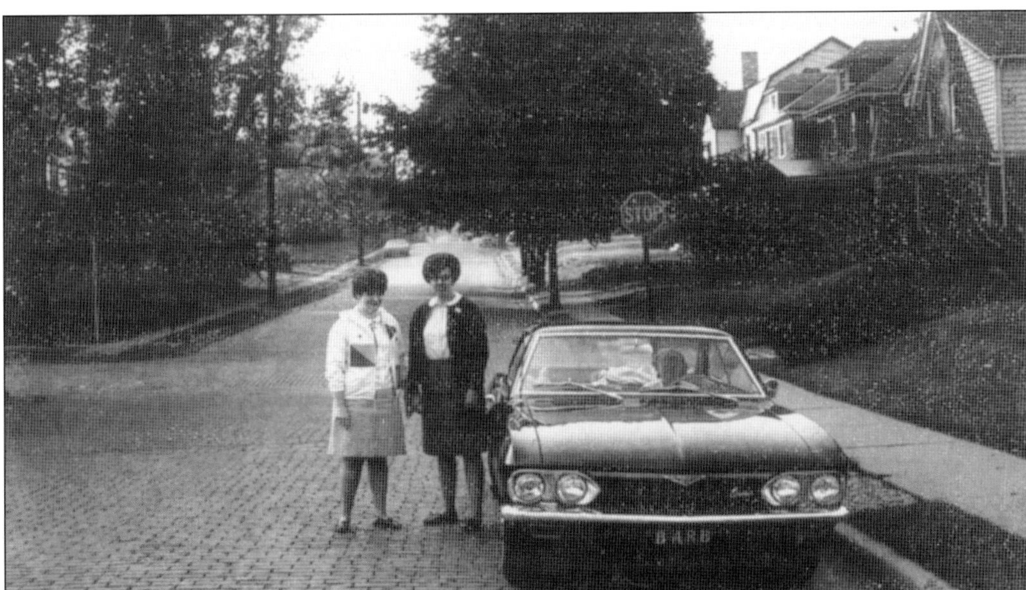

Some of the residents of Ingram can still follow the yellow brick road, as even today a number of streets have their original yellow brick streets. This mid-1960s view at the corner of North Duane and Greenwood Avenues is the last street westward in Ingram before the city line. Most streets in Ingram were of yellow-clay brick with large trees bracketing them, giving the town a very tranquil feeling.

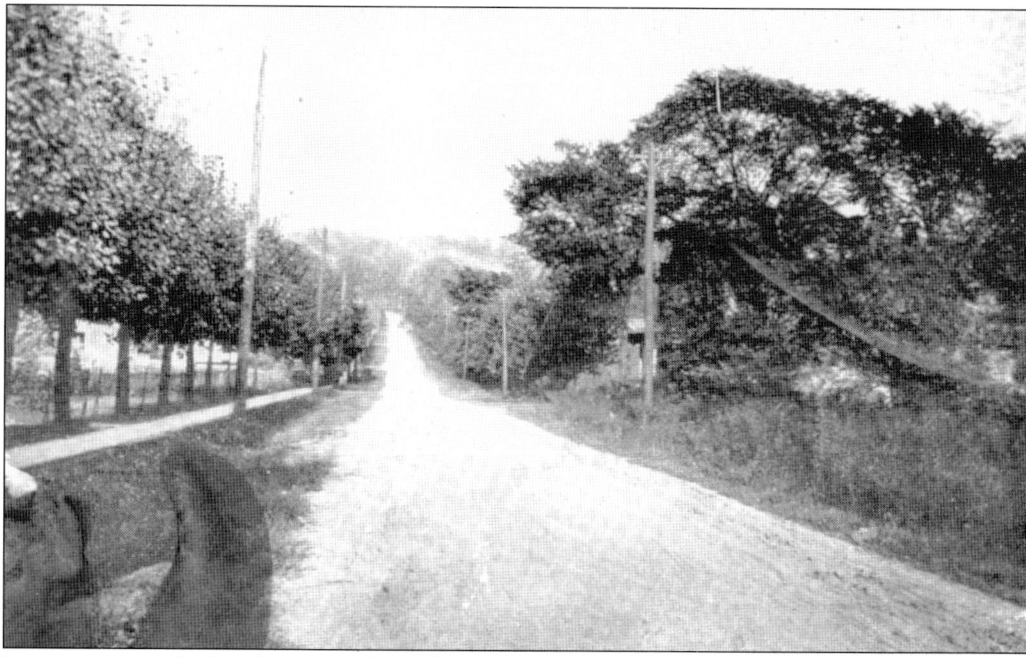

Ingram Avenue, before the surge of vehicle traffic, was a tree lined, dirt road. The road was a main artery connecting Ingram and the surrounding farms with Steubenville Pike. The pike connected Pittsburgh to Steubenville, Ohio, through farmland and wooded areas of western Pennsylvania. Shown below, paved in brick, it was the last bit of Ingram people would see on their trip "Out the Pike," through the countryside. Although the original trees are gone, new trees have been planted along the now heavily traveled asphalt avenue. (Below, courtesy of Claire Rex.)

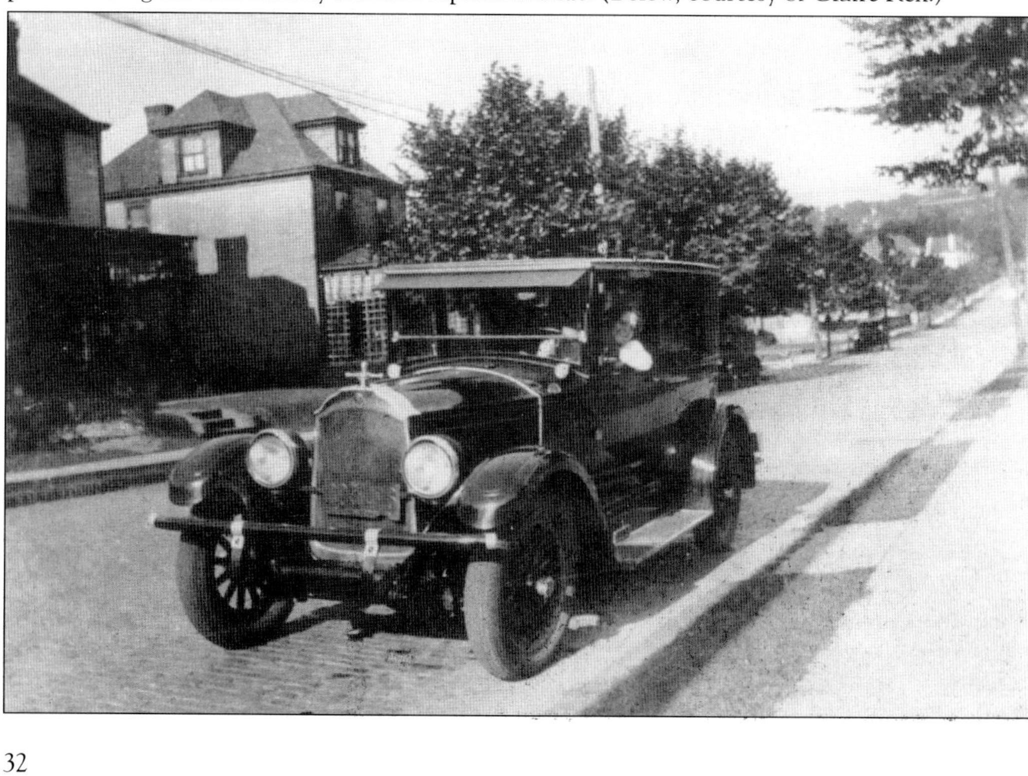

Three

Houses

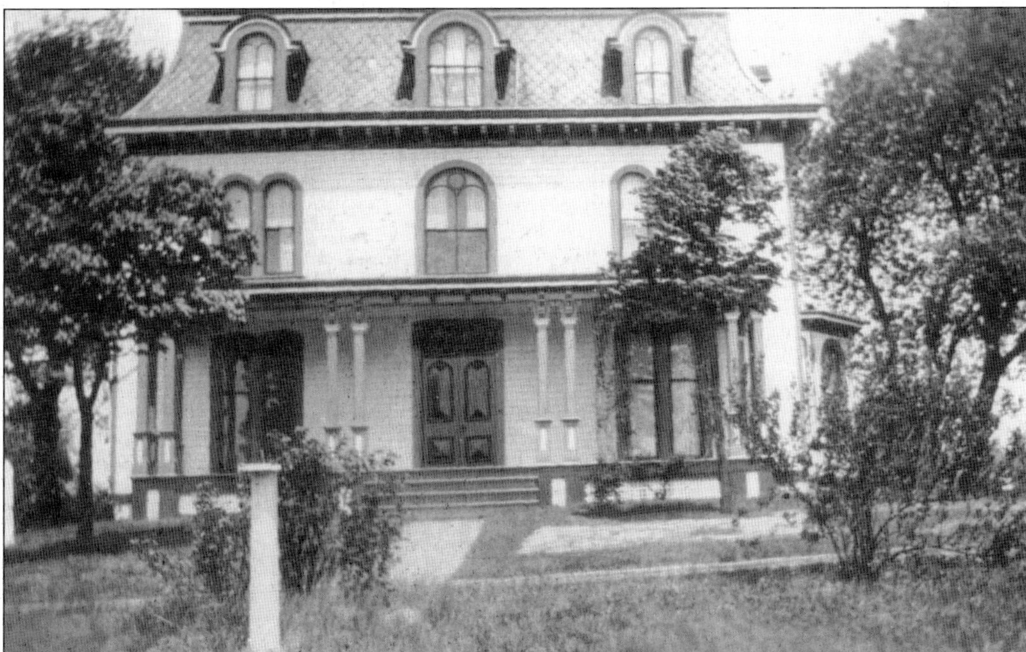

Not much is known about the construction of Thomas Ingram's home. Located on property that is now part of West Prospect Avenue, only part of the original driveway to the home still exists. Until 1890, building was slow in Ingram—only 17 houses were contained within its boundaries according to a development brochure of the time. However, a building boom occurred after 1890 when the railroads began to add many commuter lines, as many as 90 a day. This allowed Ingram to become a bedroom community for the city of Pittsburgh and development began in earnest. With the further development of trolleys, building lots were quickly snatched up. Today Ingram is filled with fine examples of homes from every era of architectural development, even to today's modern townhomes.

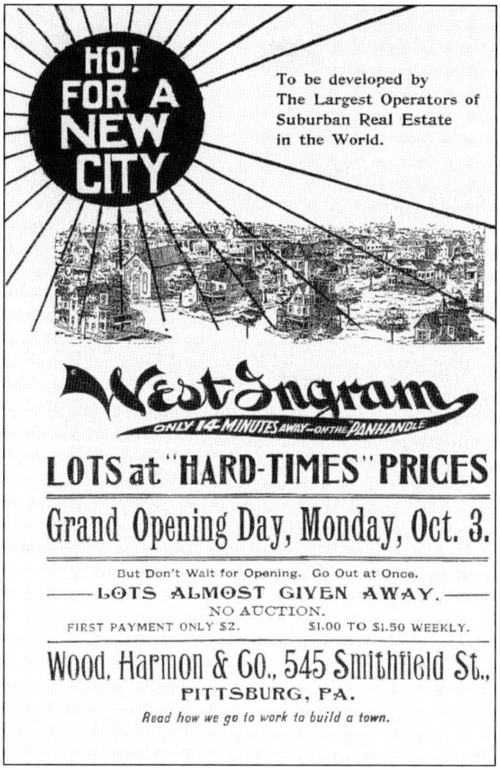

Here is an advertising circular from 1897 enticing people to move to Ingram. Lots could be purchased for only $2 down, with weekly installments of $1.50. City conveniences, such as gas, electric, and telephone, were promoted and the business, schools, and churches praised. New macadam roads were a high point of technology. Ingram's proximity to Pittsburgh allowed development to burgeon from 17 homes in 1896 to over 1,600 households in 2007.

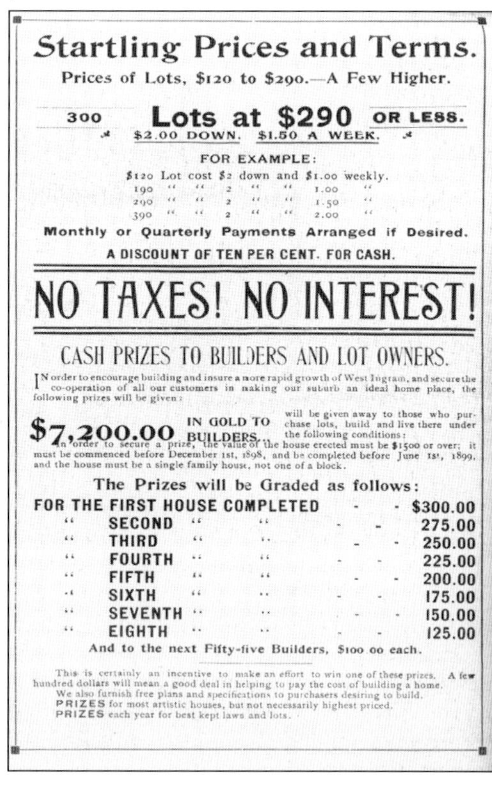

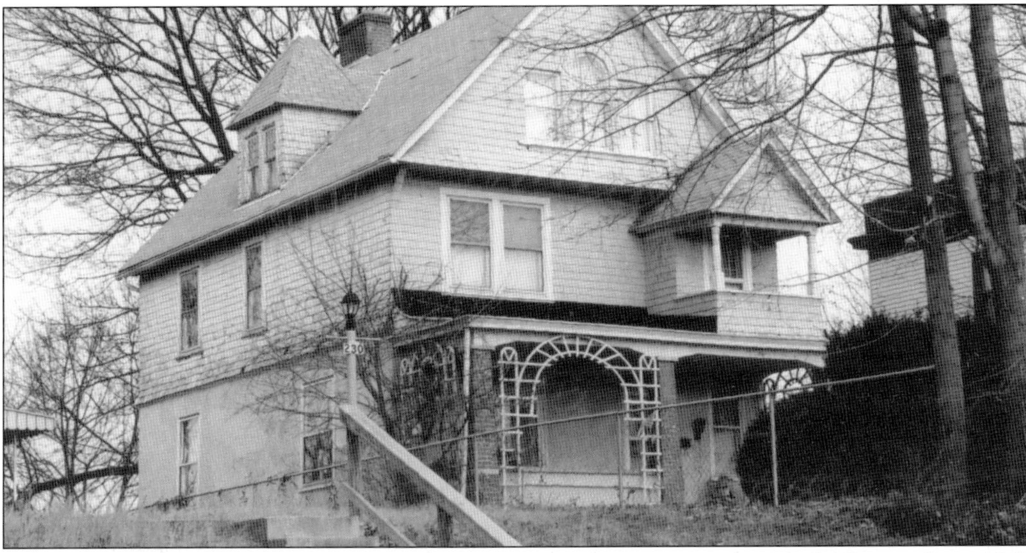

This home is rumored to be the oldest house in Ingram, tracing its origins back to at least 1865, and perhaps even older. It is part of the Belmont Plan, one of a series of railroad development plans that subdivided Ingram. Little is known about the original owners of the home, only that they were two brothers employed by the railroad. This two and a half story stucco and shingle home retains much of its original interior woodwork and glass. The detached garage once served as outhouse for the home. In searching for hidden treasures in the attic, the owners found a bamboo fishing pole with its line still attached, perfect for whiling away the hours at nearby Chartiers Creek.

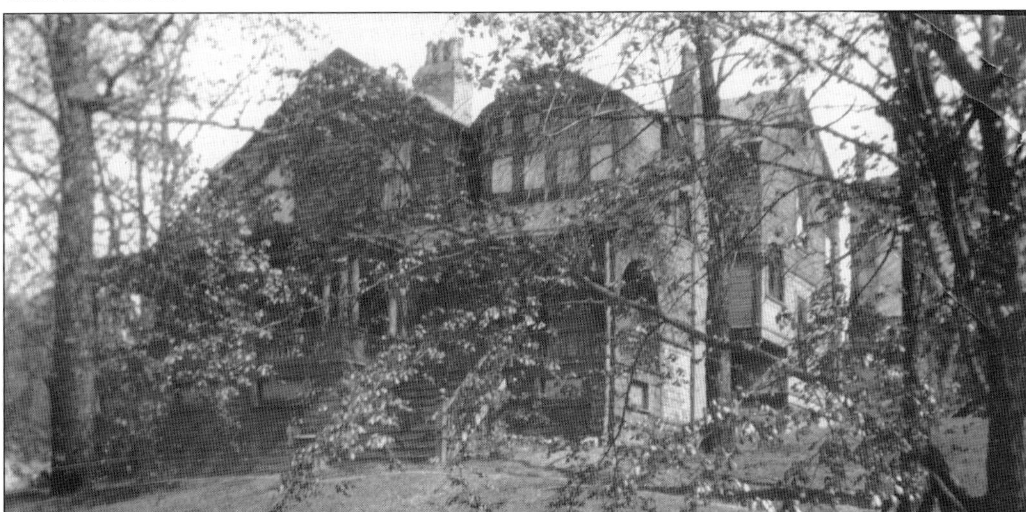

Charles Craft, for whom neighboring Crafton is named, sold a lot and two-story structure at this location in 1894. How long it existed before that is anybody's guess. Although the wood siding has been covered with asbestos shingles and the wooden porch replaced with a concrete one, Victorian elements, such as the bay windows, are still visible on the exterior of this home. As with many old homes, some features are lost while others are discovered. The home has a side entrance, but the curved entryway baseboards and original front door were found in the basement. Stacked fieldstone creates the basement walls and the removal of a drop ceiling revealed that the floor supports were tree trunks. These materials are common in many Ingram homes.

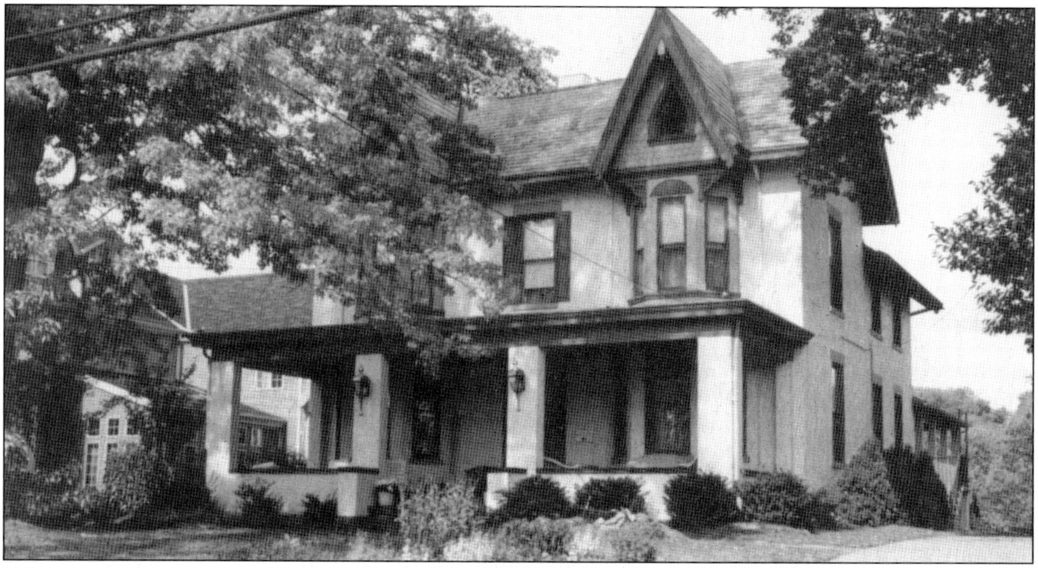

West Prospect Avenue served as the address for many prominent professional people. "On the Ridge" was one way of describing this street by old timers in town. A level area located between hilly upper Ingram and flat lower Ingram (near Chartiers Creek), this street afforded residents a view down a sloping hillside to the creek. Edward Stotz chose to build his home here. Born just further down the ridge, he did not stray far. Edward and his brother Charles were world renowned architects, designers of Point State Park in Pittsburgh, as well as several other buildings in the city. They also led restoration efforts in Old Economy, a Harmonite society, and Fort Ligonier. Even the borough building was designed by the brothers. Edward's home is quite large with a slate porch encompassing the entire front of the home. Built in a more Edwardian style of the early 1900s, this home's features are simpler in design detail, but still spectacular. Two large parlors, a dining room with stained-glass windows, large kitchen, and butler's pantry are located on the first floor. Five bedrooms on a second floor and several bedrooms on the third floors servant's quarters finish the home. Even the basement is divided into several rooms. Recent owners have added a great room and large integral garage to the home. The beige brick building located further down the ridge (below) is the childhood home of architects.

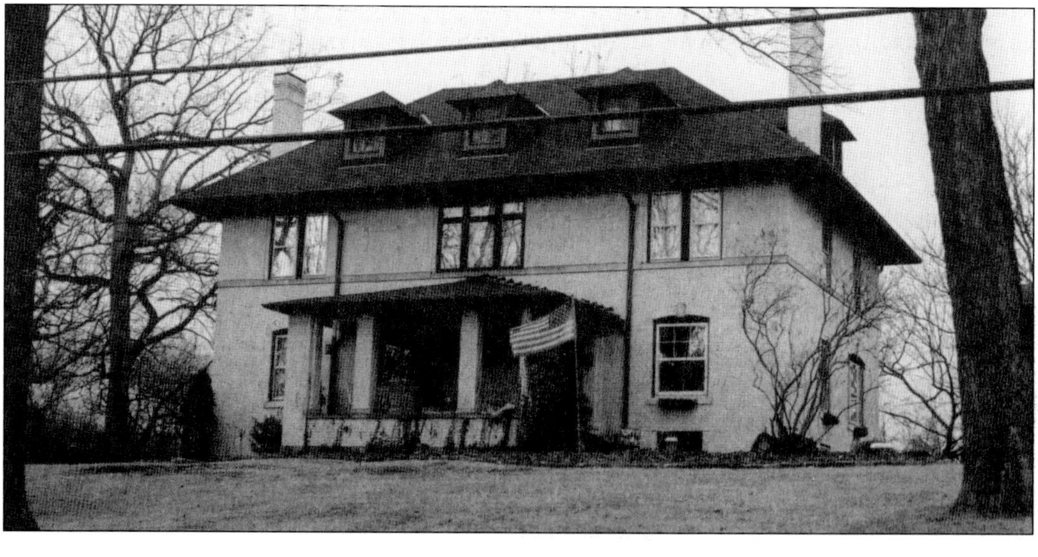

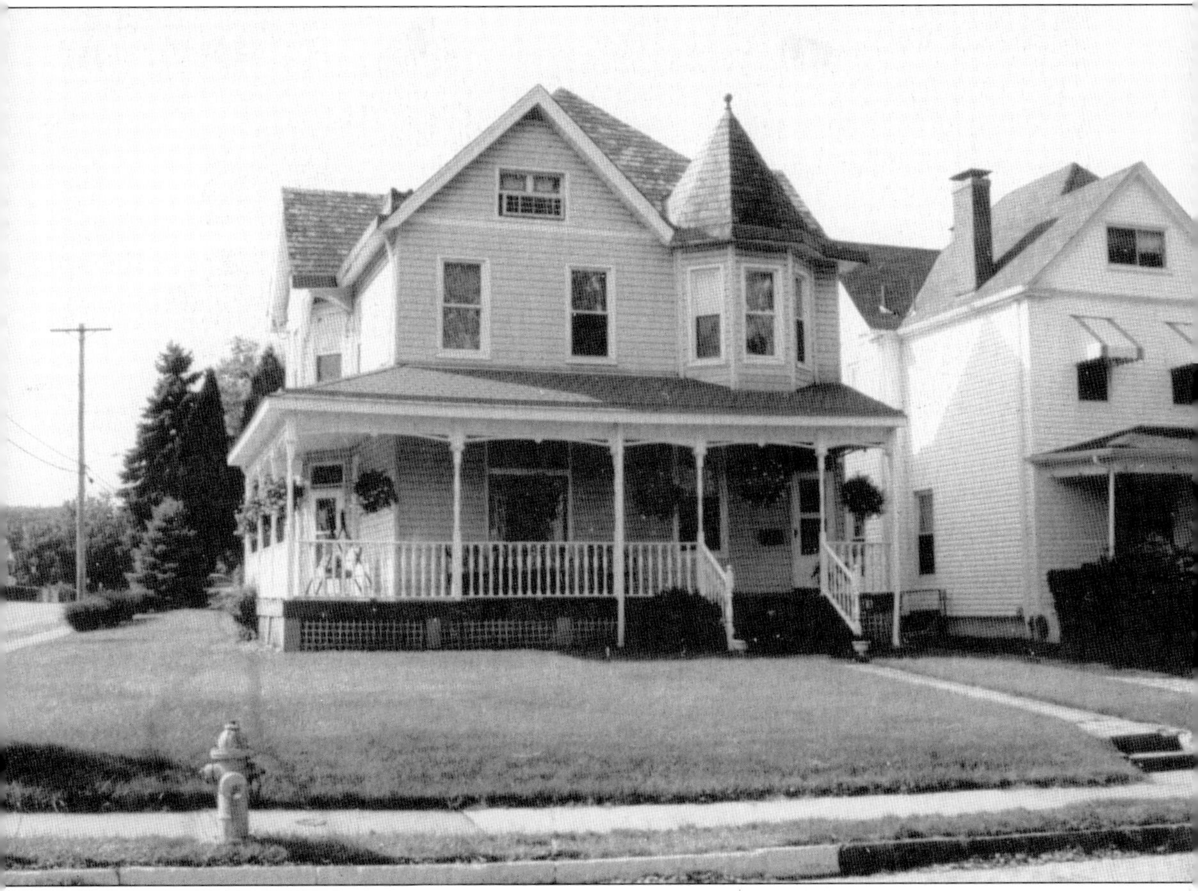

Ingram is fortunate to have so many fine examples of Victorian architecture to admire. Part of the Belmont plan, a development sponsored by the railroad, and built in 1895, this beauty retains most of its original interior design. Stained-glass arches above the first floor windows, servants' staircase, and small nooks and crannies adorn the interior. The wrap-around porch showcases the exterior of the house and, at Christmas, is beautifully decorated. Many residents make a point to see its magnificent Christmas tree that illuminates the porch during the holiday season.

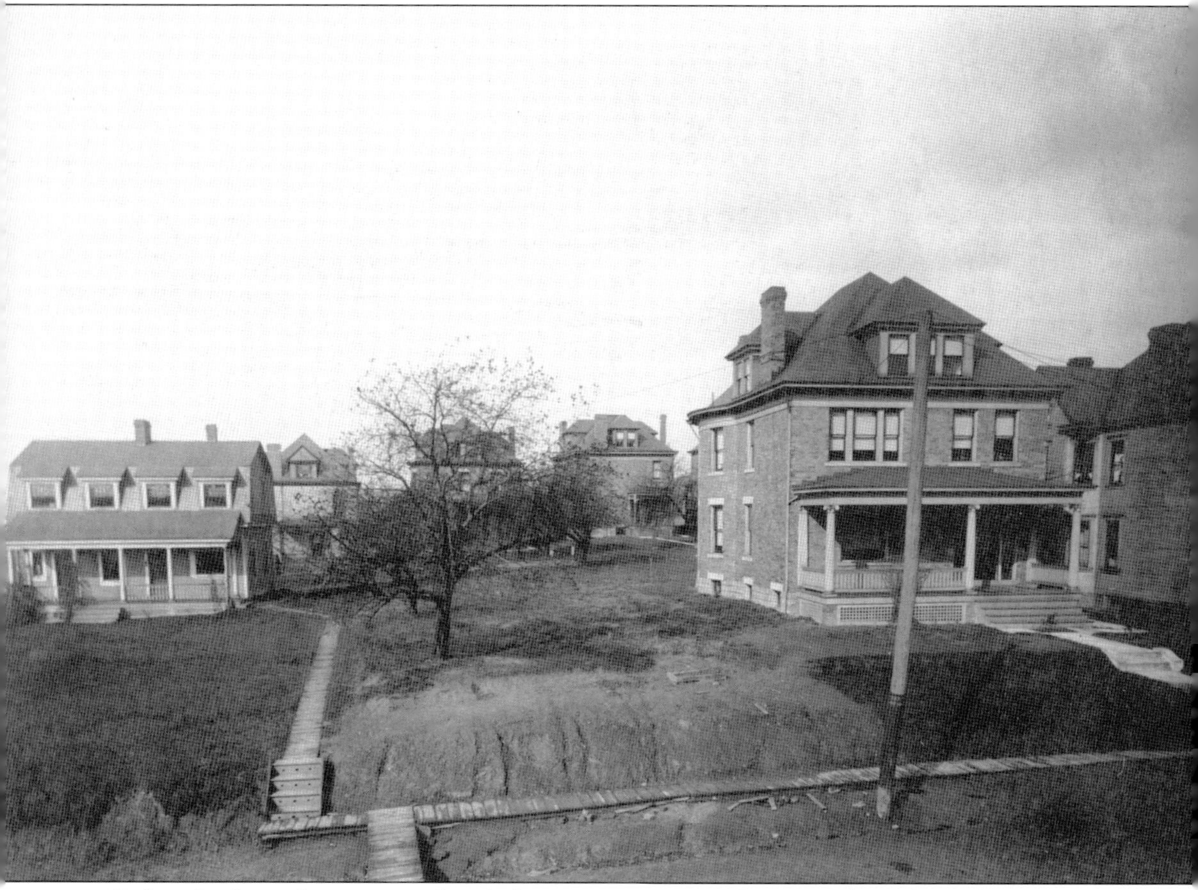

Before the days of concrete and asphalt, most streets were dirt or cinders. Shown here are homes located on Vancouver Avenue. There were no sewers at the time so ditches were dug along the roads. Notice that these are not concrete sidewalks but instead boardwalks, which were not uncommon at this time in Ingram's history.

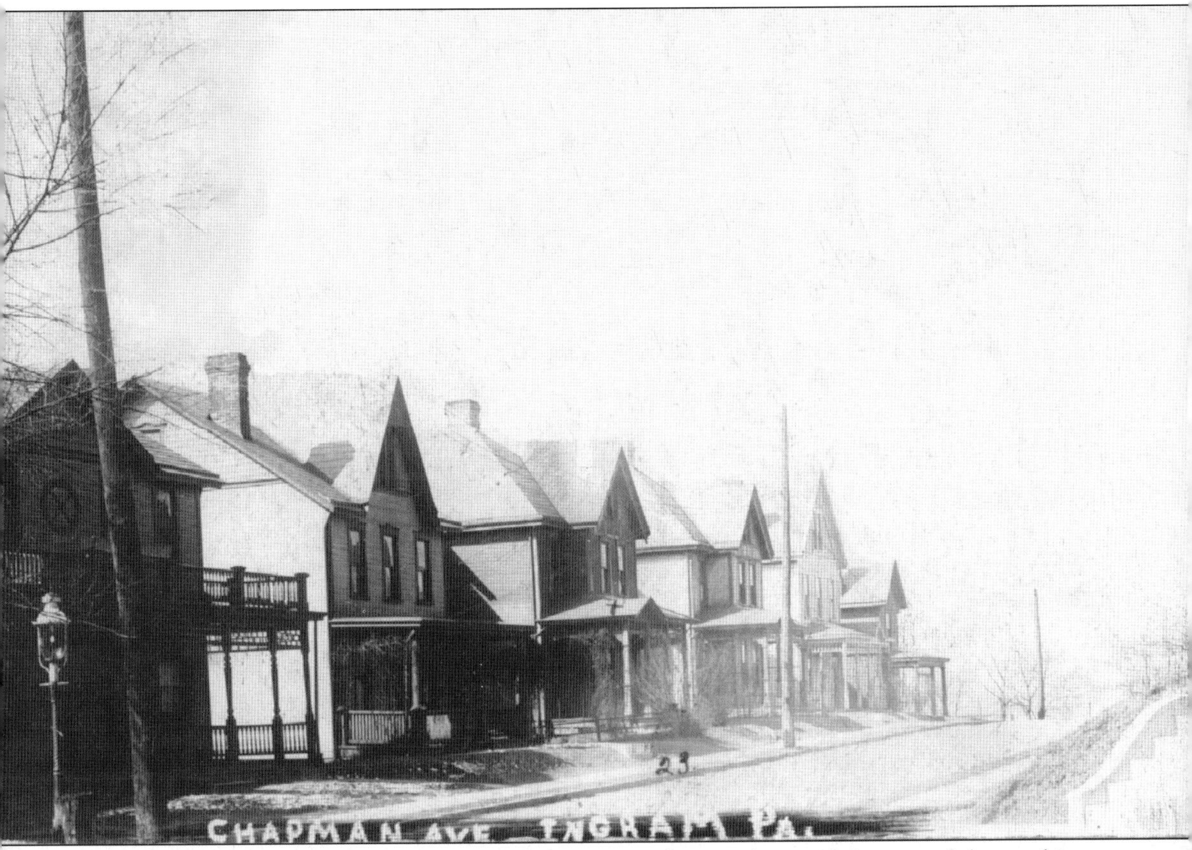

Houses in Ingram varied from mansions of the upper class to the meek homes of the working man. This picture of a section of Chapman Avenue was taken in 1919 and shows a sampling of houses commonly seen in the working man's area of Ingram. Chapman Avenue is a dead-end street that leads to an overlook of the town. Note the brick street and gas lamps. The concrete sidewalks were a new feature for this period of time. This area was a welcoming home for the working man needing to be close to Pittsburgh but away from the city smoke.

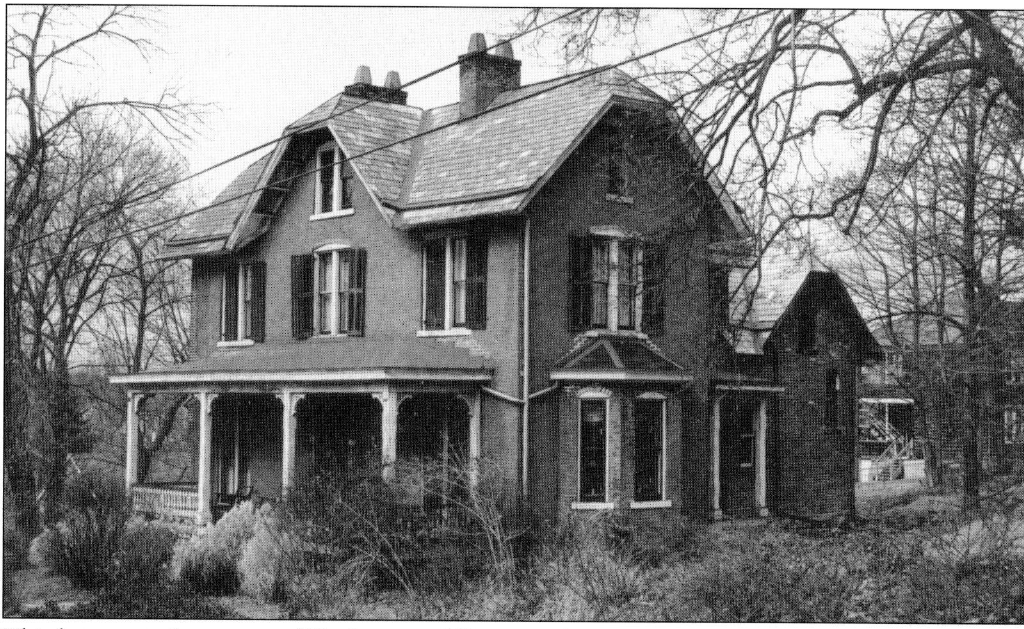

This home, on the corner of Hodgson and Danvers Avenues, was part of the Craft Plan. Charles Craft's sister Caroline Bloomer sold this piece of property to the Markam family in 1880. The original house is in tact and restored with original parquet floors and fireplace. The attached kitchen burned in 1930 and was rebuilt with the original brick. The slate roof and original shutters have been replaced.

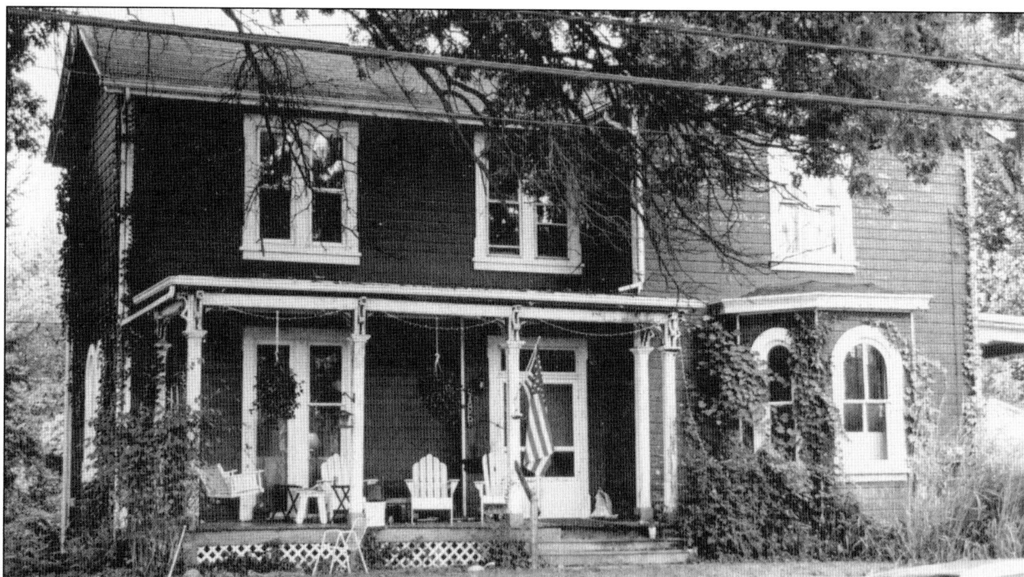

Known to local residents as the Parsons house, this red frame home, built in 1872, was the locale for many a piano lesson given in the early 1900s. Mary, a renowned concert pianist who had studied in Europe, and her sister Martha Parsons, daughters of the original owners, gave lessons in both parlors of the home. The house has elements of the Italianate period of design with its tall, narrow windows dominating the front and straight porch rails and trims. Missing are the gingerbread curlicues that are associated with later Victorian design.

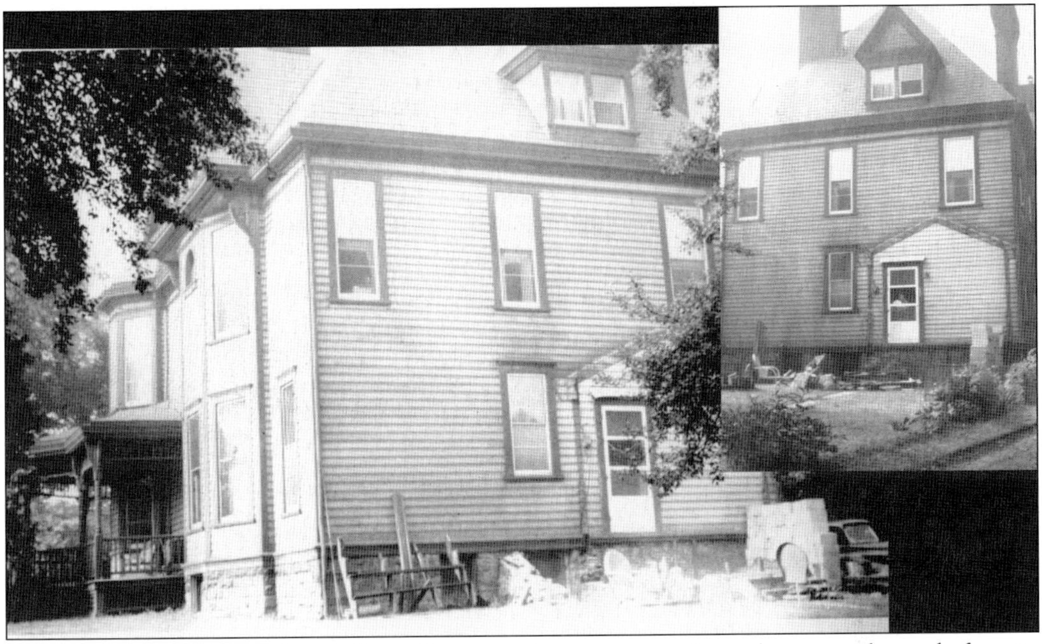

This house, built in 1873, on West Prospect Avenue went through many phases before its final look. This back view of the house shows the beginning of its first transformation. The wraparound porch was still intact as well as the gingerbread under the eaves. The back porch had been removed.

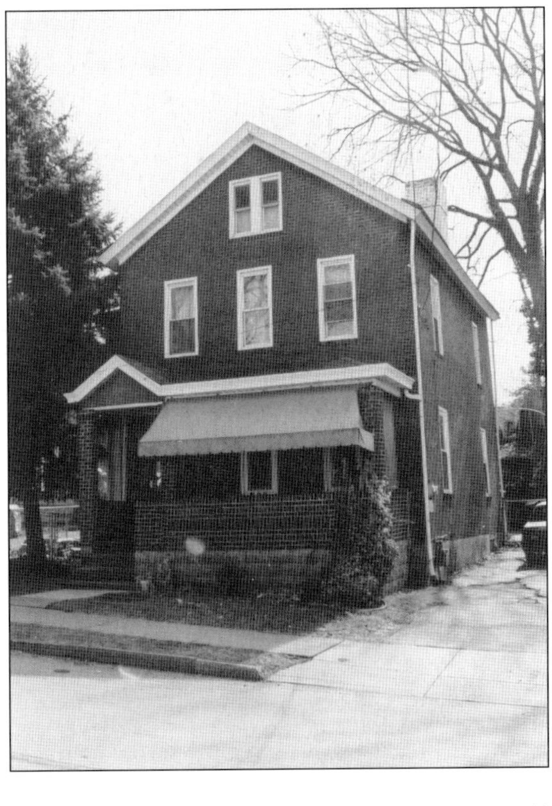

This street, part of the Steger Plan (after builder Charles Steger), contains homes built for many of the working class of Ingram. The trolley line traveled Hodgson Avenue, giving its residents easy access to their jobs. A resident, researching the home in an old telephone directory, discovered that Pascal Lawson, a bookkeeper, lived in the home in the 1920s. In old directories not only is the number listed, but the person's occupation as well. Another clue to the home's past was found in Sanborn fire maps. A resident thought there had been additions to its original design, only to discover that the maps gave the same dimensions as the current house. Although there is nothing unusual in its design, it is typical of the working-class homes that so greatly number the hilly slopes of upper Ingram.

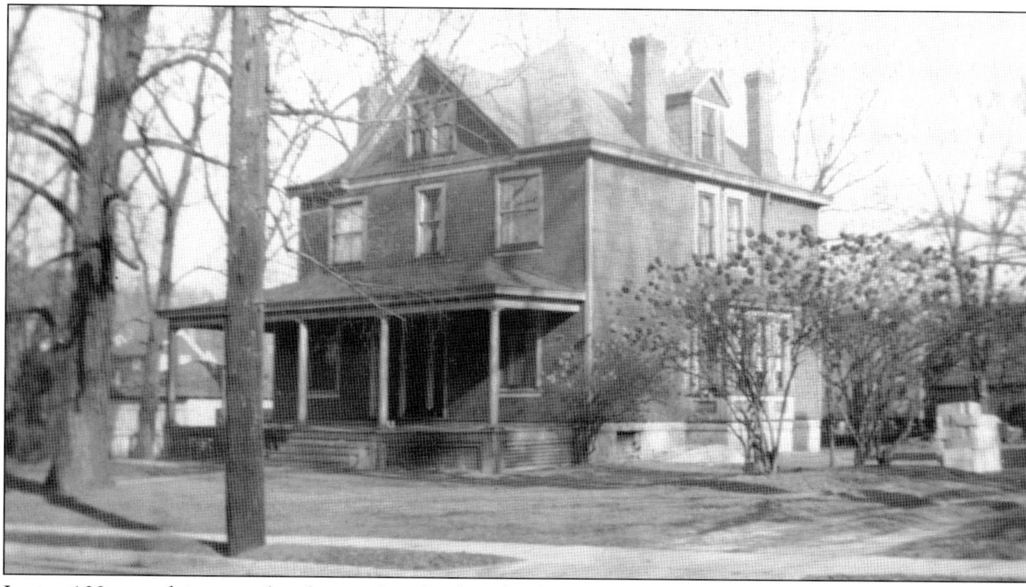

In its 102-year history, this home has had only three owners. The current owner dreamed of living here as a child, made his wish known, and proved dreams can come true. This Victorian home retains its exterior charm, however much of its interior design was lost. Converted back from two apartments to a single family home in 1989, the only original items salvageable in the interior were leaded glass panes above the front two windows, the mantle in the living room of the home, and a stained-glass window from the staircase landing. Original log beams in the basement had to be replaced with modern steel ones, pocket doors were replaced because of missing tracks, and a third floor chimney collapsed into the basement. Often such sad events occur when old homes are not properly cared for. The large wraparound porch still serves as a reminder of slower days and is the perfect place to laze around on a summer afternoon. (Above, courtesy of Claire Rex.)

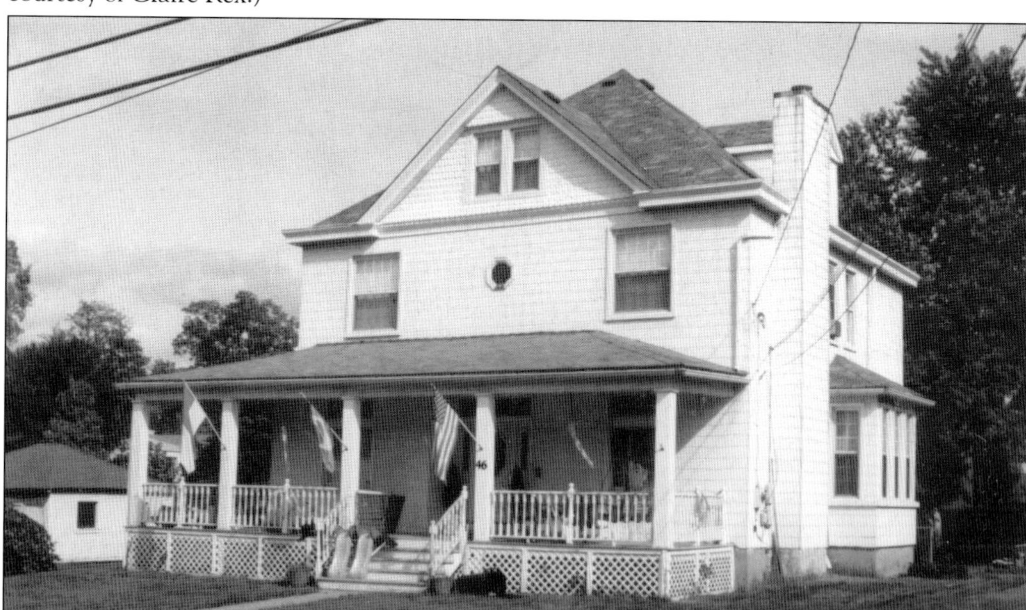

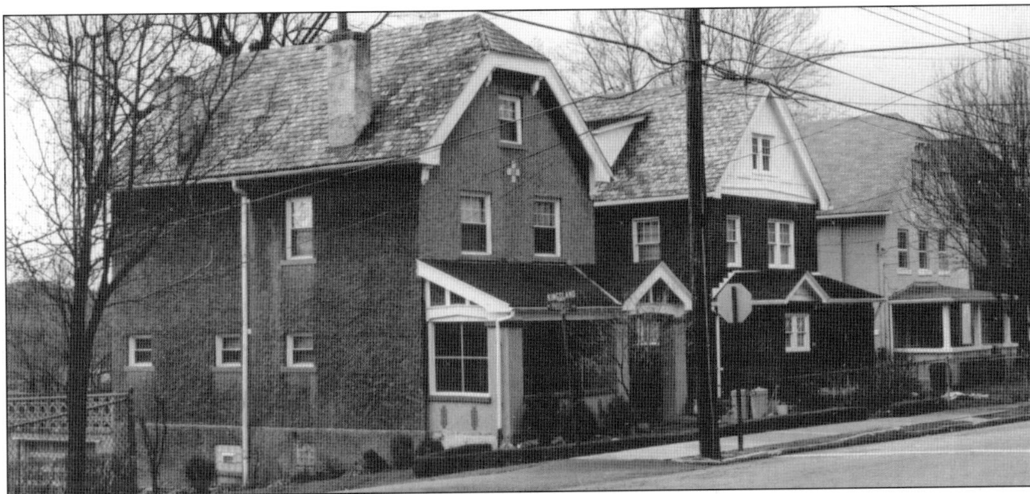

This quintuplet of homes, built about 1910, is quite unique in the fact that they contain no wood framing. They are internally constructed of Natko tile, a type of fired ceramic block–type material, each block being approximately two feet long and eight inches wide. This material was created for the construction of one-story commercial buildings, such as stables. An episode of "This Old House" showed a one-story Florida home constructed of Natko that had withstood Hurricane Andrew. In framing the homes, a wall of tile was laid, as air space allowed, then another line of tile. The exterior of these homes are covered in brick, stucco, or a combination of the two. To add electrical or plumbing lines can be a nightmare, the fired tile is extremely strong and resists intrusion. On the benefit side, termites are not even a consideration.

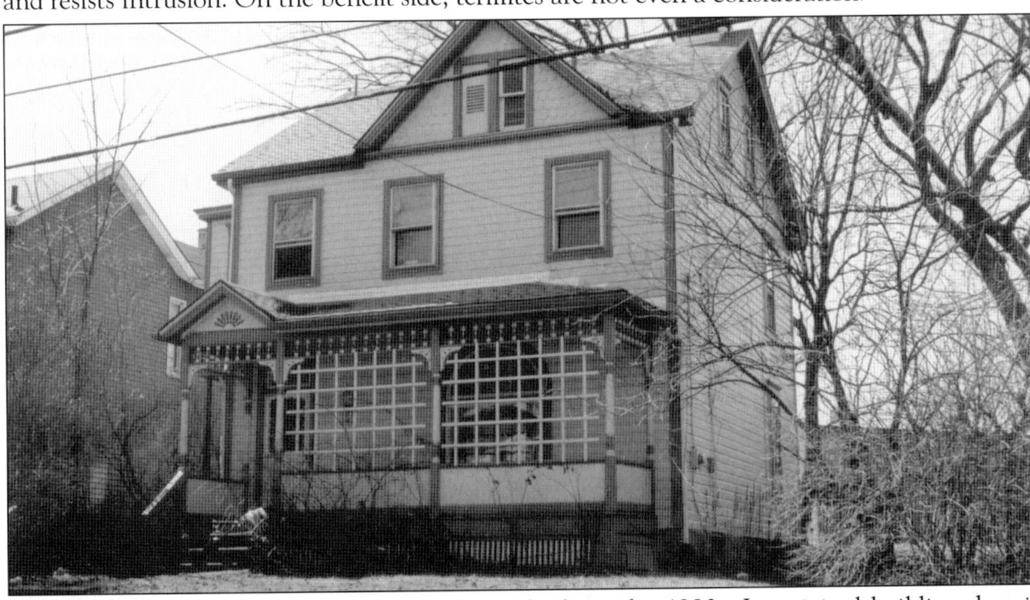

This house is typical of a working-class home built in the 1880s. Its original building date is unknown but the owners found a letter during interior renovations dated 1888. The clapboard siding and decorative exterior woodwork are original to the home. However, like many old homes, the owners spent months hand-making missing porch spindles and pieces of porch fretwork to get an identical match. During the renovation of a small back room, old gas pipes were found; longtime former owners solved the mystery. A summer kitchen once existed there, built to avoid heating the house during the hot summer.

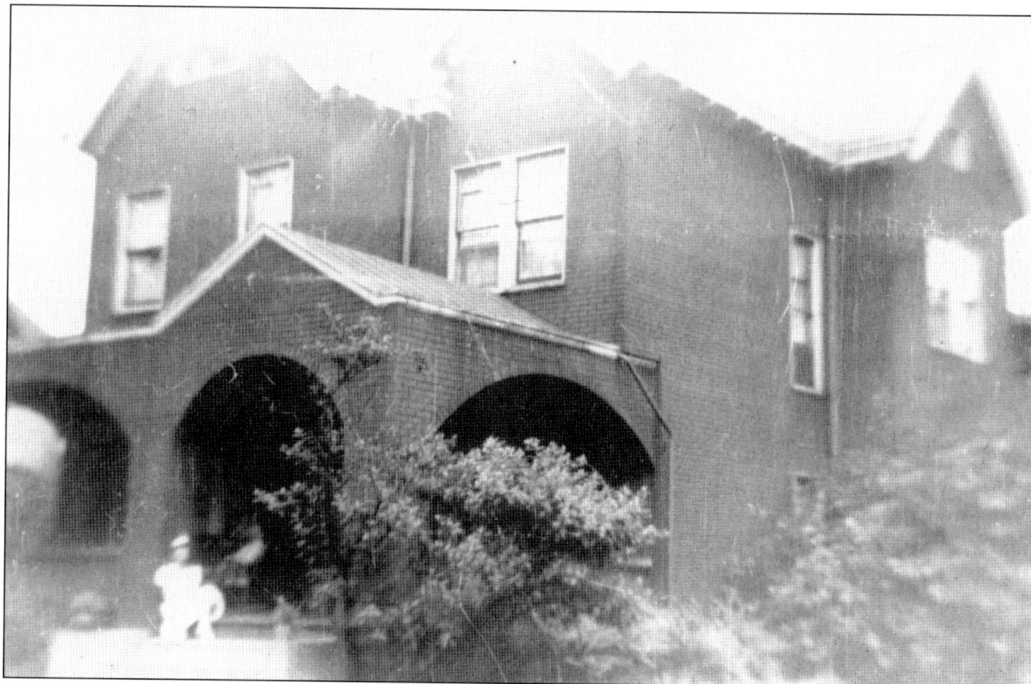

This home, at 112 West Prospect Avenue, originally belonged to Judge Swearingen. It had a stuccoed exterior but in later years the house was covered in red shingles. The large porch in the front was unusual with its large curved archways. This house was demolished in the 1970s in order for two apartment buildings to be built.

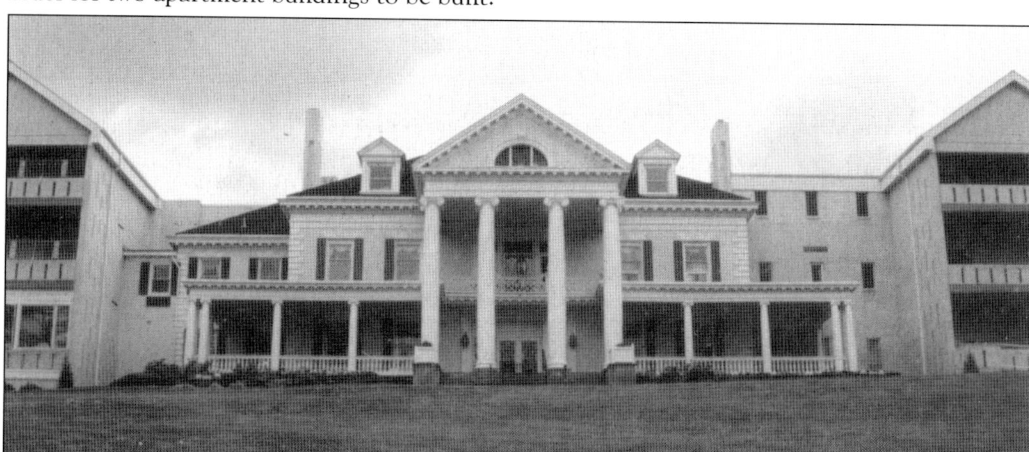

John M. Yohe, an early resident of Ingram, supervised the construction of the stately residence of George M. Von Bonnhorst. Von Bonnhorst had this mansion built for his fiancée who unfortunately passed away before the wedding. When, in the late 1890s, the residents of Ingram decided to incorporate their community as a borough. Von Bonnhorst, a political czar of the region, defeated the measure. When the petition was again submitted to the courts, Von Bonnhorst's property was left outside the proposed property limits. The mansion eventually became the Pittsburgh Home for Babies and is currently the Allegheny Valley School, Patricia Hillman Miller Campus. The center section of the home with the tall pillars and side porches was the original mansion. The Von Bonnhorsts were famous for the peacocks that lived on their property and were often admired strutting on the front lawn.

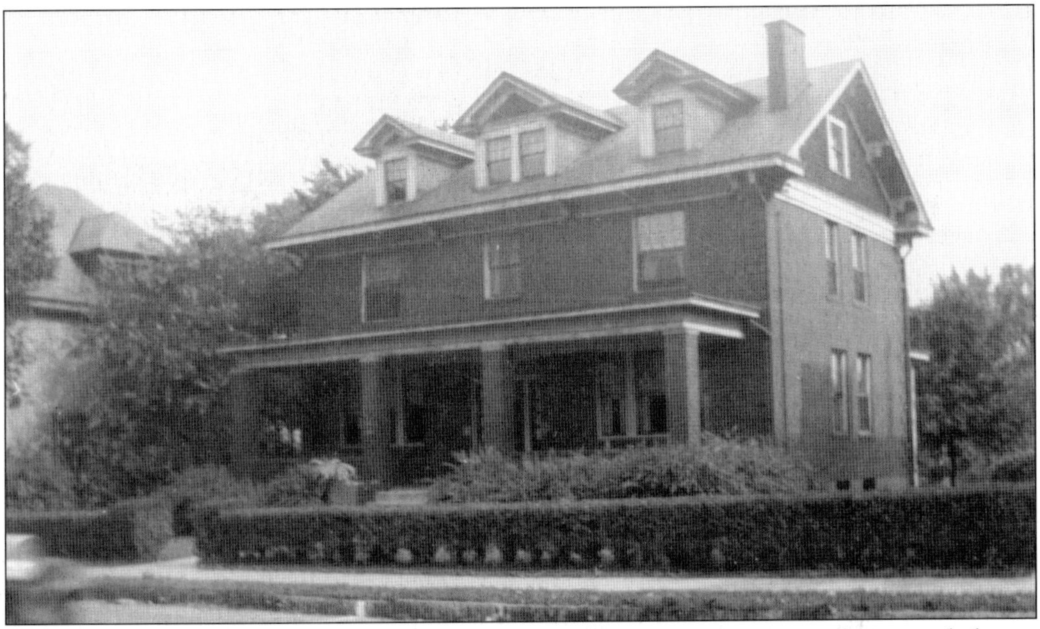

This house at 163 Ingram Avenue was built by John Rex in 1924. It is a craftsman-style house designed after a house on Cochran Road in Mount Lebanon. The Rex family lost it in taxes in the Depression era right before World War II. Not much has changed over the years except the landscaping. A new chimney was added on the opposite end of the house, and the old one was removed. (Courtesy of Claire Rex.)

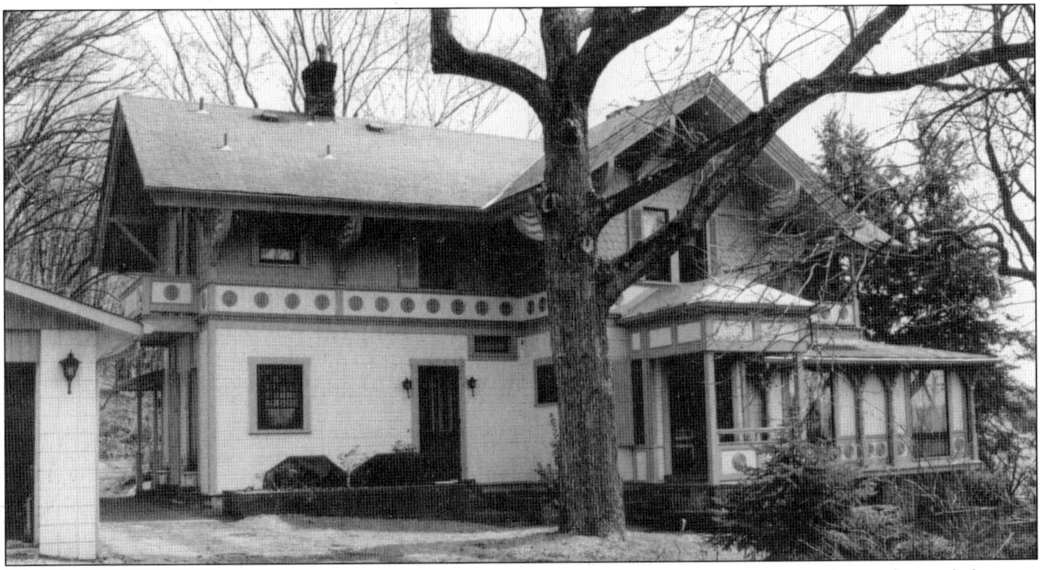

Charm and tranquility best describe this beautifully maintained, cruciform-shaped home. Built in 1865, this two story Victorian farmhouse reflects the Gothic style of architecture that was popular in Europe during the 13th through 15th centuries. Characteristics such as ribbed vaulting and pointed arches adorn this treasure as do functioning shutters on the second story windows. In 1967, a large porch was enclosed to create a functional room for year-round pleasure. Likewise, an expanded kitchen and second-floor bath compliment the original structure. During the spring and summer months, flowers provide a blaze of color to the surrounding landscape.

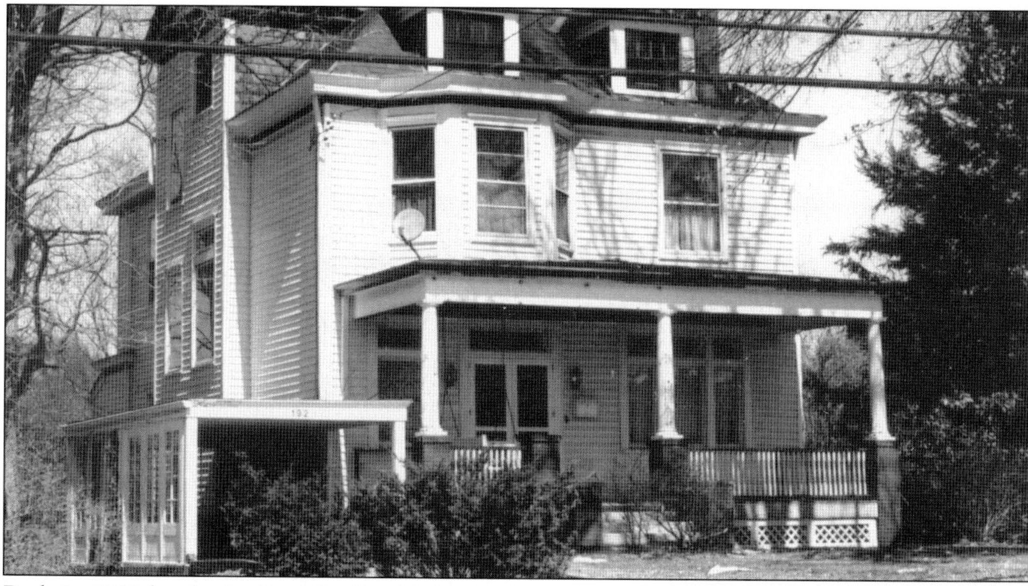

Built in 1902 by the McIlroy family, this home was occupied by their daughter until her death in 1976. She expressed a desire that it not be broken into apartments, but that it continue on as a single family home. This is a beautifully preserved home of its era. The entryway is large, and light from the surrounding leaded windows adds special sparkle. Each room contains fireplaces with original copper hoods and distinct tile. Interestingly, wallpaper samples from the homes entire life were found layered upon each other when the resident began to remodel. The only change to the home has been the combination of the kitchen and a small parlor into a larger, more practical kitchen.

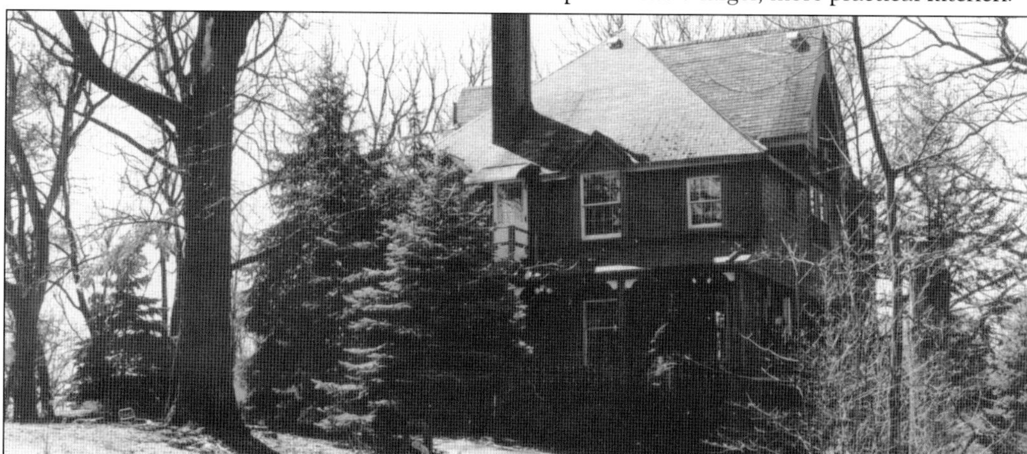

The deed says this home was built in 1887, but reliable neighbors say the date is 1879. No matter, this house is a fine example of the Queen Anne style of architecture. Legend has it that many parties and weddings were held on its grounds, with peacocks proudly strutting among the guests. Around World War I, the home became the property of a German immigrant, Mrs. Van Felt, who added the kennels to the property to house her prize German shepherd. In use until the mid-1990s, a later owner raised champion Doberman pinschers, one of whom appeared in the opening of the Jerry Lewis movie *The Bellhop*! The entryway boasts 26-foot-high ceilings, with a music room and parlor just off the entrance. A multileveled staircase leads to five bedrooms; the most unique one is located in the turret and contains curved seating. Each bedroom even contained a direct communication line to the butler's pantry.

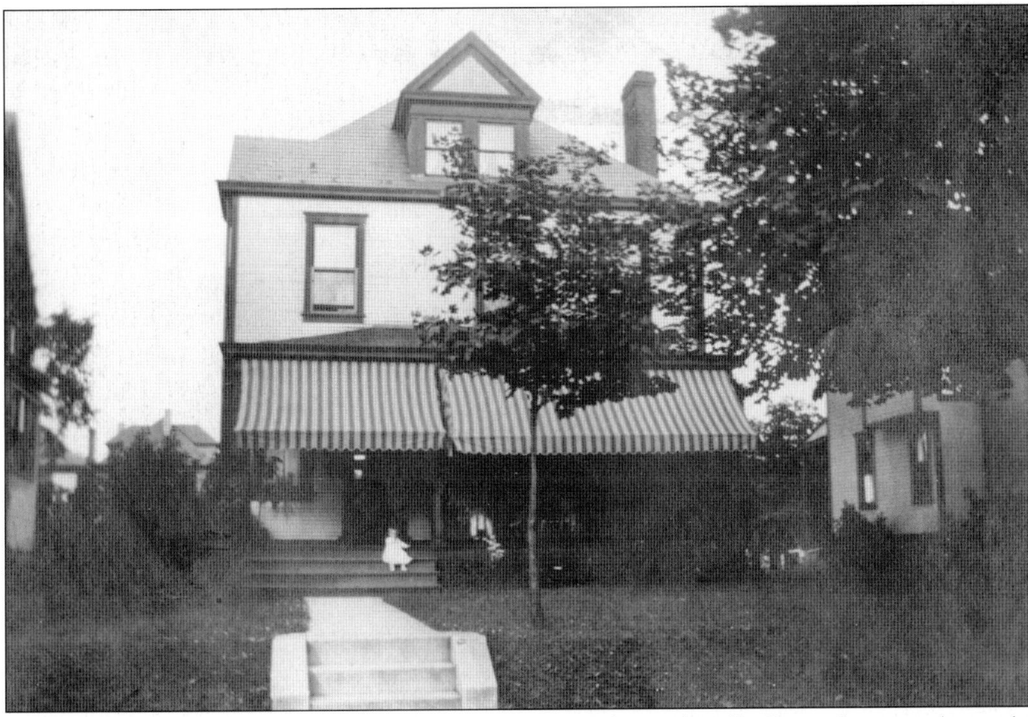

This house, with the striped awning, was the home of John and Nellie Rex, who moved into the house after their marriage in 1899. They remained in the home, where their children were born, until they built a new house on Ingram Avenue in 1924. A new porch was later built onto the house, replacing the awnings with a permanent roof.

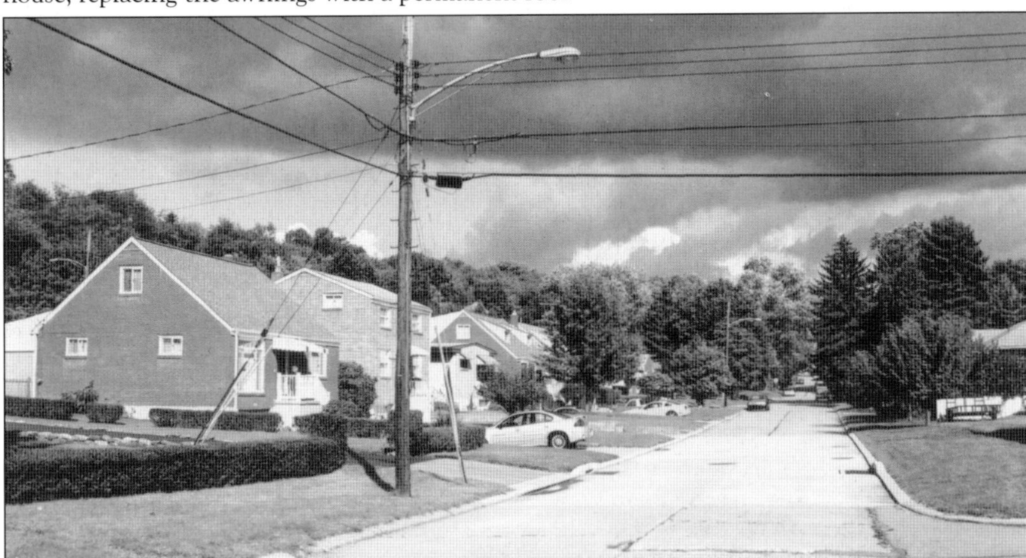

When the GIs returned home following World War II, the main objective was to secure a job, marry, start a family, and settle into a new home. This area, which came to be known as New Ingram, was perfectly suited for achieving the American dream. During the early 1950s, new homes were constructed and modern two-lane concrete streets were laid out. Unlike most of the borough, New Ingram became known as a thoroughly modern, postwar community.

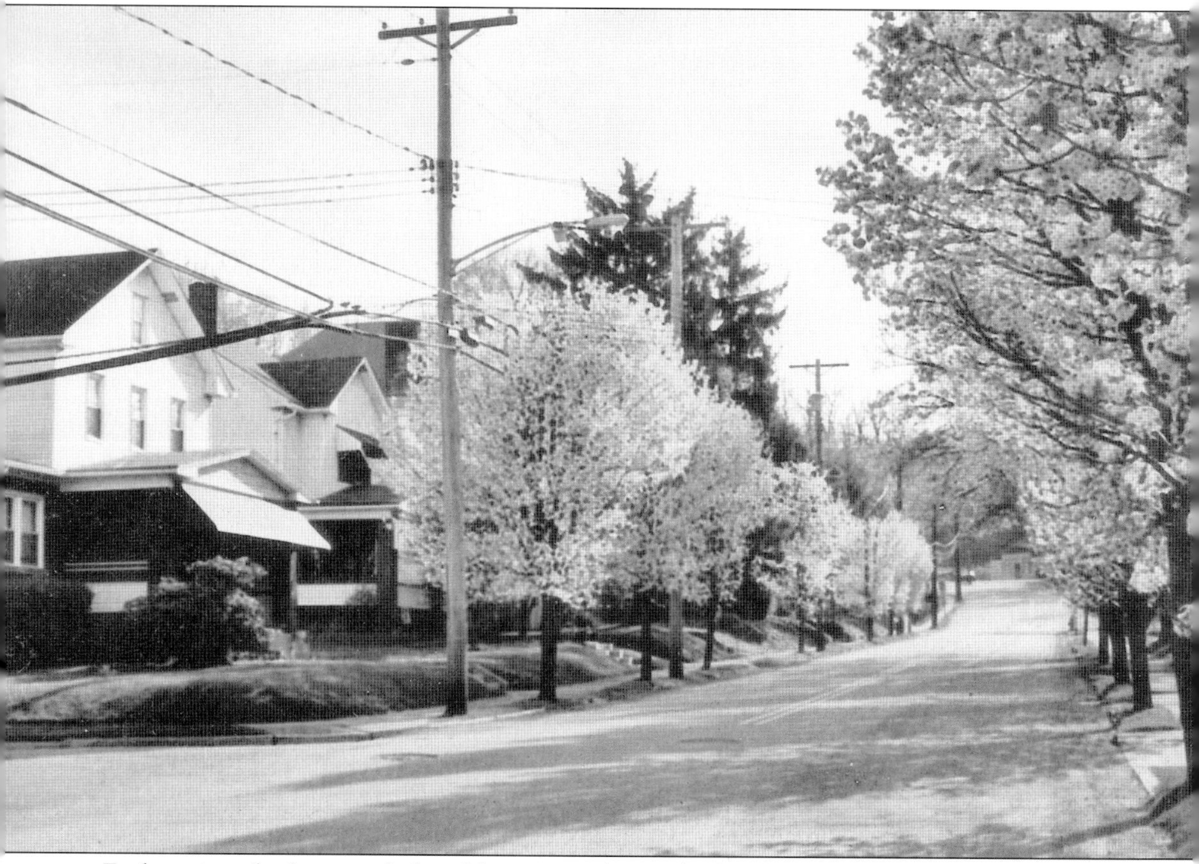

Each spring, the beauty of white blossoms, enhance both sides of Ingram Avenue for borough residents and motorists alike. This recent photograph looking east on the avenue reveals the beautiful Chanticleer Callery pear trees that were planted by the Ingram Garden Club in conjunction with the Public Works Department, in 1992. The Ingram Avenue residents maintain these trees.

Four

CHURCHES AND SCHOOLS

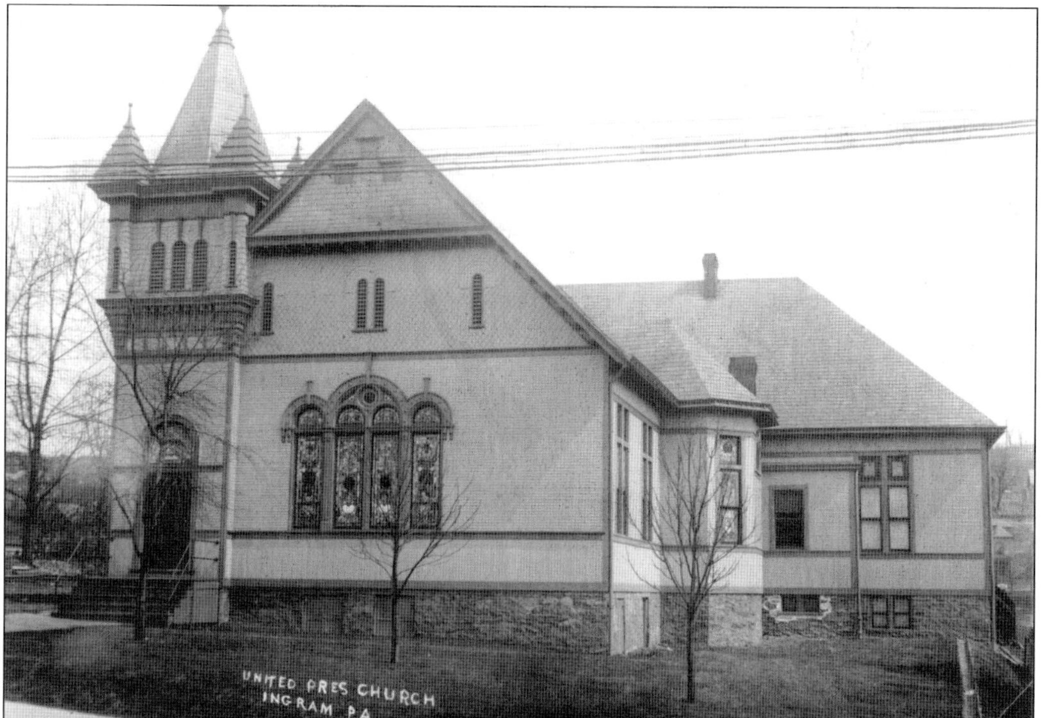

In February 1888, a group of 23 people who had been meeting in the Old Mission Chapel purchased ground on the corner of West Prospect Avenue and Thorndale Streets. The United Presbyterian Church of Ingram was granted a charter on May 19, 1888. In September 1888, ground was broken for the original church building. In spite of the catastrophic collapse of the framework due to a January 9, 1889, windstorm, the church was completed and dedicated on June 9, 1889. In 1895, and again in 1916, additions to the original structure were added. Due to the growth of the congregation, it was decided that the building be razed and a new church built on the same site. This photograph shows the church in its heyday, in the early 1900s.

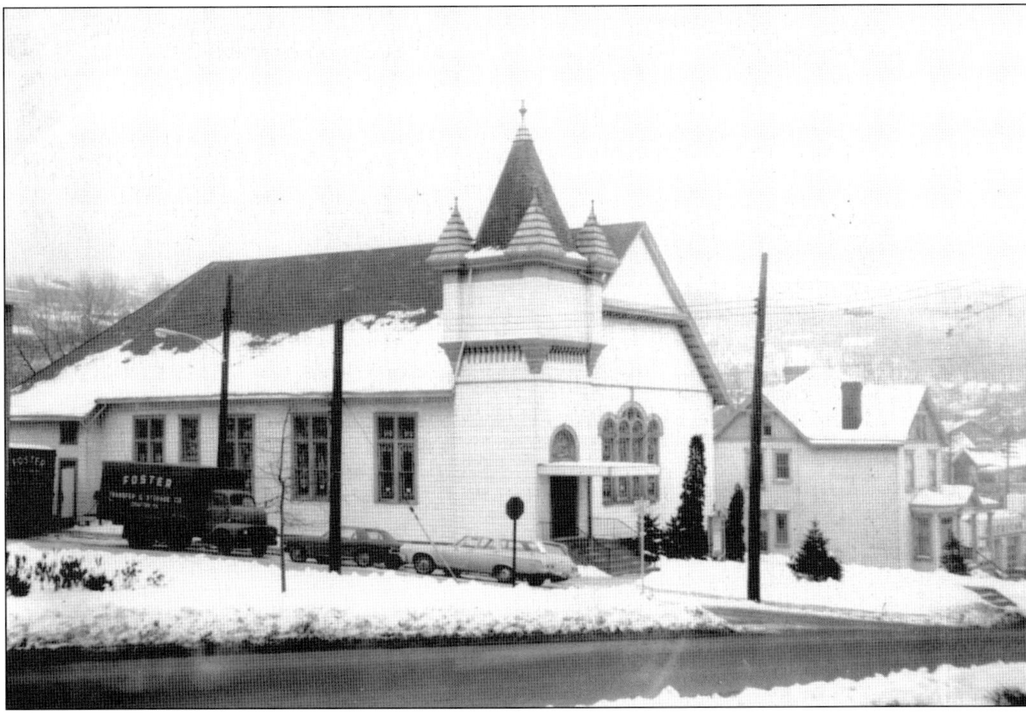

This is how the former United Presbyterian Church of Ingram looked when the last service was held on January 23, 1966. It shows some minor additions but more importantly, the manse that was torn down for the development of the new church building. The new building was just another step in the modernization of Ingram, as the borough building (just out of the picture to the left) had been in place for nine years and the American gas station, at the far right next to the house, had taken the place of the Rex Building. (Courtesy of John Sacco.)

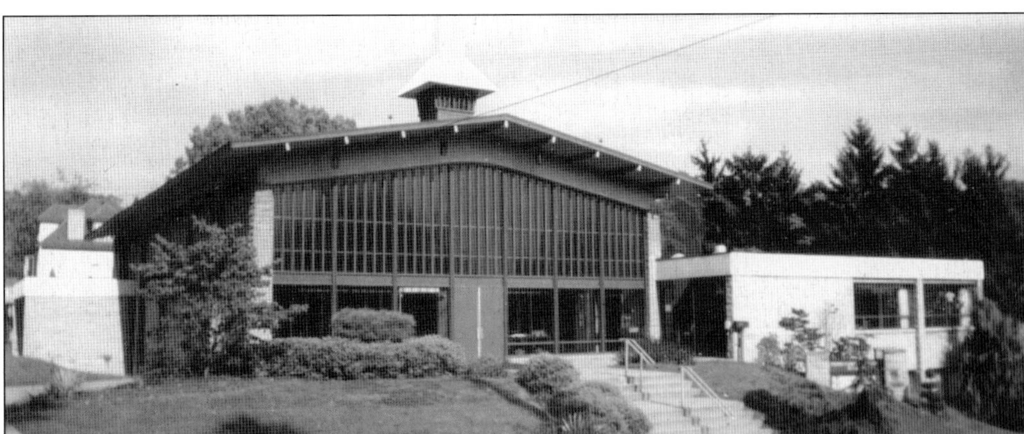

The present United Presbyterian Church represents the merging of two congregations—the Ingram First Presbyterian and the United Presbyterian Churches in 1971. The present church building held its first service on Christmas Eve, 1966, after the original deteriorating building was demolished in January 1966. The church has remained active in the community providing both religious and social programs for the area.

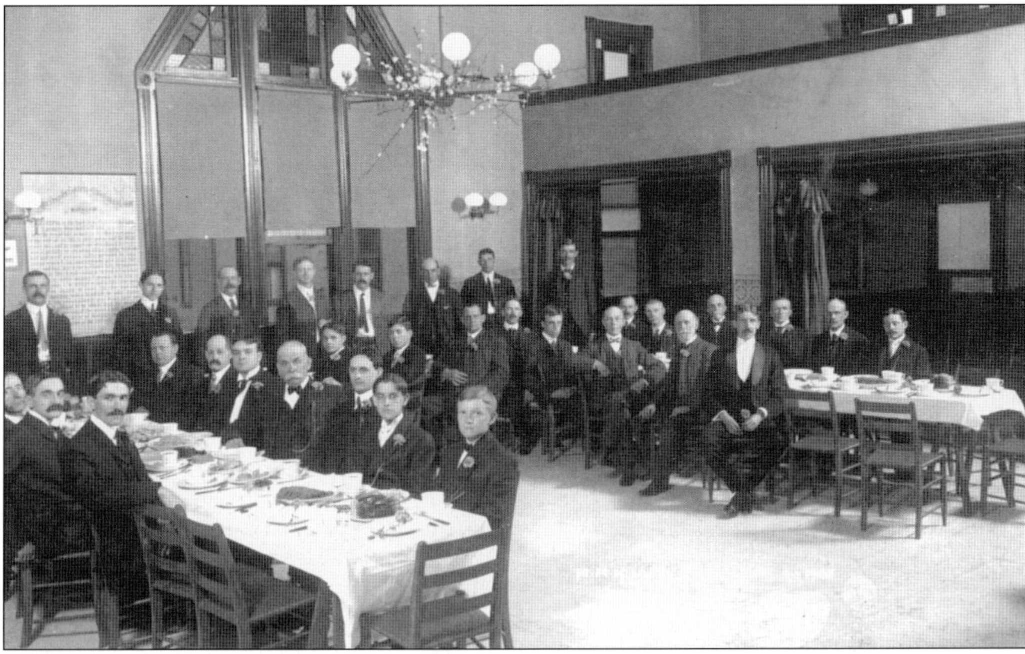

The churches were the center of social life in Ingram at the beginning of the 20th century. Men's clubs were common forms of social interaction before the days of television and major league sports. Pictured here is a banquet for the Men's Association of the United Presbyterian Church. The picture was taken on May 4, 1905.

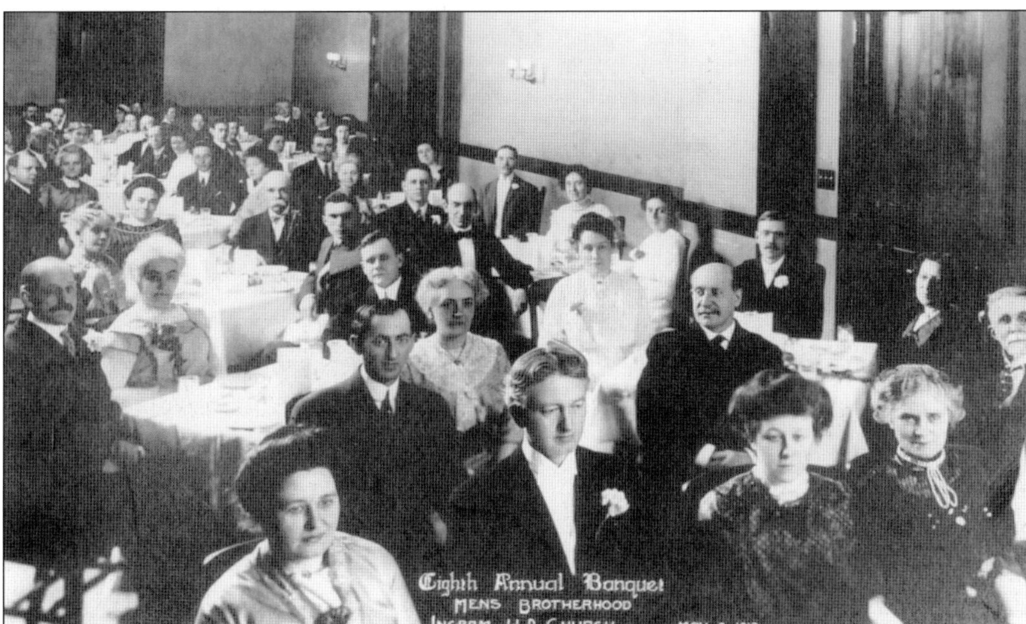

Another social group that was started in the early 1900s was the Men's Brotherhood. This is a photograph of the eighth annual banquet of the Men's Brotherhood held in the Ingram United Presbyterian Church on May 2, 1912. Seated in the front row of the group, from left to right, are Dr. and Mrs. Harry Welsh, Gertrude Welsh, and Valerie Welsh.

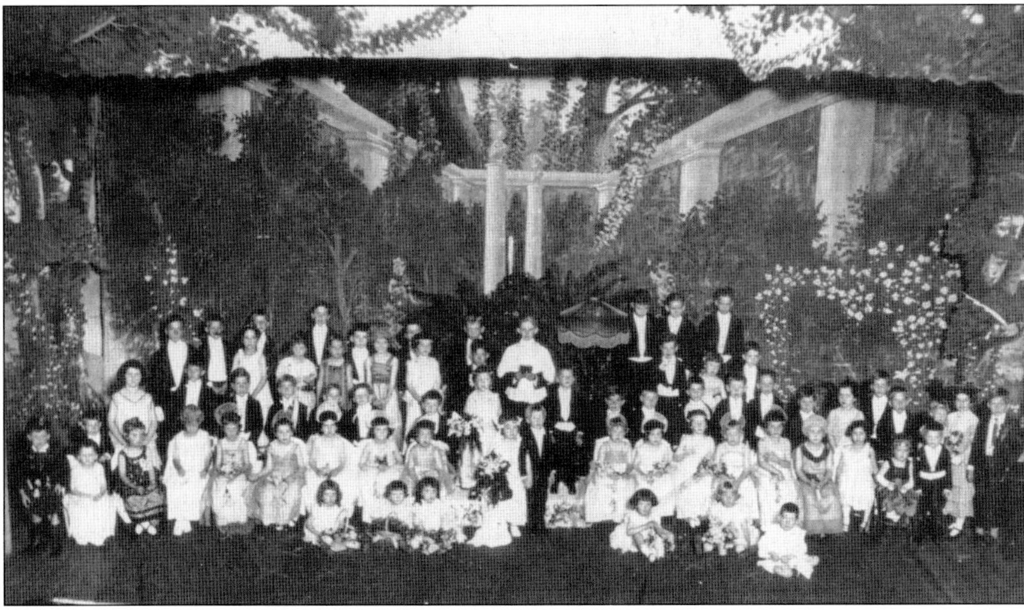

Tom Thumb weddings were once a popular program in the Ingram churches. These programs involved all of the children from toddlers through fifth or sixth grades. Each child took part in the wedding ceremony and costumes were assembled. Wedding guests portrayed famous people of the times and were each announced before preceded down the aisle. The bridal party was announced, wedding music sung, and "I dos" were exchanged. It was quite the celebratory event of the day. The elaborate scenery was borrowed from professional Pittsburgh theater companies.

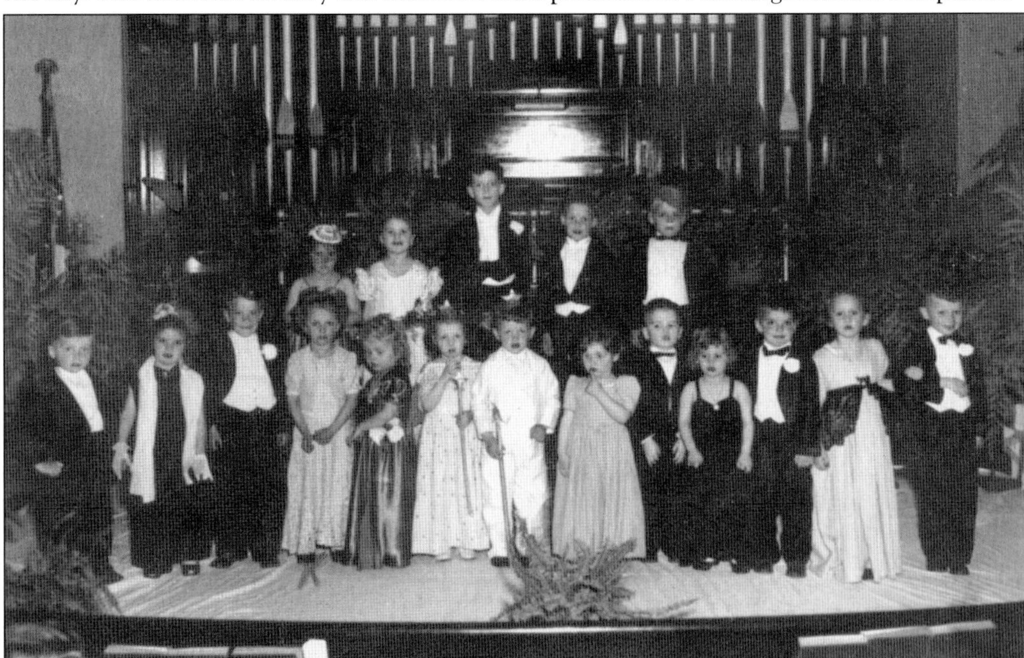

In most cases, the church organists and members of the choir were also included in the Tom Thumb weddings and musical numbers were introduced throughout the wedding ceremony. Seen here is a wedding held in the United Presbyterian Church in 1958.

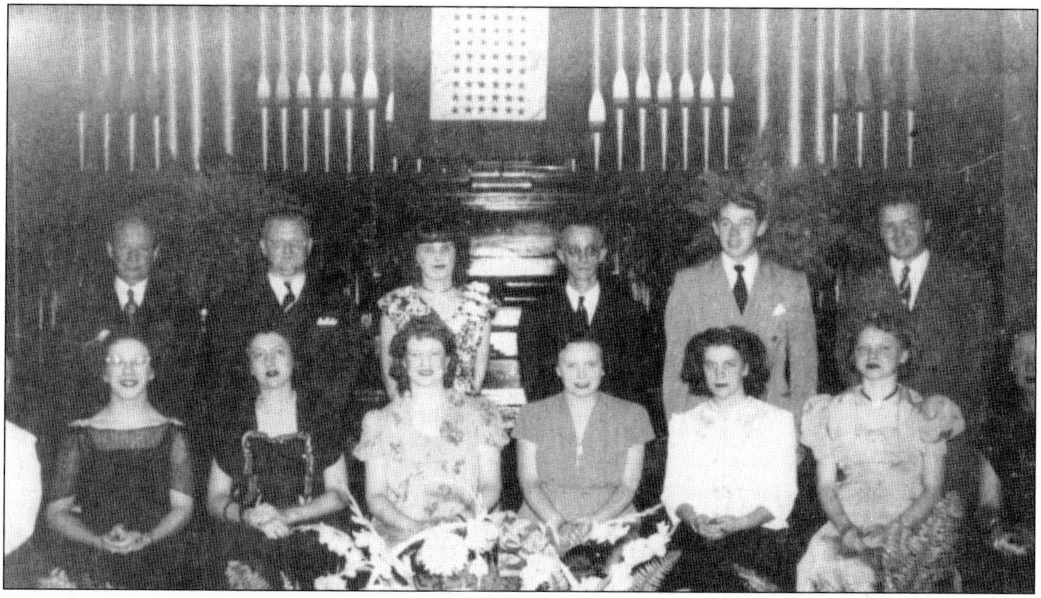

This picture, taken in the late 1940s, shows the Ingram United Presbyterian Church Choir sitting in front of the church's organ and its magnificent set of pipes. The members are, from left to right, (first row) Mary Jane Curtis, Betty Wallace, Dorothy Alm, Jean Skiles, Jean English, and Ruth Hurst; (second row) Ray Long, Wilmer Lucas, Ruth Evans, Lloyd English, Dave Nelson, and Jim Hawtree.

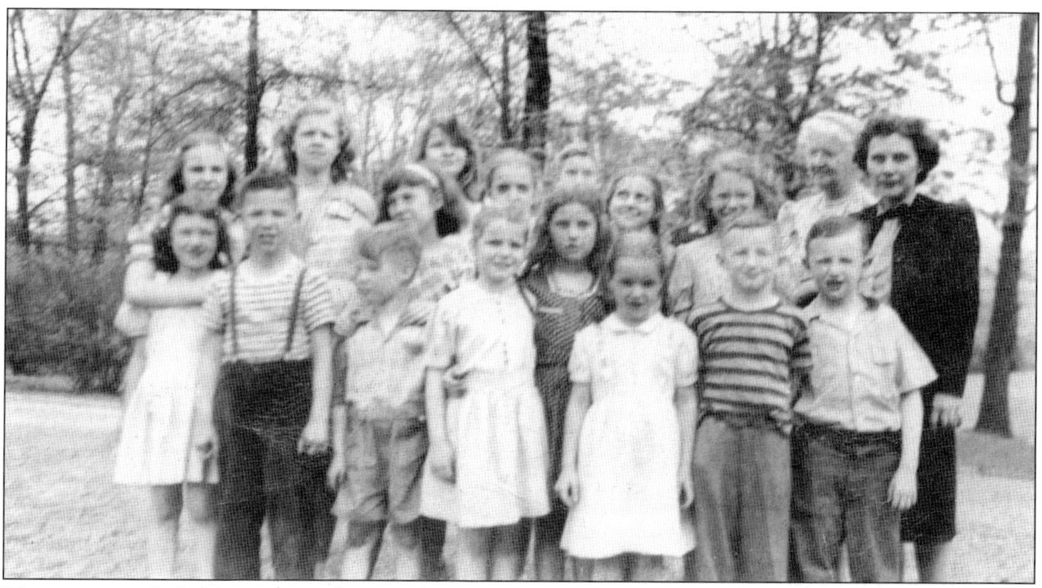

This group of children is made up of members of the Junior Missionary Society. Each year, Mrs. Edward Stotz, the leader of the group, entertained them at her home on West Prospect Avenue. She was assisted by Margaret Upstill, who was a teacher at Ingram elementary school. A favorite project was raising money and contributing to the Japanese interred in this country.

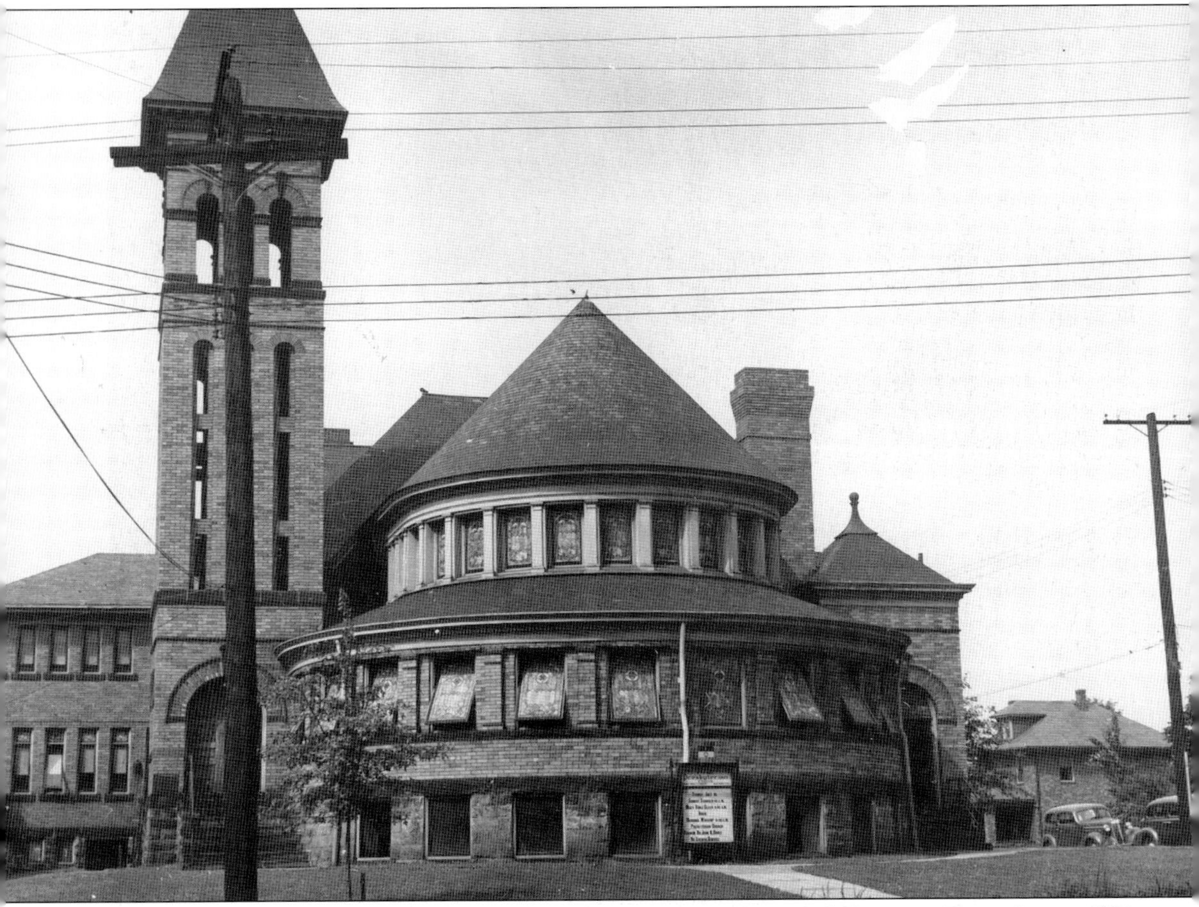

A Sabbath school was organized from the Christian Association of Chartiers Township in 1891, as chapter members of a new church. On January 8, 1892, the name of the church was chosen as First Presbyterian Church of Ingram, and by 1899 ground was broken for a new building on West Prospect Avenue. The first services were held and the church was dedicated on June 24, 1900. This shows the church as it looked in the 1930s, and it remains much the same today. The last service was held in 1970, after that the two Ingram Presbyterian churches united. The building was purchased in 1975 by the Guyasuta Lodge of the Free and Accepted Masons, who then upgraded and remodeled the building, adding seats purchased from the demolition of Pittsburgh's Nixon Theater for only $1 per chair. The building is registered with the Pittsburgh History and Landmarks Foundation.

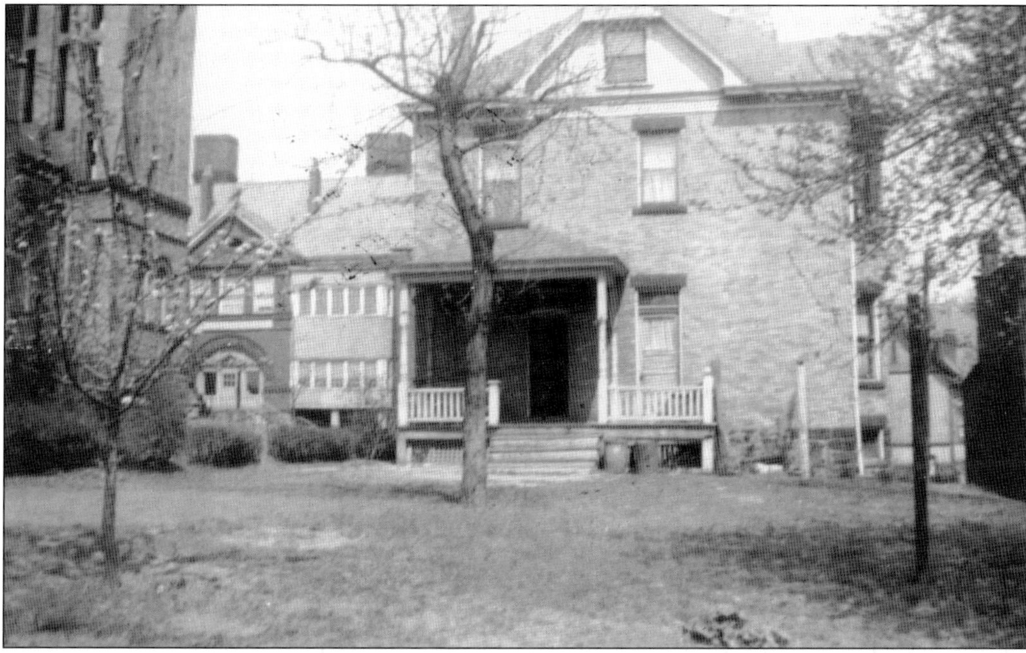

Originally used as the manse for the First Presbyterian Church, this building, at 31 West Prospect Avenue, is now a private residence. Ruth Craig was a tenant for a time before it was purchased by Joseph Sacco Jr. Ingram's Scully school can be seen between the two buildings. Showing the connection between church and state was very close in this town.

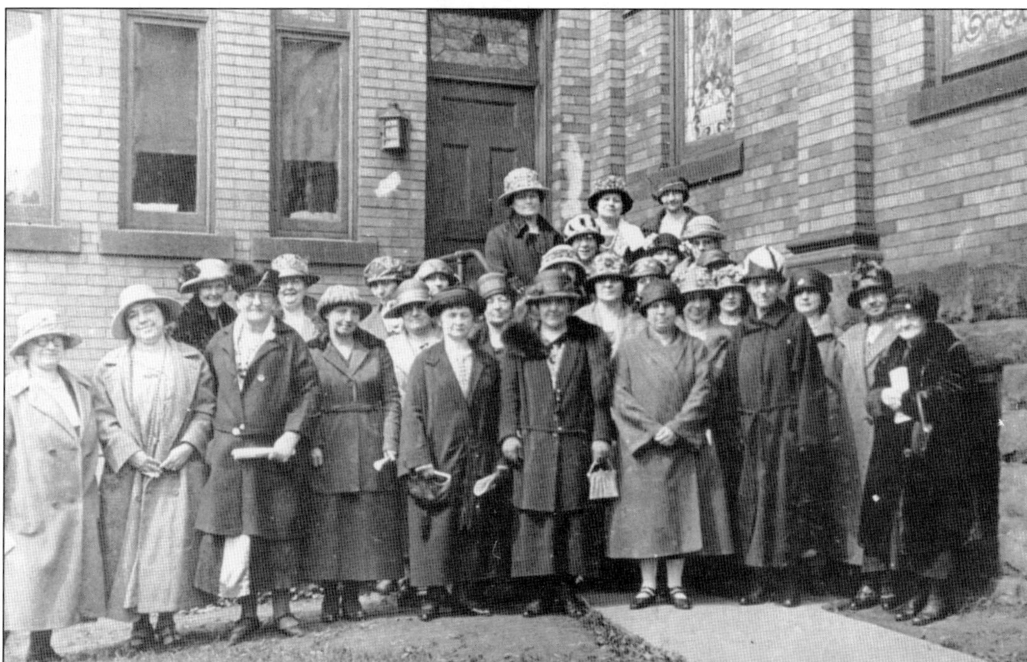

Women also enjoyed the social atmosphere of church groups. Pictured here is a women's group in front of the First Presbyterian Church. As was the fashion of the 1920s, no one attended Sunday services without a hat.

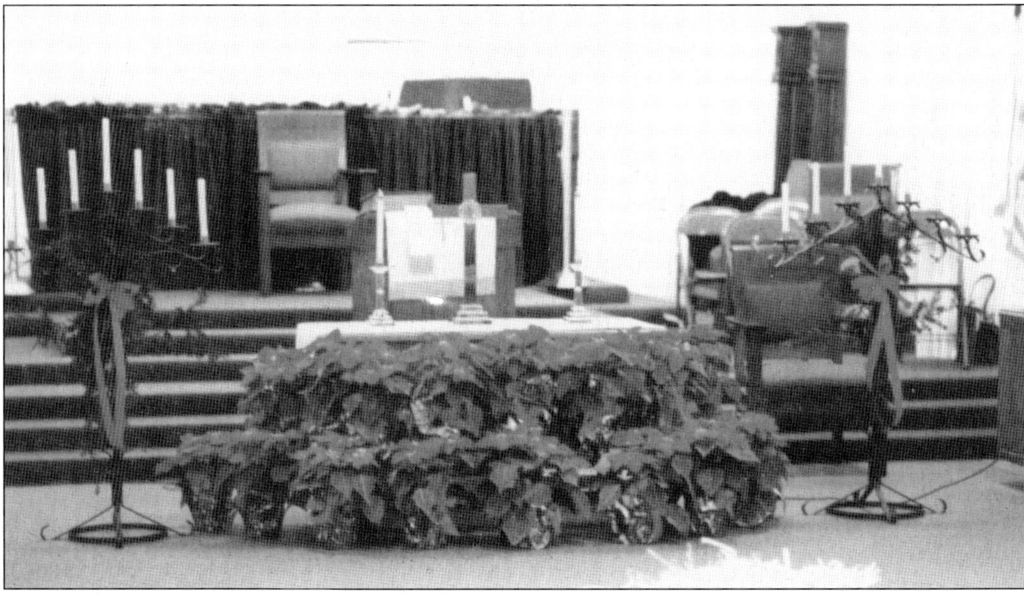

The Ingram Community Church was a non-denominational worshipping group that met in the Ingram Masonic Hall (the former First Presbyterian church). The first gathering of this independent body was on June 18, 1978. It was started as the Temporary Sunday Association, then the Sunday Association, and finally incorporated as the Ingram Community Church in March 1979. The church dissolved in 1990. This Christmas picture shows the altar decorated with traditional poinsettias.

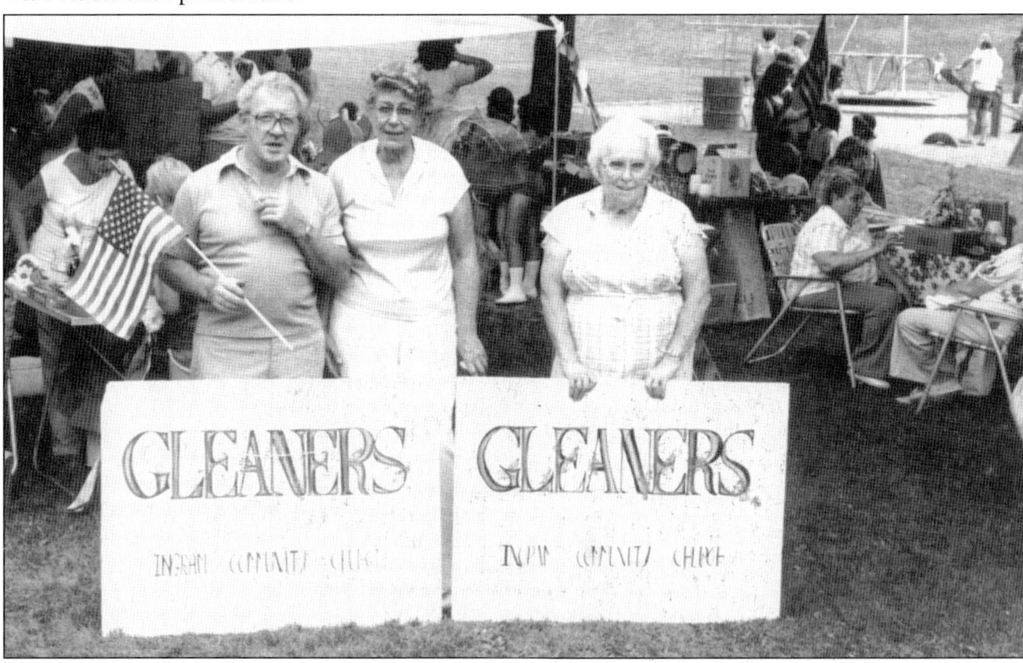

Gleaners was a name taken from the Book of Ruth in the Old Testament and used by the woman's organization of Ingram Community Church. They met for fellowship as well as work projects. Pictured here are members of the Gleaners with helper Ray Nolte taking part in the 1982 Ingram Days celebration.

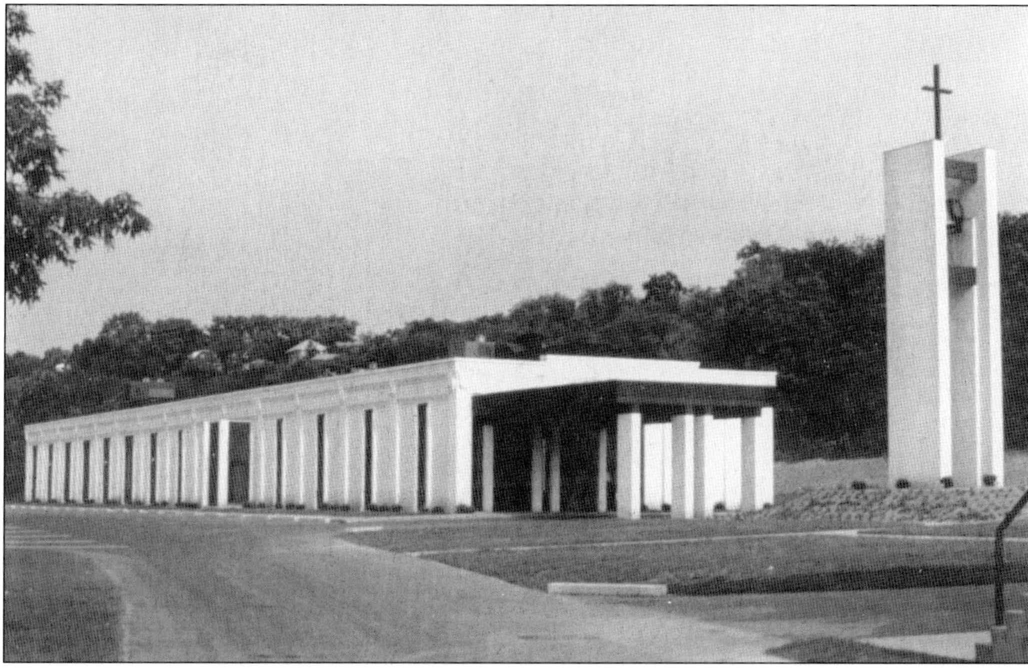

The soaring bell tower in the foreground, which can be heard throughout the borough, makes a great statement as it reaches toward the heavens. Behind the tower is the entrance to Ascension Church. Pictured below is the renovated office building, formally belonging to the Pittsburgh Railways Company, which now accommodates Sunday school classes and the parish office of Ascension Church. The architects who changed the dingy, red brick building into a bright modern one are Edward Harley, Robert Murray, and D. Donald McGervey.

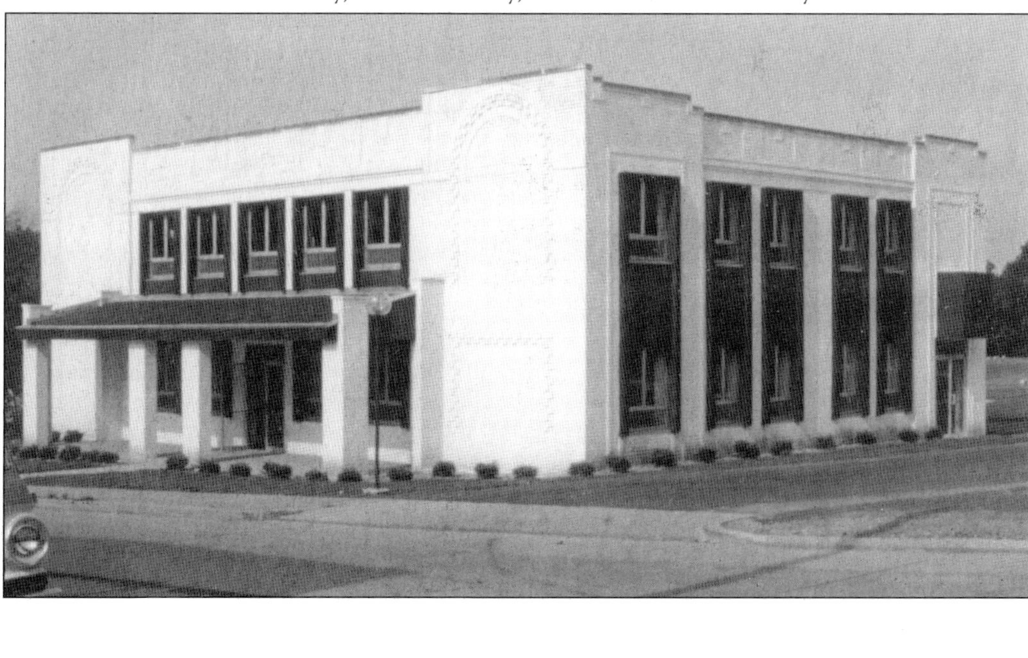

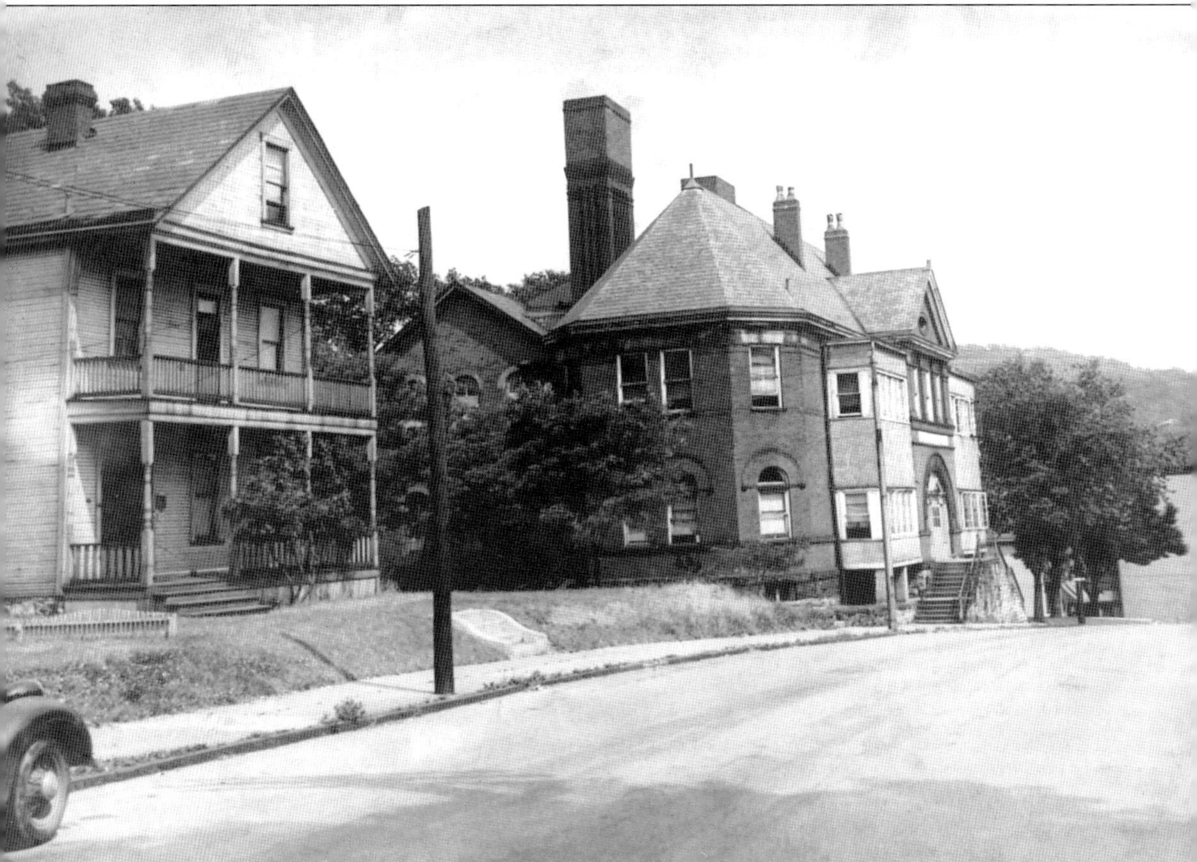

Ingram's first school was a one-room facility located in Steger Hall, which stood on the corner of Hodgson Avenue and Center Streets. Miss Ryan served as the first teacher, earning a salary of $25 per month. It was not until 1890 that the borough's first school building was erected at West Prospect Avenue and Thorndale Street. Originally the brick building had four classrooms but was enlarged to include eight classrooms with an office over the hallway. The building was named Scully Public School in honor of Mr. Scully, who generously donated the stone used in its construction. After the borough was incorporated in 1902, it was renamed Ingram Public School. The old schoolhouse faithfully served the community for 24 years. When the new Ingram Public School opened in 1914, Scully Public School was converted into apartments. It was razed in 1956 for construction of the new Ingram Borough Building. This 1930s view, looking down West Prospect Avenue, shows Scully Public School as an apartment building. Just beyond the school are the former Ingram United Presbyterian Church (hidden behind the trees) and the Rex Building.

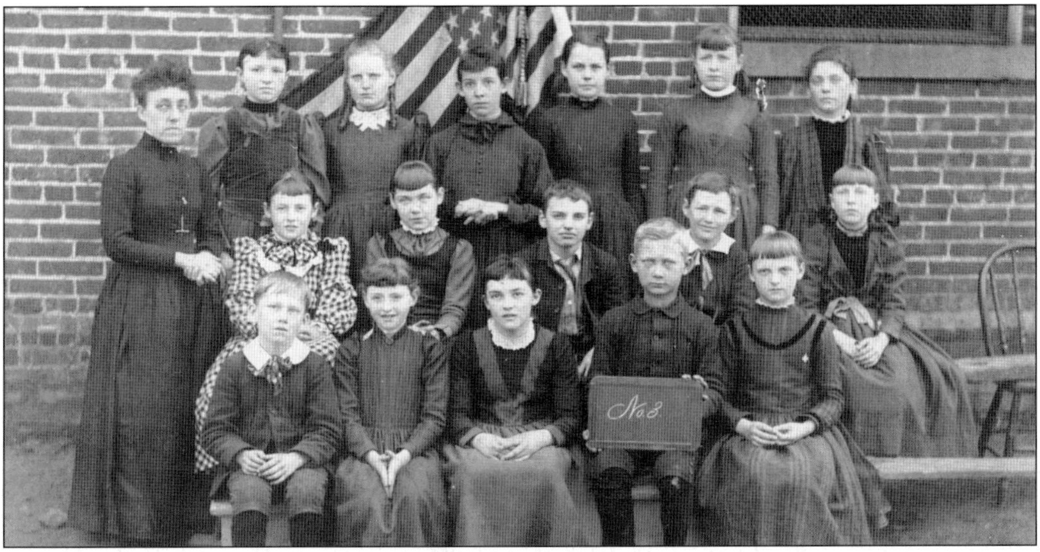

The first class in the Scully school building included several grades. The pupils in the class include, from left to right, (first row) Fred Parsons, Eleanor Rex, Margaret Phillips, George Benedict, and Edith Ohl; (second row) Florence Petrie, Mary McCoy, John Rex, Lewis McCoy, and Edna Wright; (third row) Bertha Boyle, Bertha Forrest, Ella Cunningham, Carrie Gilmore, Edna Dilworth, and Bella Irwin. The teacher is Miss Shaw. The boys and girls looked very somber. Most little boys wore knickers and knee socks with high laced shoes. Bangs were very popular with the girls, along with a lot of braids and an occasional long curl.

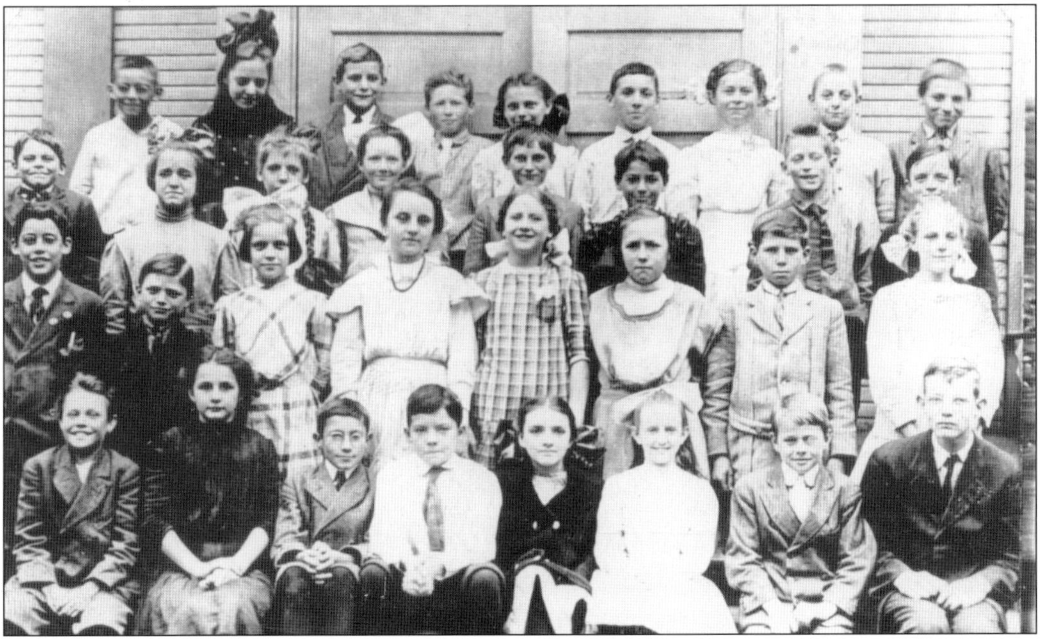

This group of students gathered in front of Scully Public School in 1905. This was a one-room school for grades one through six. The school was later modified into apartments and eventually torn down. On this site, the Ingram Borough Building was erected in 1957. The few students identified in this photograph are John Sacco in the fourth row on the right, Joseph Gensler in the same row fourth from right, and Calvin Steele Lucas in the first row on the right.

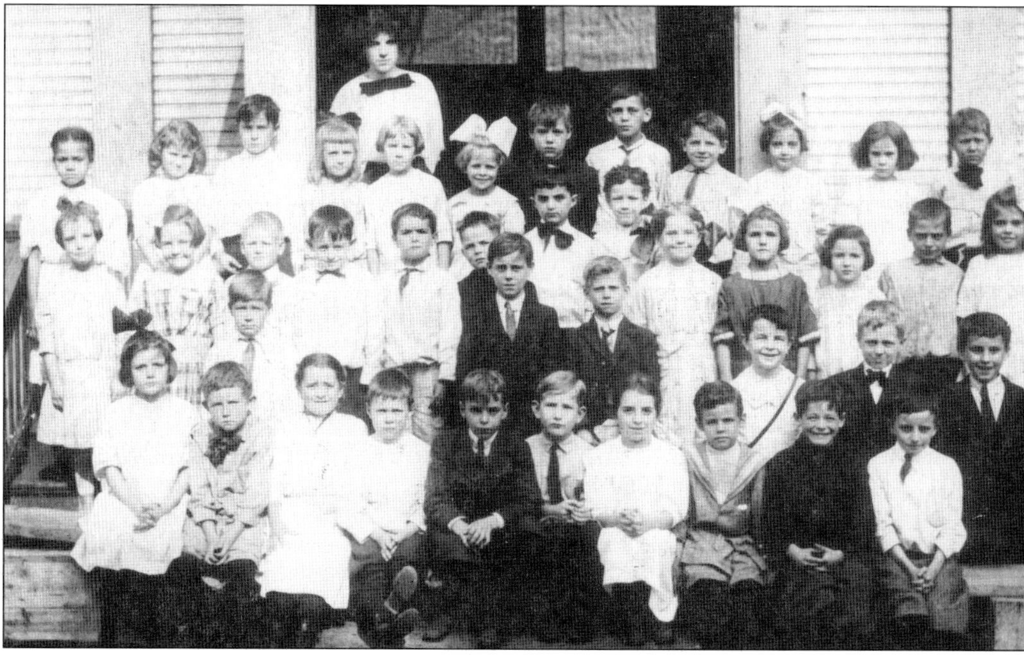

Scully Public School grew with the town of Ingram until 1914, when the new Ingram Public School opened. Pictured here is Ingram Public School's second-grade class in October 1913. They would be among the last students to graduate from this school.

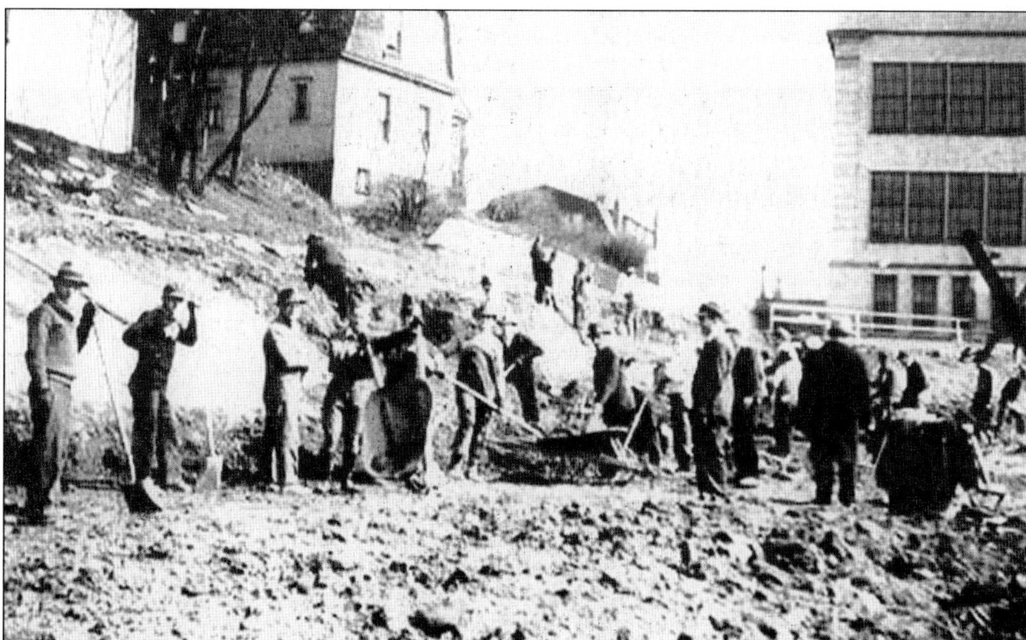

Here is the construction of the Ingram Public School playground. Note the hand labor. The original playground was a grass and dirt surface, later replaced by concrete and asphalt. Today's modern safety surface has play equipment provided by the Ingram PTA and painted designs by art students from Montour High School.

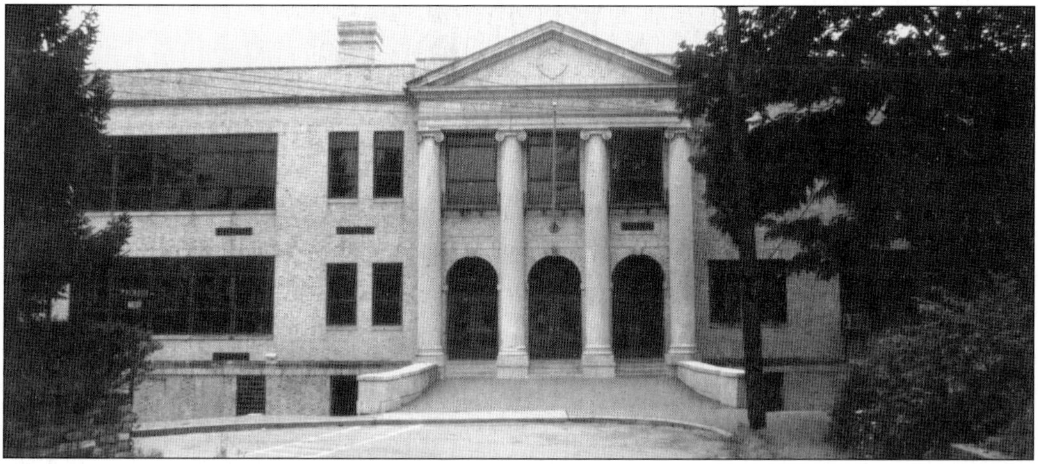

With much fanfare, the new Ingram Public School at Vancouver and Marcross Avenues opened its doors in 1914. While Dr. Melvin A. Steiner served as principal, grades 5 and 6 were departmentalized, and grades 7, 8, and 9 were incorporated into junior high. In 1925, a 10th grade was incorporated into the school's curriculum. Throughout the years, Ingram Public School has been enlarged to include a gymnasium in 1926, additional classrooms, and a kindergarten in 1930. After completing grade 10, students attended either Langley or Crafton High Schools for their junior or senior years. In 1961, Ingram Public School became part of the Montour School District and was reclassified as an elementary school. Playing an important role in the district, the renamed Ingram Elementary School underwent a major renovation, which included new windows and replacement of its old wooden floors. In 1988, the building received much publicity when it was awarded historical landmark status by the Pittsburgh History and Landmarks Foundation. Today Ingram Elementary School stands as a beacon of knowledge and development for tomorrow's leaders.

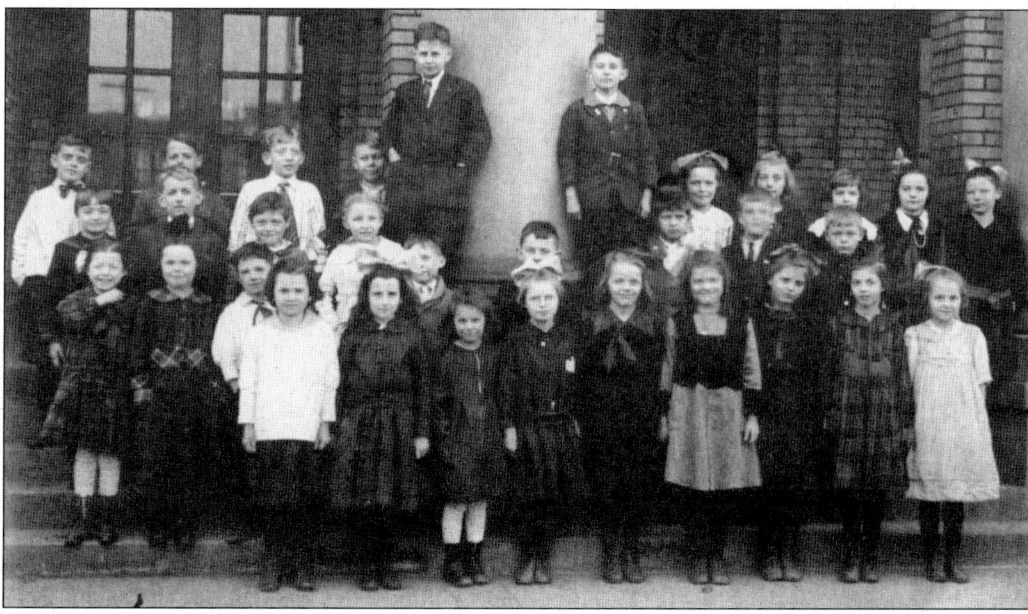

In this picture of students grouped in front of Ingram Public School in 1918, the girls are seen wearing the common-style jumpers or dresses with long stockings, usually dark. Hair styles varied with pig tails and long curls held by large bows, while boys wore long trousers or knickers.

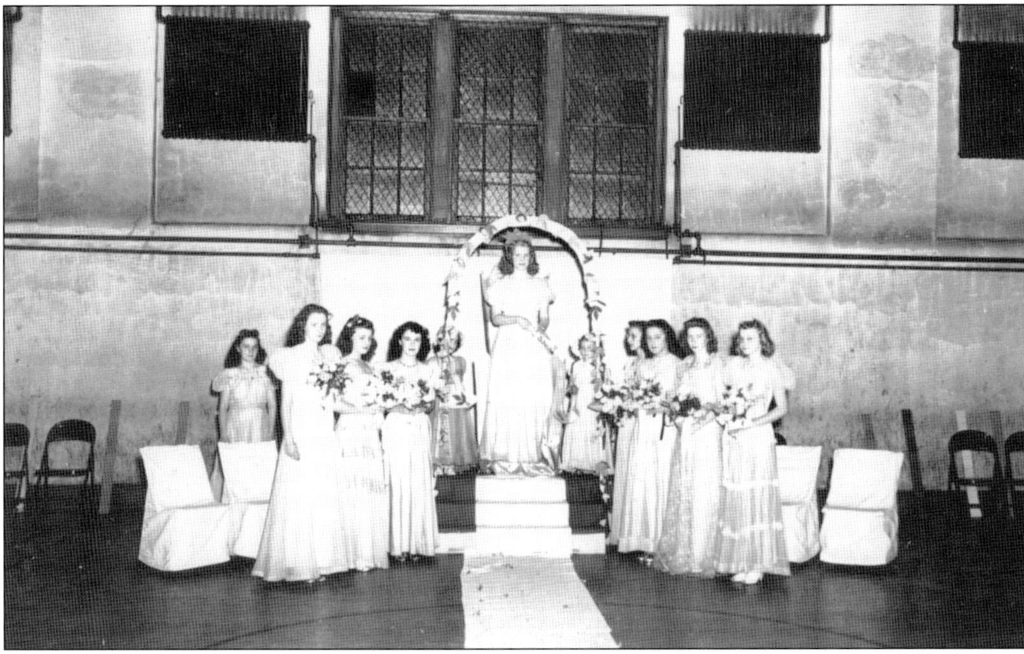

Ingram Public School's first May Day celebration was held in the gymnasium in 1941. A queen was selected while the other girls served as attendants or members of her court. The queen and her attendants all carried lovely bouquets and wore soft, long dresses. The queen was photographed under a trellis with her maids grouped around her.

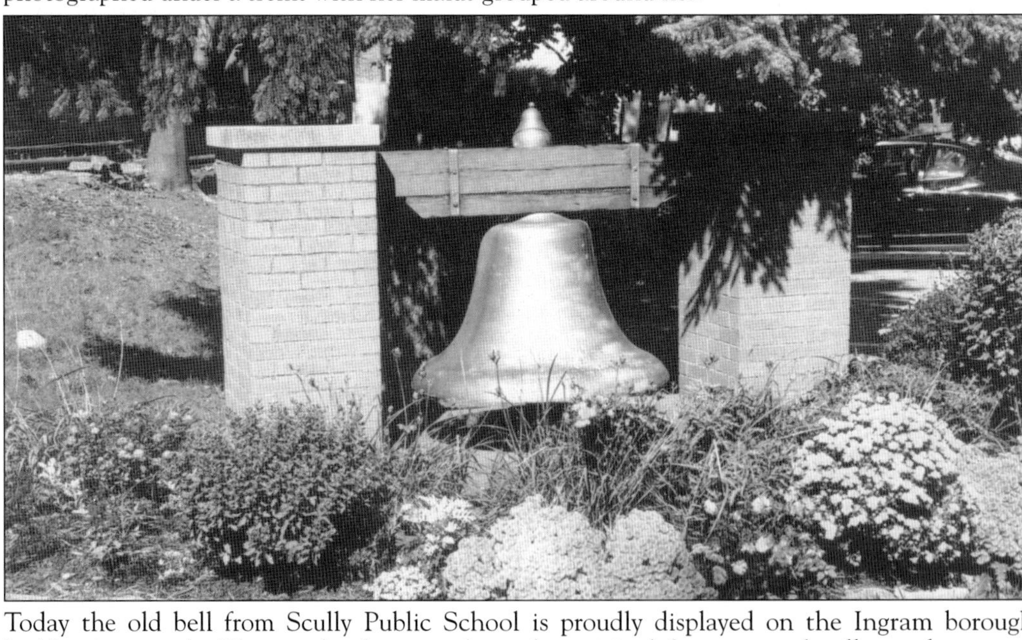

Today the old bell from Scully Public School is proudly displayed on the Ingram borough building's grounds. This marks the site where the original four-room schoolhouse known as Bonney School once stood. The bell was mounted in the belfry of the old schoolhouse and called neighborhood children to school each day. It was also used as a fire bell by the Ingram Volunteer Fire Department until 1926. It rang when Pres. William McKinley was assassinated, and it tolled to announce the end of World Wars I and II.

Five

BUSINESSES AND STORES

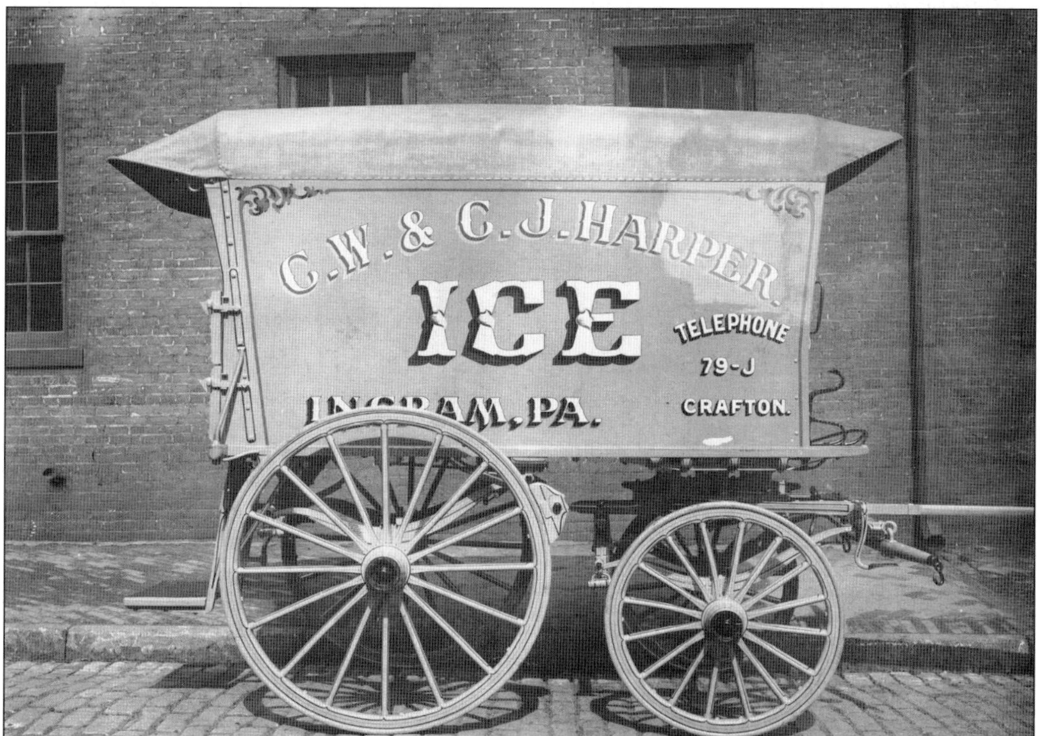

Before the days of electric refrigerators, a visit from the iceman was essential for preserving food. A heavy block of ice was carried into the house using a large pair of tongs and placed into the upper compartment of the icebox to keep food cold. A pan under the icebox collected water from the melting ice. It was important to check the pan regularly to avoid an overflow onto the kitchen floor. During the late 19th and early 20th centuries, the C. W. and C. J. Harper Ice Company wagon was seen making deliveries throughout the borough. The ice company was one of Ingram's first businesses.

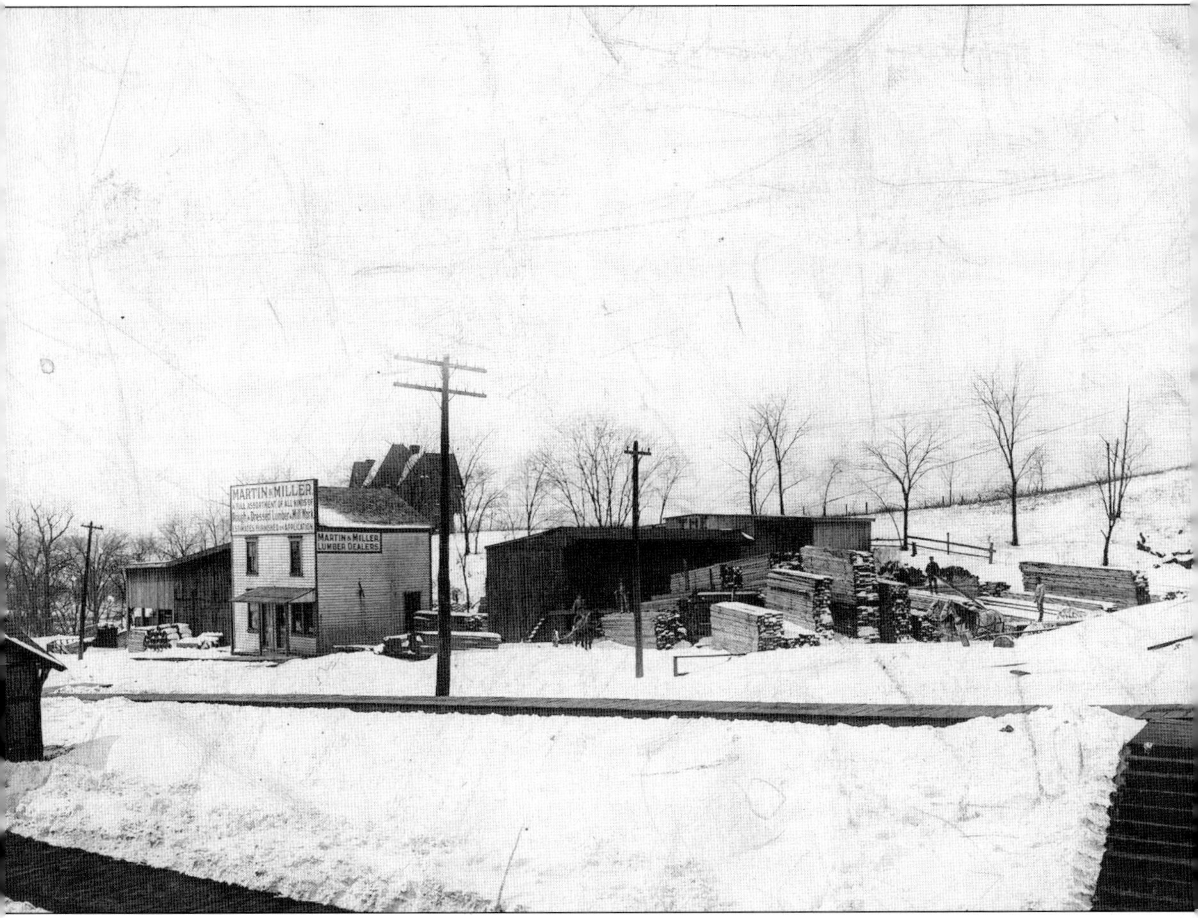

This early-20th-century photograph shows the Martin and Miller Lumber Company, which was located near the top of Ingram Avenue. The hill directly behind the lumber yard is the site of the present Ingram Elementary School. The wooden steps, boardwalk, and building at the bottom of the picture belong to the railroad, which served the lumber company with their team track across Ingram Avenue.

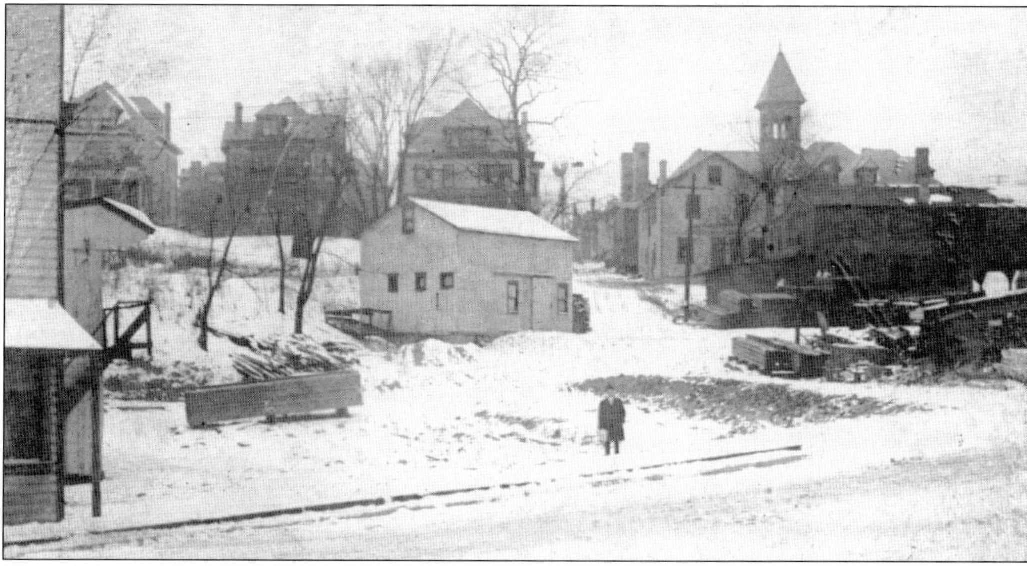

This photograph shows Craig Way from Ingram Avenue on a cold winter day during the early 20th century. To the right is the Martin and Miller Lumber Company, which supplied much of the building materials for the early Ingram houses. To the right is the bell tower of the Ingram Presbyterian Church. The homes above the yard are on Vancouver Avenue. Looking closely at the crest of Craig Way, the windmill from a neighboring farm can be seen, making this a good example of the transition from farmland to a residential area that Ingram would experience early in its history.

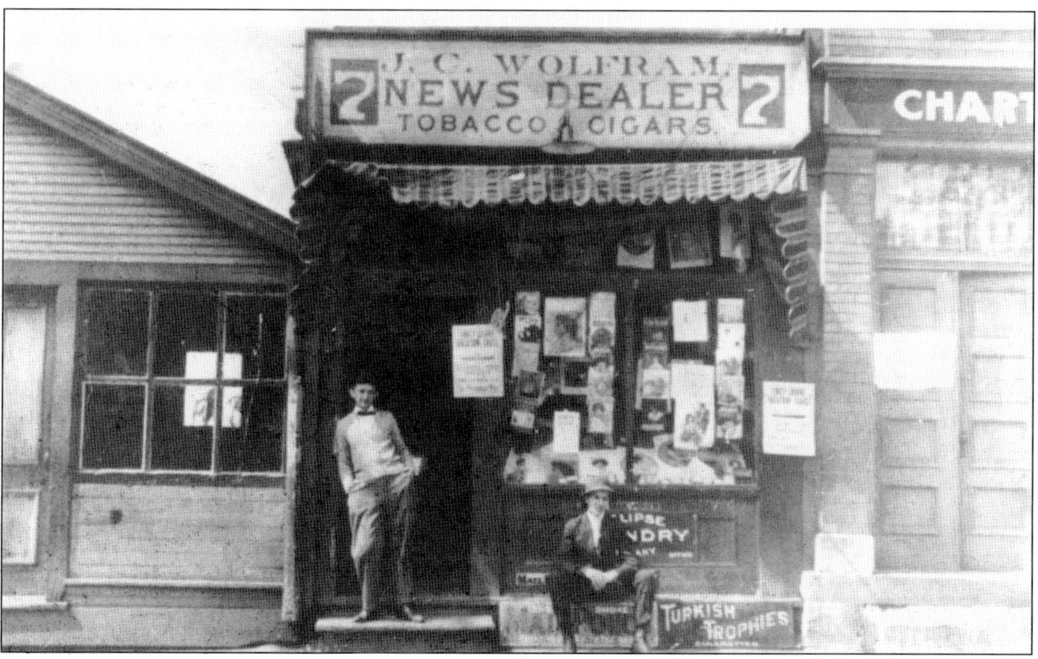

At the beginning of the 20th century, the J. C. Wolfram store was the place to go to purchase a newspaper and catch up on the current happenings about town. Located on Center Street near the railroad station, people would often stop and pick up a morning paper to read on the train. Wolfram's also sold magazines, penny candy, tobacco, and cigars.

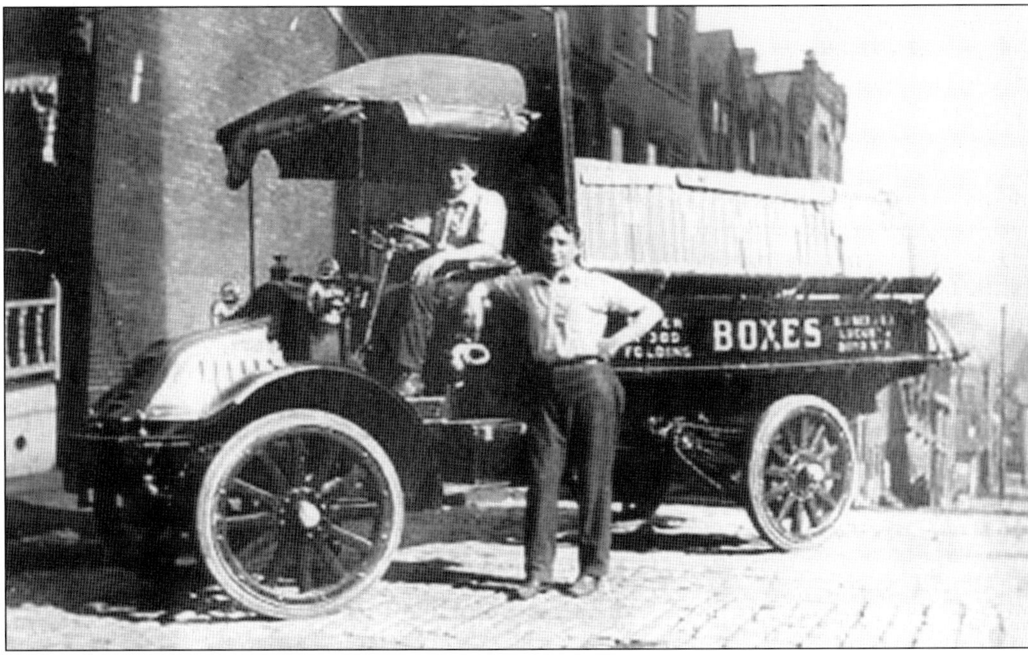

The D. J. Rex Iron City Steam Paper Box factory was formed in 1873. The factory produced paper boxes of every sort, tea caddies, and cigar boxes. The proprietor, David Rex, was a longtime Ingram resident and the first burgess of Ingram. Pictured here is the box truck, often seen on the streets of Ingram.

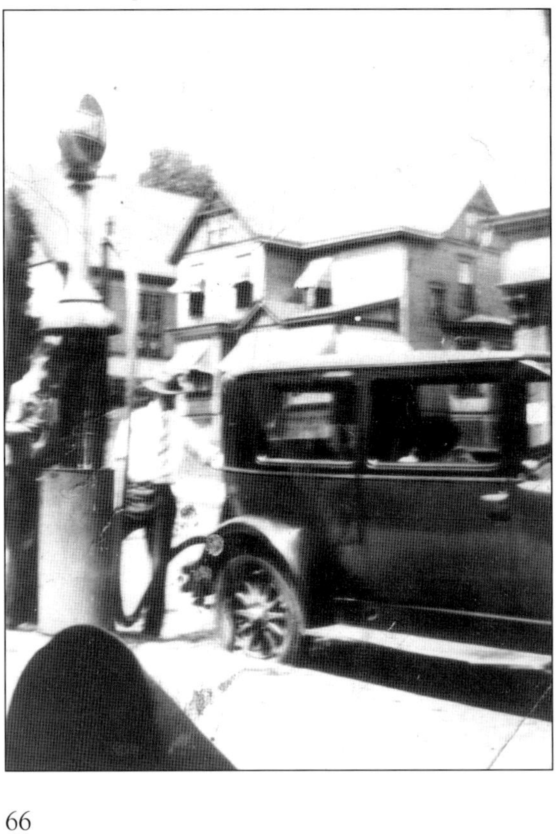

On December 1, 1913, Gulf Oil Corporation opened the very first drive-through gasoline station in the world. The station was located in Pittsburgh's East End at Baum Boulevard and South St. Clair Street. Prior to that, gas pumps were located on the sidewalk. Automobiles would pull up to the curb for service. This scene from September 5, 1925, shows an unidentified man filling up at the curb on West Prospect Avenue.

Like many communities, Ingram had a number of small, independent grocery stores to serve its residents. Mary Shafer Lauer operated this store at 59 Schley Avenue, in the lower part of Ingram. The shop was later owned by Ethel Davis and remained a favorite stop for many residents on the surrounding streets. Unfortunately most other stores in Ingram were not photographed, and memories are their only historical documentation.

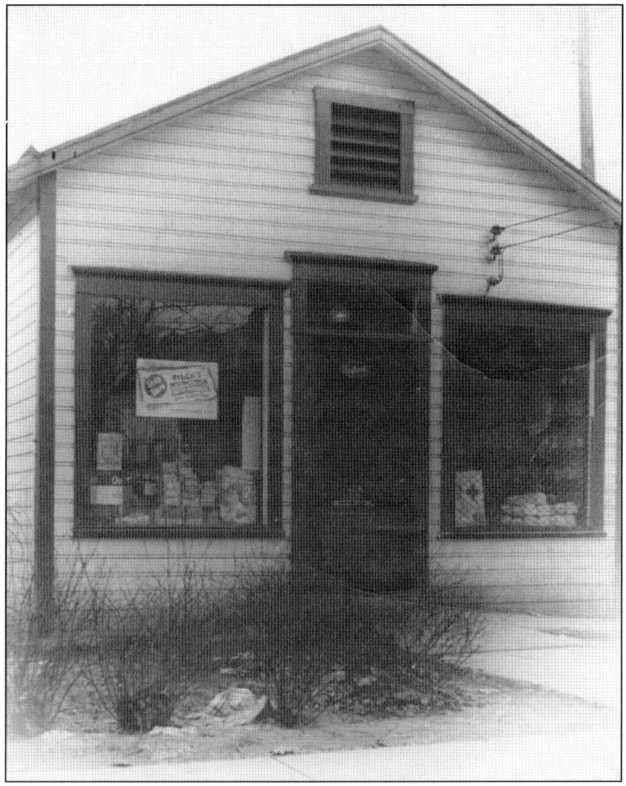

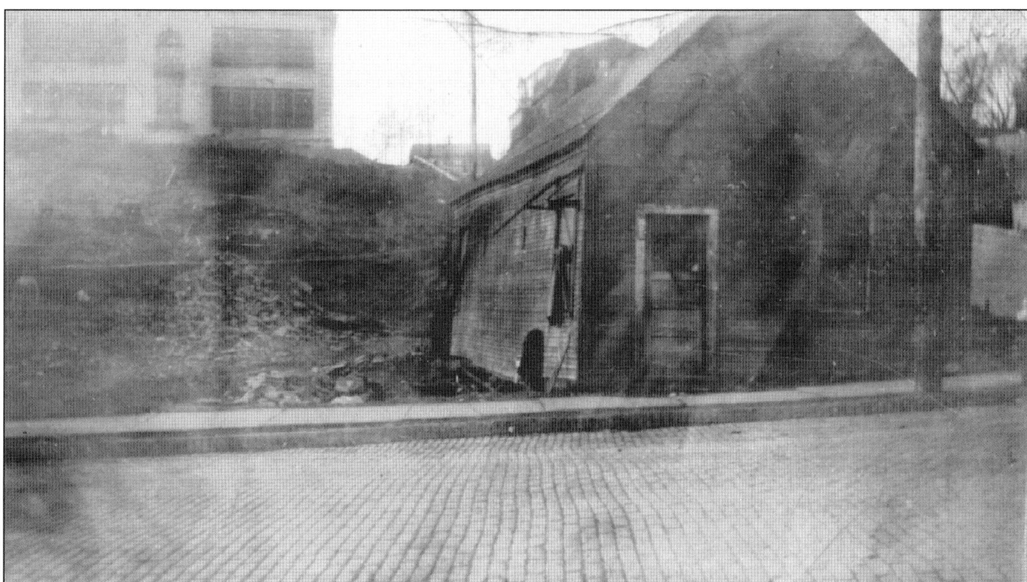

As the business community began to develop, many small establishments located near the railroad. This Chinese laundry on Ingram Avenues was one of two serving the early Ingram residents. The new elementary school stands in the background. This old frame structure would soon be torn down to make way for Sacco's Ingram Garage, which would quickly become a big business in Ingram. (Courtesy of John Sacco.)

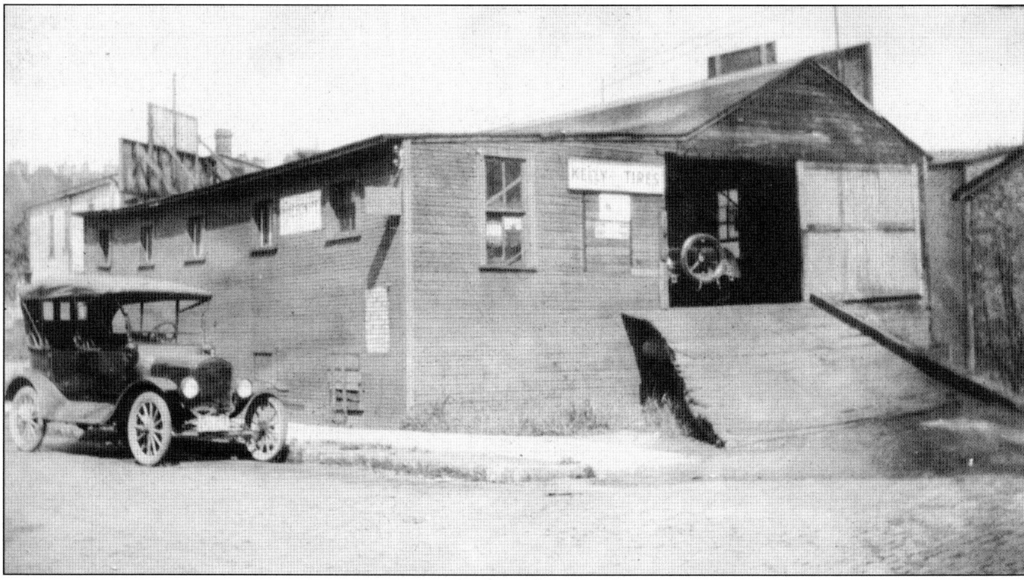

An early entrepreneur who became fascinated with automobiles was John A. Sacco. His first garage covered a one block piece of land bound on three sides by West Prospect Avenue, Vancouver Avenue, and Craig Way. This photograph shows the rear of the building on Craig Way. Note the extremely steep ramp that motorist used to enter the building. (Courtesy of John Sacco.)

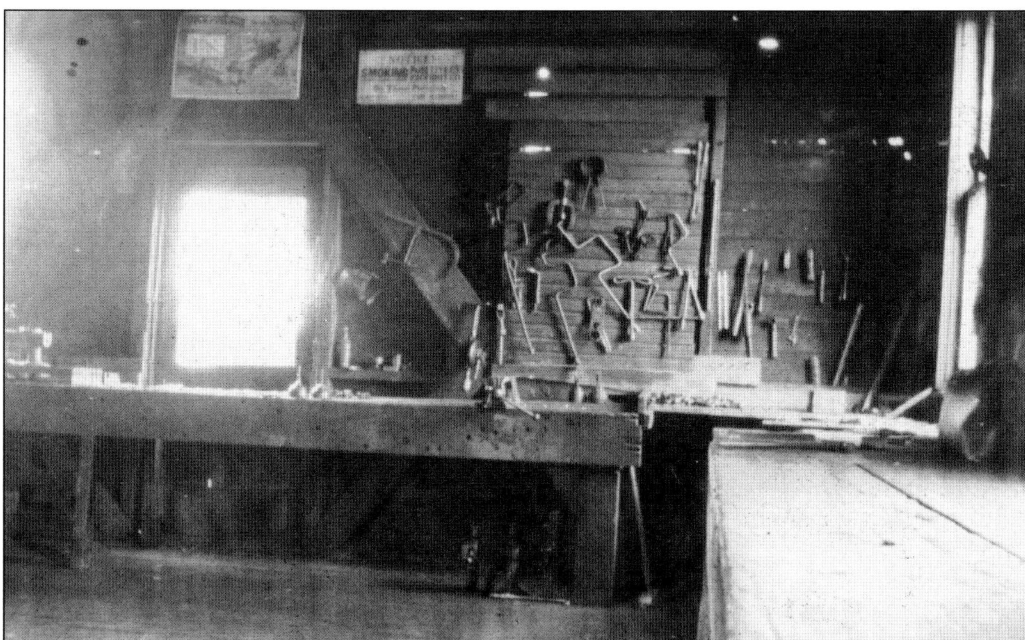

Inside Sacco's Garage is what might be described as the service department. In the early days of motoring, it took ingenuity as well as skill to keep the tin lizzies running. Sacco made it a point to keep clutter away from the work area. Tools of the trade were always arranged in a neat and orderly fashion. (Courtesy of John Sacco.)

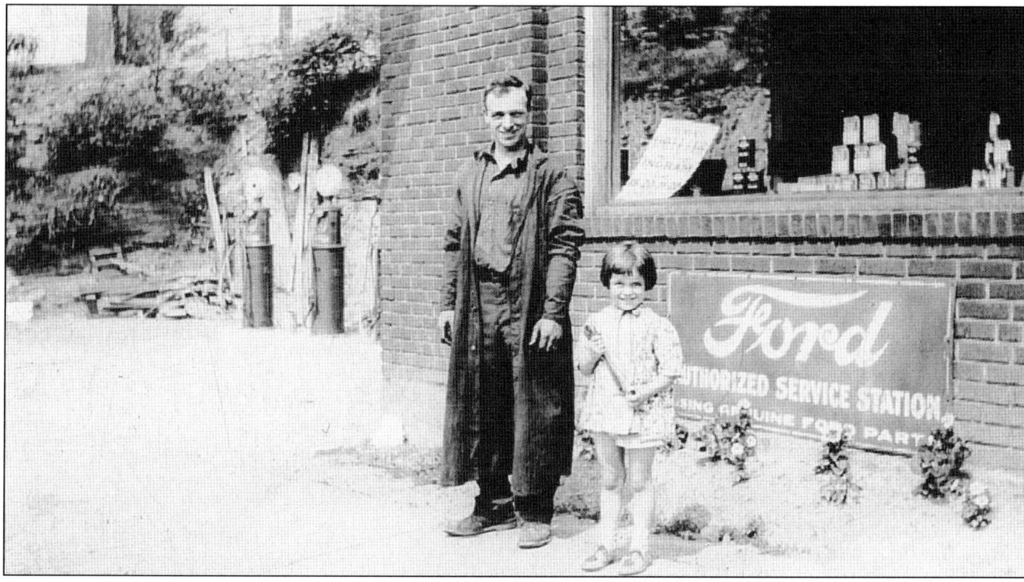

On October 1, 1908, Henry Ford introduced a revolutionary new vehicle known as the Model T. Always looking ahead, Sacco purchased property where one of Ingram's Chinese laundry's stood, on Ingram Avenue, built a modern garage and began selling Fords. Unlike his old garage on Vancouver and West Prospect Avenues, the new dealership was a one-story brick building with a modern service bay. This photograph shows John with his little sister Helen in front of the dealership. Helen would become a founding and active member of the Ingram Historical Society. (Courtesy of John Sacco.)

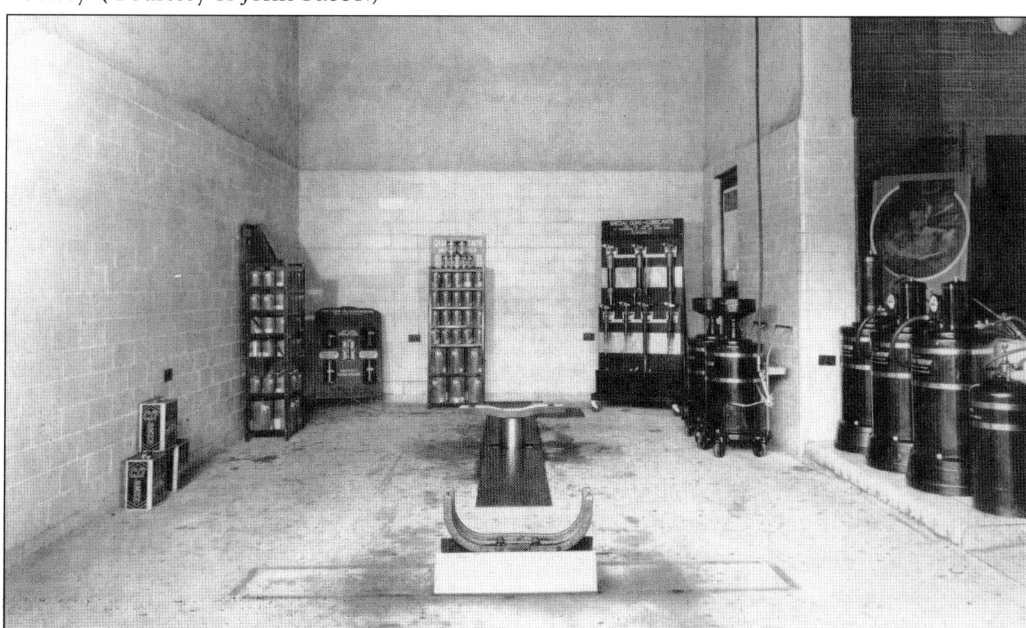

This interior shot of Ingram Garage shows the bay where cars were brought to be inspected, serviced, and cleaned. Maintenance included oil changes, lubricating the chassis, and battery and tire changing. It was important to Sacco that the shop be clean and organized since the showroom was adjacent to the service bay. (Courtesy of John Sacco.)

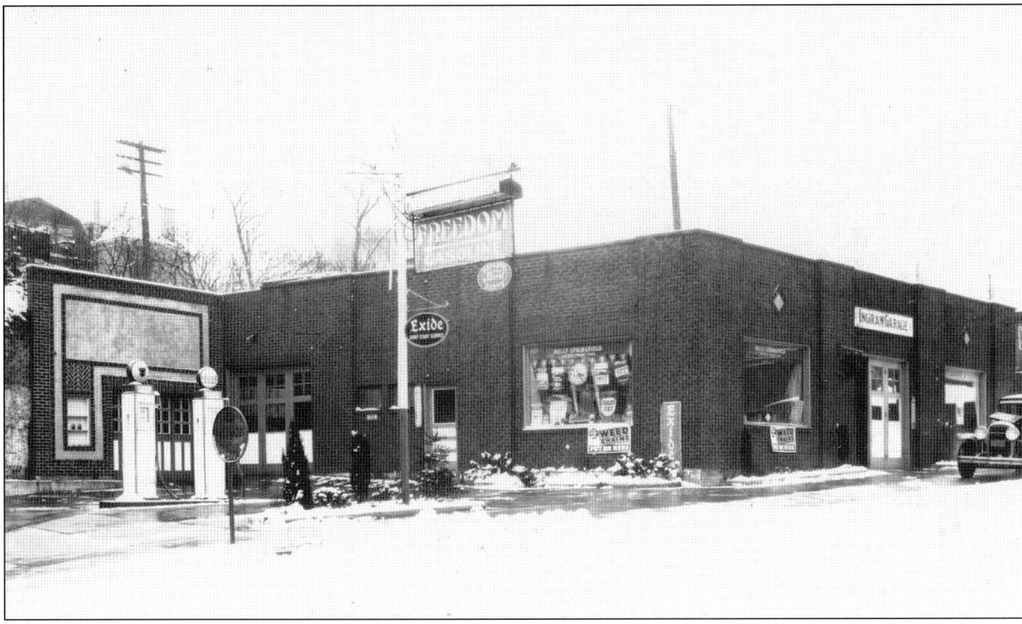

In 1924, John A. Sacco opened his new Ford dealership in a single-story brick building at 30 Ingram Avenue. The new building had a well-appointed showroom, service department, and drive-through gas pumps. After 12 years of selling Fords, the Ingram Garage became a Pontiac dealership. Another 12 years would pass until a second story was added. The lubrication room is the garage built into the hillside on the left. (Courtesy of John Sacco.)

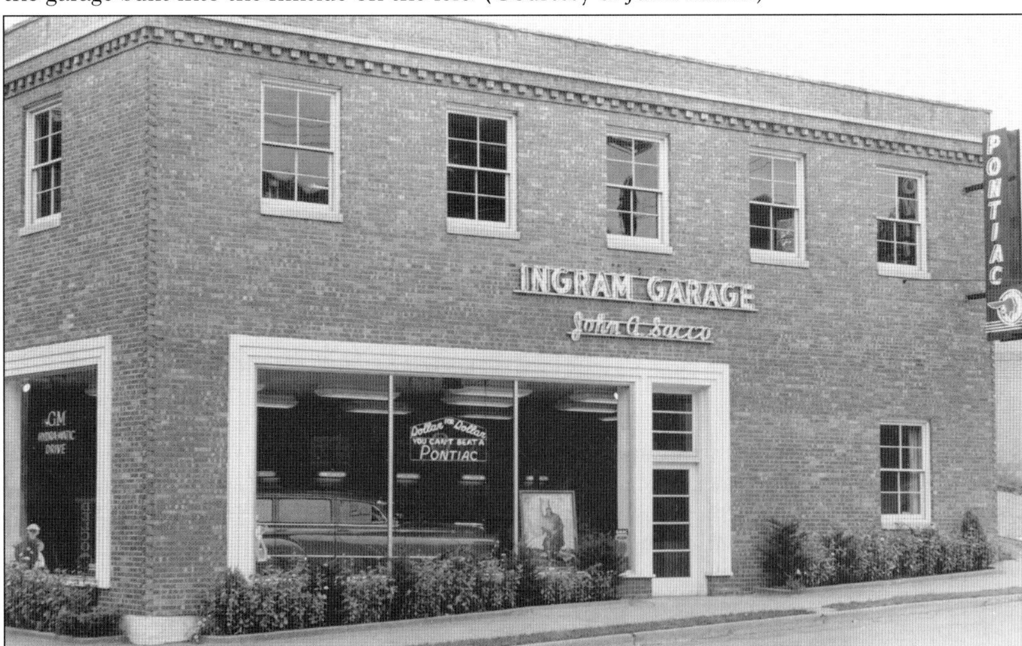

In 1948, Sacco began enlarging his business at 30 Ingram Avenue to include a second story and modern showroom. Dedicated in 1949, reigning Miss America Jacque Mercer, made an appearance to introduce the new Pontiacs. This photograph shows the dealership in the early 1950s. (Courtesy of John Sacco.)

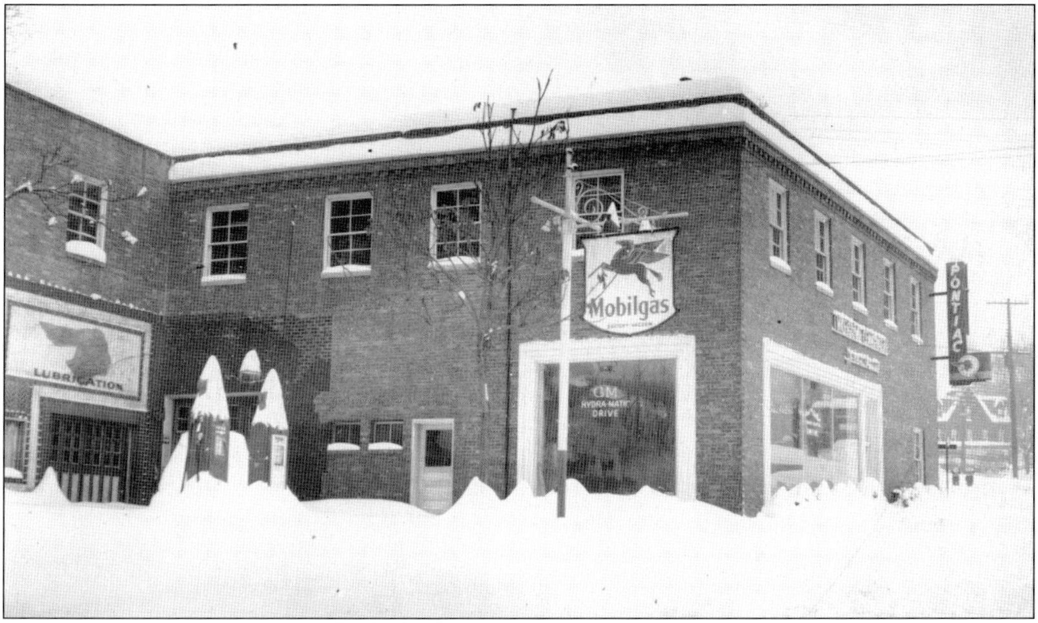

This winter scene shows the Ingram Garage after Sacco added a new brick facade and a second story to his building. On November 23, 1950, Pittsburgh was buried under 30.5 inches of snow. This record-breaking storm brought the city to a standstill. Automobiles were stranded, streetcars were stalled, and businesses remained closed for several days. There was little for anyone to do but dig out. (Courtesy of John Sacco.)

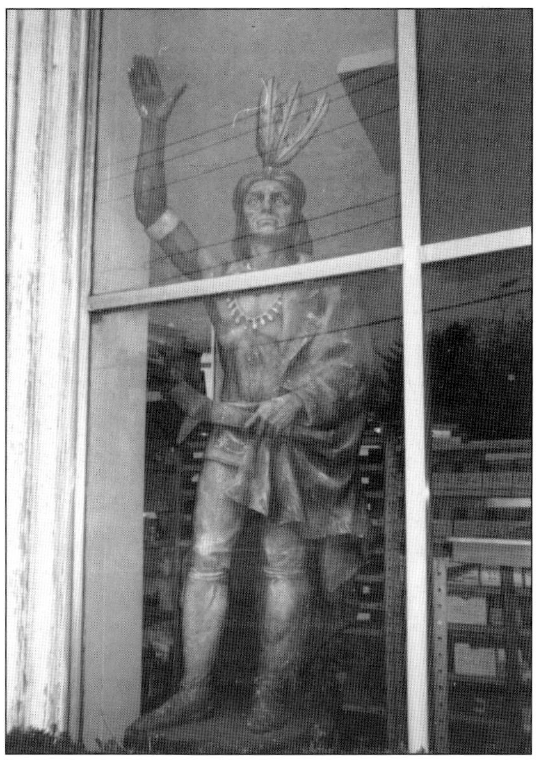

Standing in Sacco's garage was a 6-foot-tall plaster-of-paris replica of Chief Pontiac. The Pontiac Motor Division adopted Chief Pontiac as a symbol for their cars. The real Chief Pontiac was of the Ottawa tribe, located around present-day Detroit, Michigan. The Sacco family purchased the statue from Pontiac Motor Division in 1953, one of only three statues in the Pittsburgh area. When the garage closed in 1959, the building was converted into a hobby shop. (Courtesy of John Sacco.)

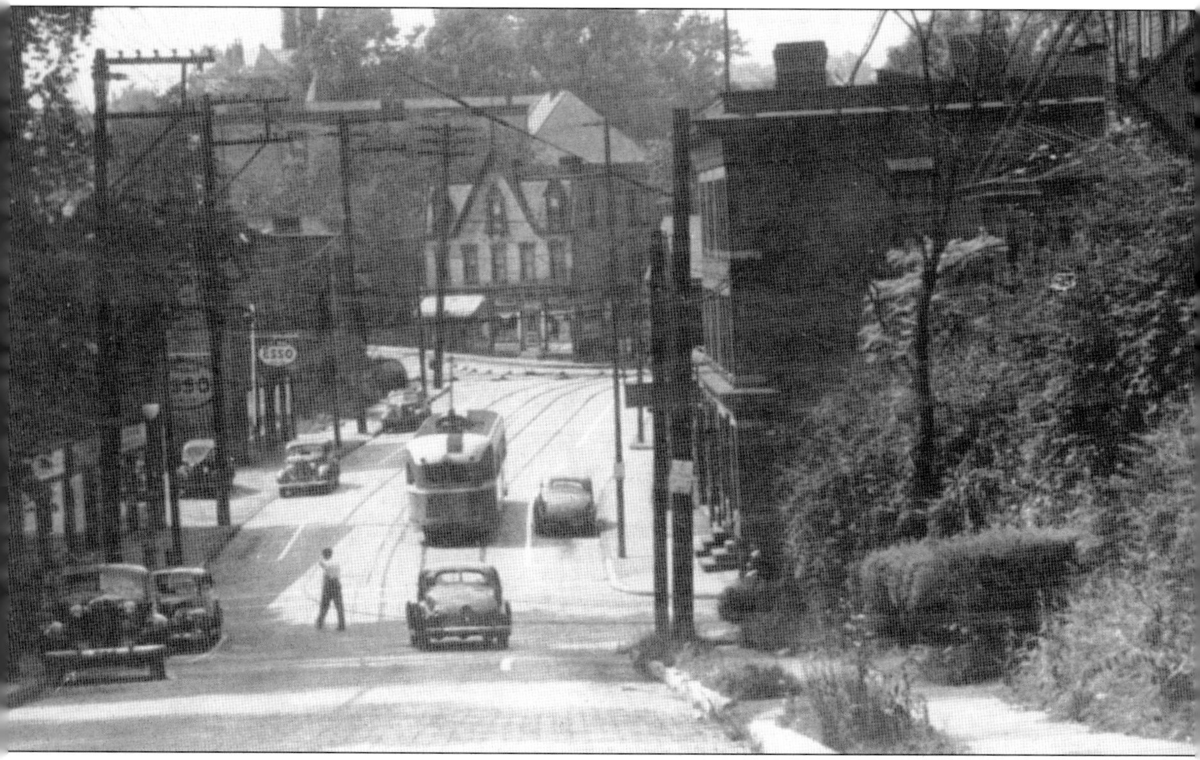

The Pennsylvania Railroad operated in a culvert through the center of Ingram's shopping district. After Conrail abandoned the tracks in the early 1980s, the right-of-way was paved into a private road for buses, known today as the Port Authority Transit West Busway. Two bridges span this culvert on East Prospect Avenue and Center Street. This *c.* 1941 view of Center Street (named for its position in town) shows more landmarks where residents went to shop. The building directly ahead of the streetcar was Marx's Dairy Store. Marx's was more of a general store for all of the residents shopping needs. The train station was directly across the street at the East Prospect Bridge. Before the days of self serve gasoline stations, Ingram Service Station (left) was an Esso dealership. Attendants in uniforms came out to a person's car, pumped the gas, checked the oil, and washed the windows. While the streetcars no longer clang their way along Center Street, much of this scene remains the same today. As shopping habits have changed over the years, many new establishments occupy these buildings.

Before the opening of the Crafton-Ingram Shopping Center, most of Ingram's business establishments were centered around the railroad station. It was customary in those days for merchants to patronize each others stores. One such establishment was Bill Appel's Dairy Store, located at 2701 Center Street. While many went to Appel's for a quart of milk or a loaf of bread, others dropped in for a sandwich, a bowl of soup, or an ice-cream cone. This photograph dates back to the 1950s.

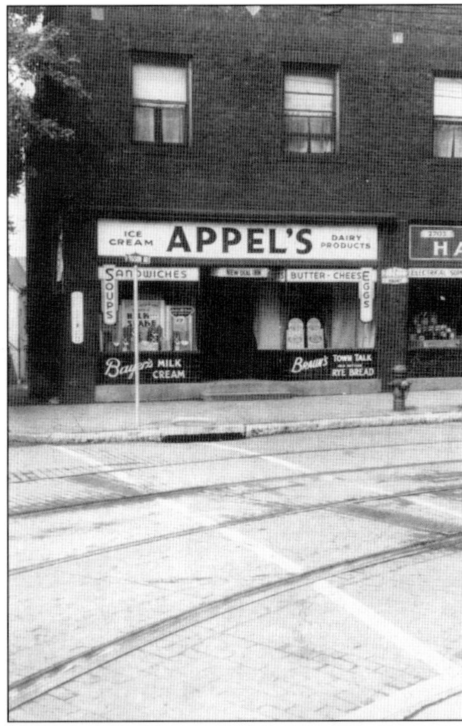

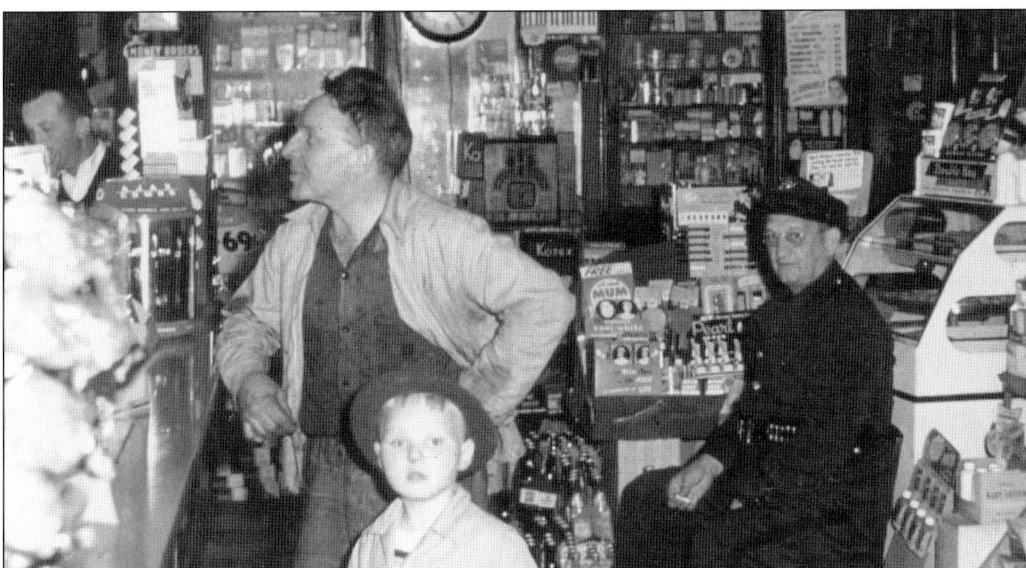

Here is young Joe Baur with his dad, Joseph L. Baur Jr., in Fineberg's Drug Store. Located on Center Street, across from the Ingram Service Station, Fineberg's sold just about everything from shoe polish to money orders. Many residents in the borough stopped at Fineberg's for a soda or ice cream on their way home from shopping. The gentleman seated on the right is Ingram Police chief Thomas Waugh. On more than one occasion, Louis Fineberg went to his store in the middle of the night to fill a prescription for a sick child in the borough. After retiring, Fineberg could be found playing Santa Claus at the borough building. This photograph dates back to 1958.

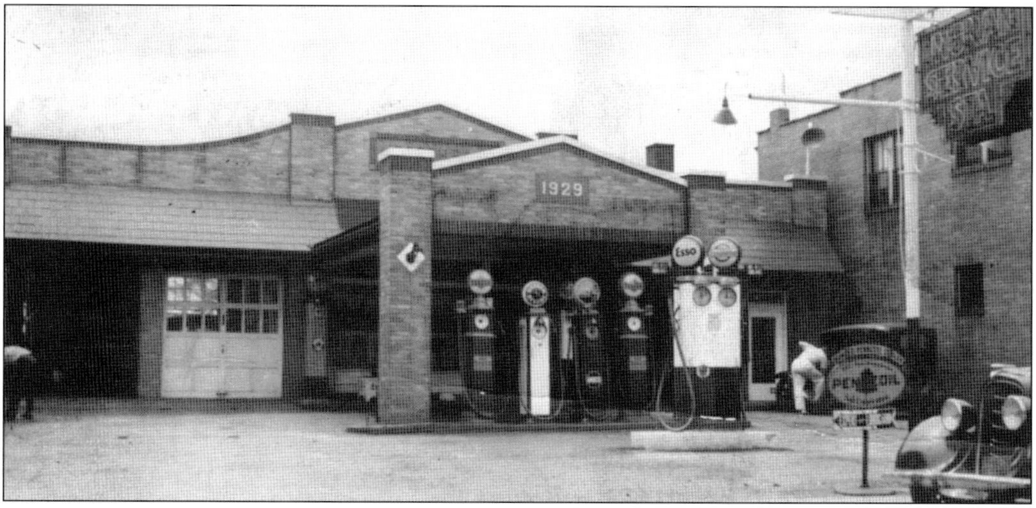

Seeing that more and more people were buying automobiles, Joseph L. Baur Sr. opened a small garage in Ingram to repair them. As his business grew and prospered, the Ingram Service Station decided to build a modern drive-through service station at 2709 Center Street. Opened in 1929, Baur originally offered several brands of gasoline. These included Amoco, Atlantic, Esso, Gulf, Pennzoil, and Sunoco. Eventually the Ingram Service Station became an Esso (later Exxon) dealer. Soon Baur's son (also named Joseph L. Baur) took over the business. He in turn passed it on to his son, Joseph A. Baur. Although the station stopped selling gas in 1980, it continues to be a stronghold in the community. Today customers are assured of the same professional service that began over 80 years ago.

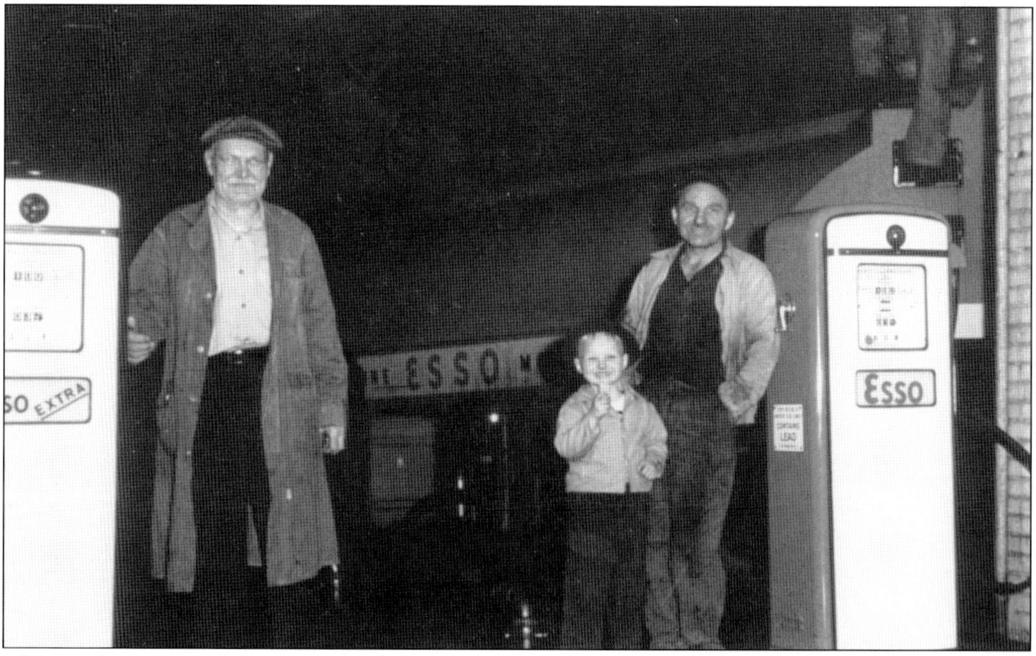

This night view, taken in 1958, shows three generations of the Baur family at the Ingram Service Station. Standing at the pumps from left to right are Joseph L. Baur, Joseph A. Baur Sr., and Joseph L. Baur Jr. Behind them is an Esso gasoline delivery truck, filling up the tanks at the station.

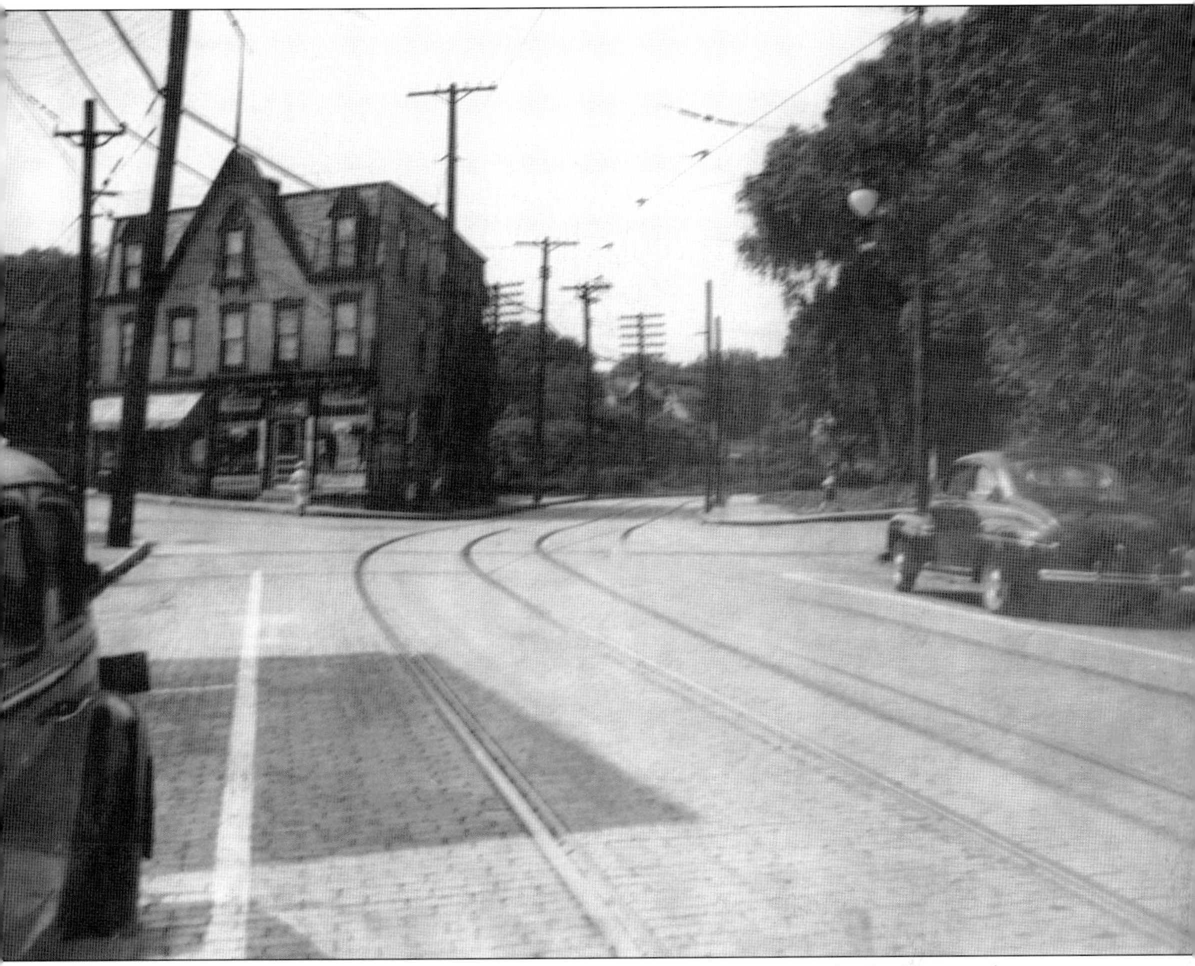

This corner mom-and-pop establishment, located on Center Street at the bridge, was known as Marx's Dairy Store. A pinball machine, snacks, and a candy counter attracted young people on their way home from school. The 30-Crafton-Ingram streetcar passed this building on its way to and from the carbarn. The upper floors housed apartments, as they still do today.

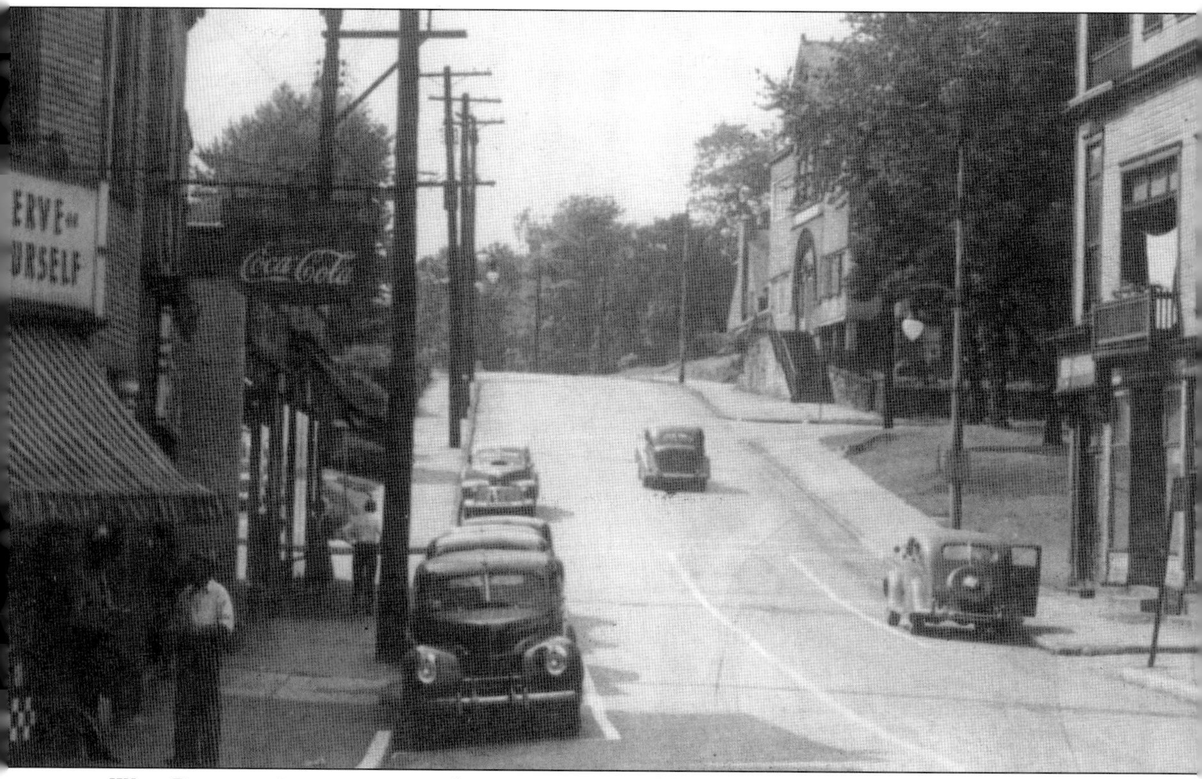

West Prospect Avenue is a good representation of downtown Ingram. Here a variety of stores could be found for the local residents' convenience. Within a small area, there were grocery stores, a hardware store, a barbershop, a pharmacy, and doctors' offices. Being a small community, shopping provided a good opportunity to catch up on the news. People always passed someone they knew walking down the sidewalk. Store owners knew their customers and prided themselves on efficient, friendly service. These establishments sustained residents between trips into Pittsburgh. Old timers often liked to stop at the service station, pull up a chair and discuss the pressing issues of the day. While the buildings on the left remain, the Rex Building (right) and Scully Public School have long since vanished from the landscape. This scene was captured in the 1940s.

The Rex Building was a large frame structure, located on West Prospect Avenue near the bridge, which carried automobile traffic over the Pennsylvania Railroad tracks. Located on the first floor was Wilson's Men's Store and Stafora's Hardware. When the new Crafton-Ingram Shopping Center opened in 1958, Frank Stafora relocated his hardware business into a large, modern store there. This photograph was taken in the summer of 1958, shortly before demolition.

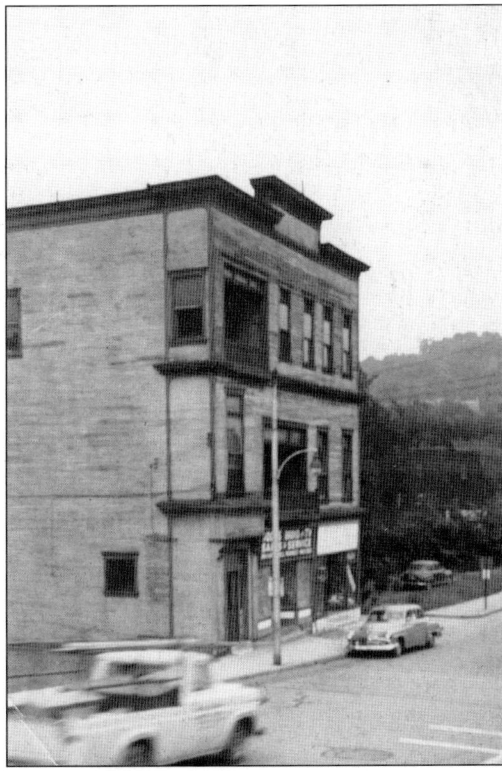

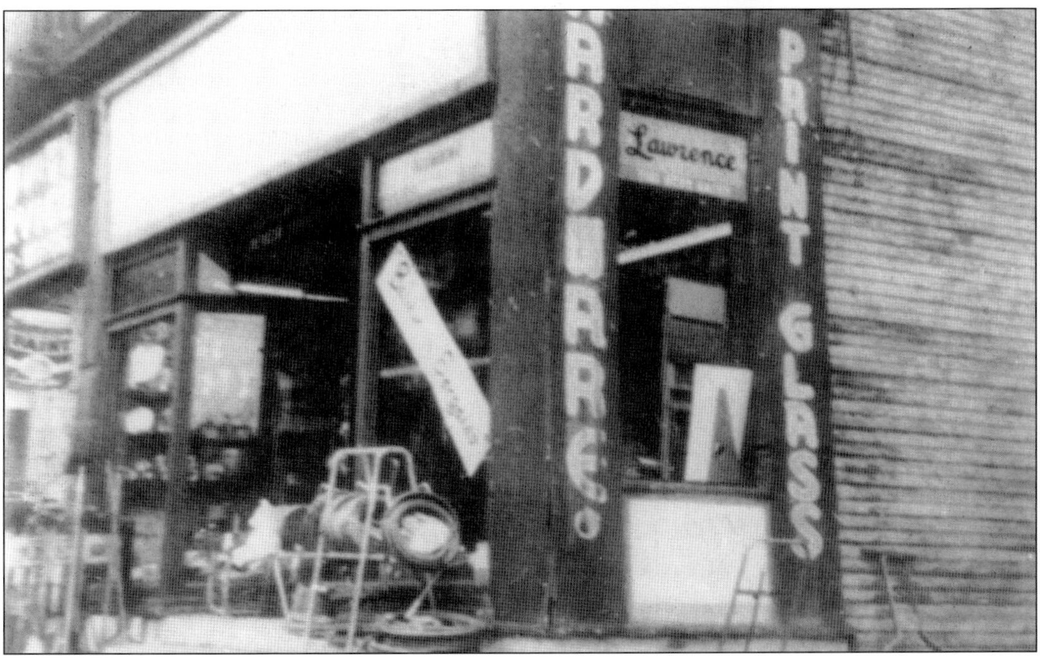

One of Ingram's early businesses was Dominick Castellucci's hardware store. The business was located on West Prospect Avenues in the Rex Building, which was later removed for a gas station. A person could literally find anything at Castellucci's who prided themselves on friendly, knowledgeable, service. The hardware store was later operated by Frank Stafora.

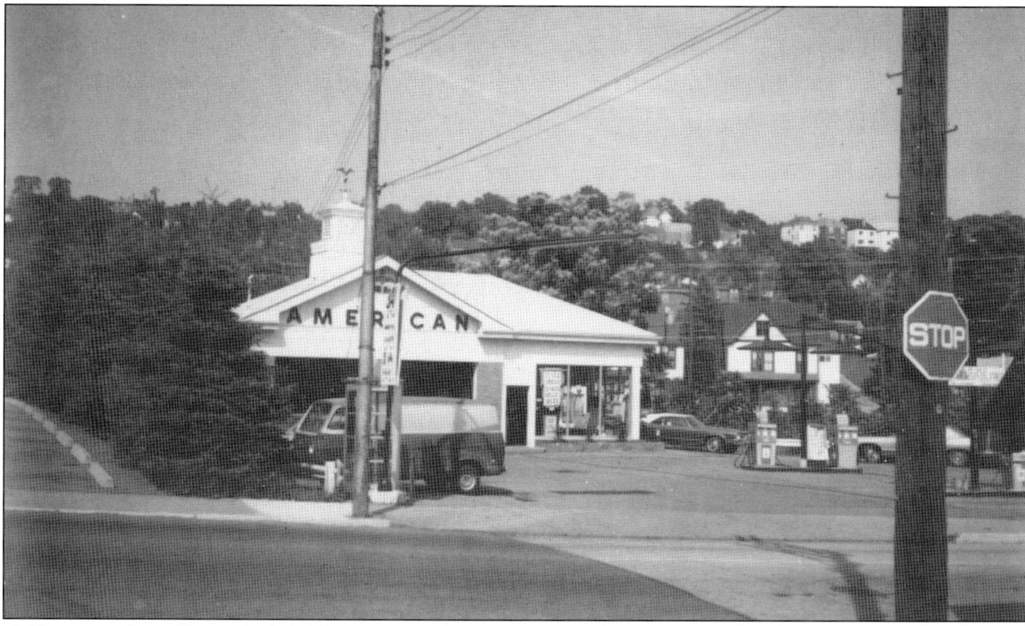

Following demolition of the Rex Building, a modern service station was built on the site. During the 1960s and much of the 1970s, gas stations still offered customers all the amenities of first-class service. At one time, there were five service stations operating in the borough. Today a gas station/convenience store occupies the site of the former Pinto's American (AMOCO) service station.

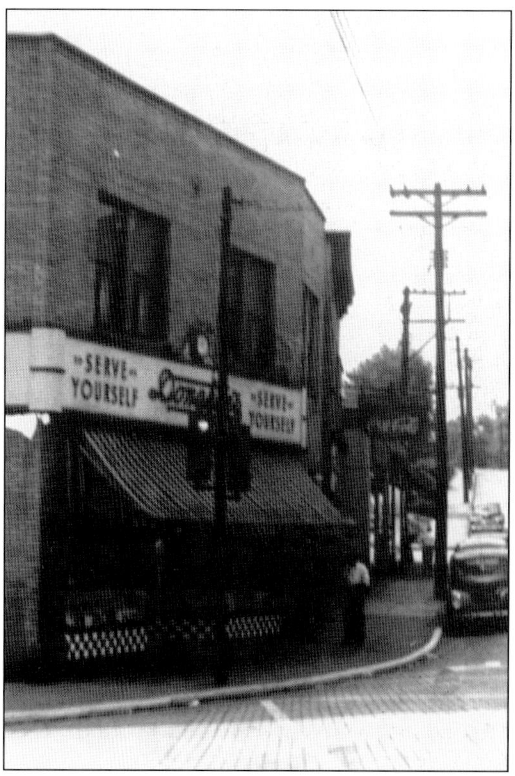

Many residents of the Greater Pittsburgh area remember Donahue's Market, which established a landmark food store, bakery, and cafeteria near the Diamond Market downtown. Donahue's was noted for their fresh foods and friendly service. In the 1940s, Ingram was fortunate to have a Donahue's Market near the intersection of West Prospect and Ingram Avenues.

Eileen's Alterations and Dressmaking shop was one of the many stores that have operated on West Prospect Avenue. In this photograph, the storefront is decorated with bridal fashions.

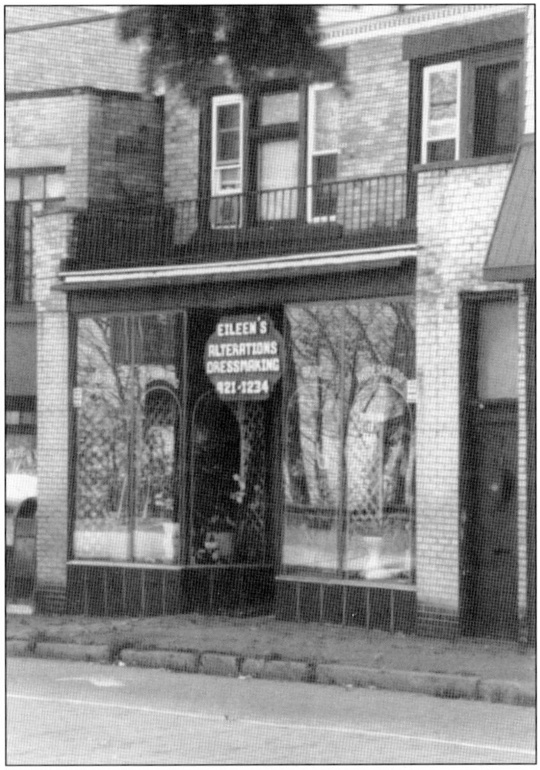

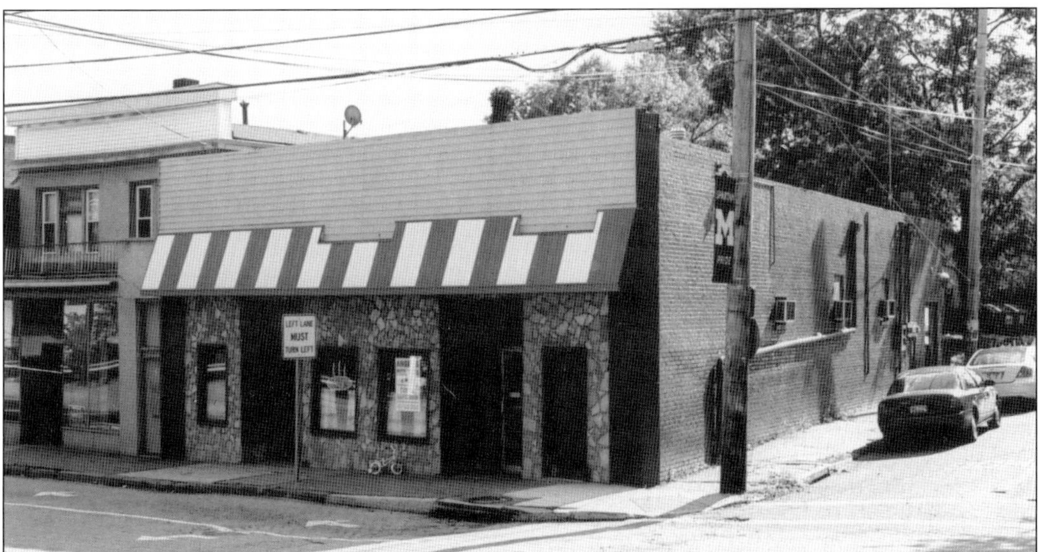

One of the first food stores to embrace the modern supermarket concept was the Great Atlantic and Pacific Tea Company (A&P). Throughout the nation, people went to A&P for their weekly grocery shopping. Like other stores, A&P had their own brand of groceries, known as Ann Page. Many remember their delicious Jane Parker baked goods and fresh ground coffee. This building, at 13 West Prospect Avenue, housed an A&P for many years before the company opened a large modern store in the Crafton-Ingram Shopping Center. Today this building houses a restaurant/pizza shop. As an interesting note, this was the site of John Sacco's first garage.

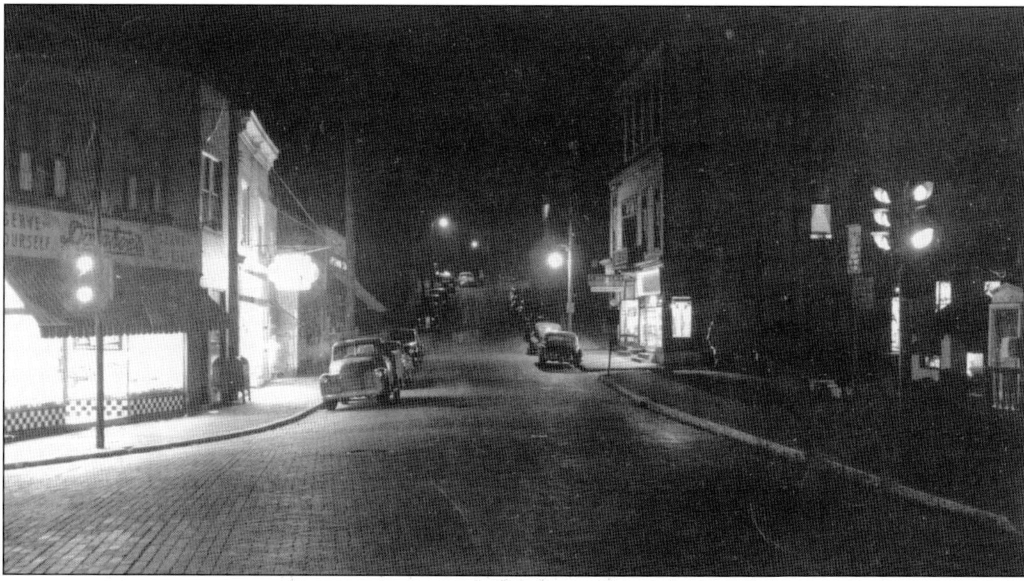

Most of Ingram's business establishments had evening hours during the 1940s and 1950s. Within this one block of West Prospect Avenue, shoppers could patronize Donahue's Food Store, Frostshel's Barber Shop, Codori's Food Store, Smitty's Barber Shop, Enscoe's Meat Market, and the A&P market. Across the street were Wilson's Men's Store and Castellucci's Hardware store. Free two-hour street parking attracted shoppers. This photograph, looking up West Prospect Avenue, was taken as a "before" picture as Ingram had new street lights installed to better illuminate the main roads for safety and style alike.

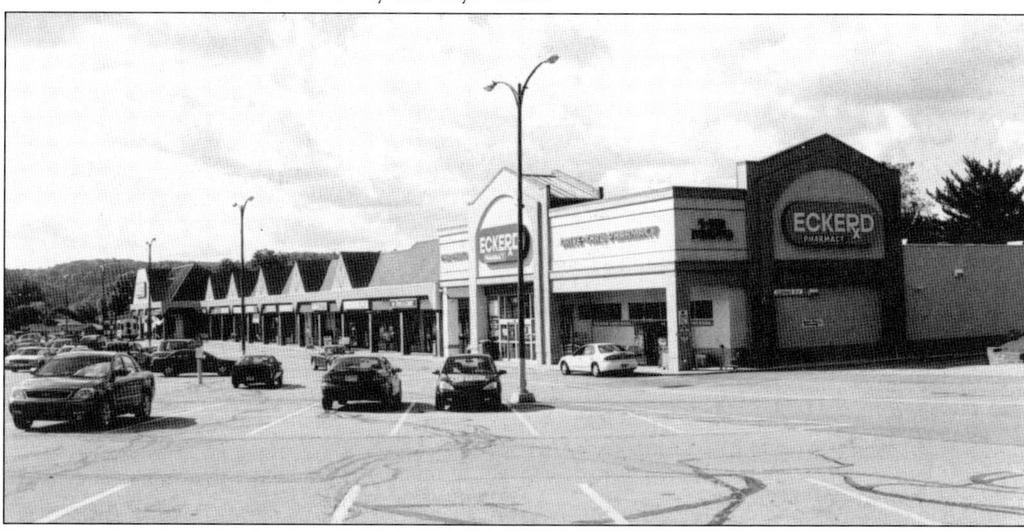

By the mid-1950s, shopping habits in the United States were rapidly changing. As American's opted for suburban living, many appreciated the conveniences of shopping in one location. Another great factor was the abundance of free parking available, at shopping centers. The Crafton-Ingram Shopping Center was built on open land situated between Steuben Street (Crafton) and Ingram Avenue (Ingram) in 1958. Originally this property was swampland used by the U.S. Army. Almost a half century later, Crafton-Ingram shopping center continues to attract shoppers from the two boroughs and surrounding communities. The Crafton Ingram Bowling Lanes, and PNC Bank (formally Peoples First Bank) are original tenants of the shopping center.

Six

THE 1968 GAS EXPLOSION

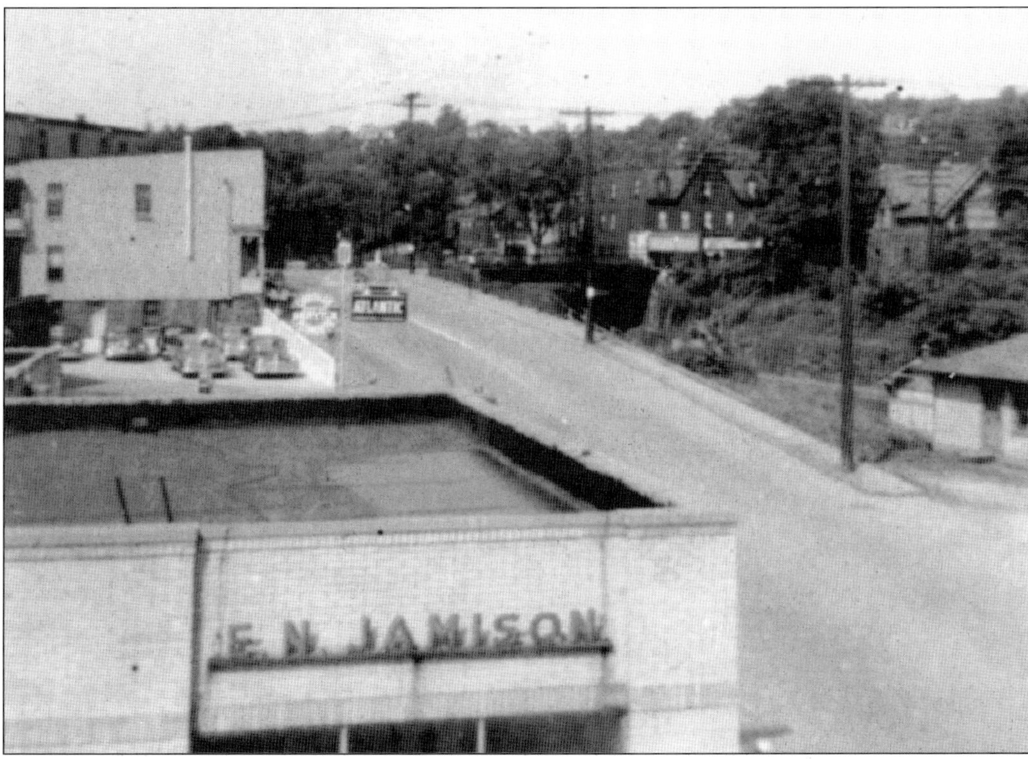

This 1940 study shows Ingram Avenue looking east. In the foreground is E. N. Jamison's Chrysler-Plymouth, one of two automobile dealerships in the borough. The small building on the far right is the Pennsylvania Railroad's freight station. Across the bridge (background) is Marx's Dairy Store (left) and the train station (right). The building to the left of the Atlantic Gasoline sign would forever change the history of Ingram. (Courtesy of John Sacco.)

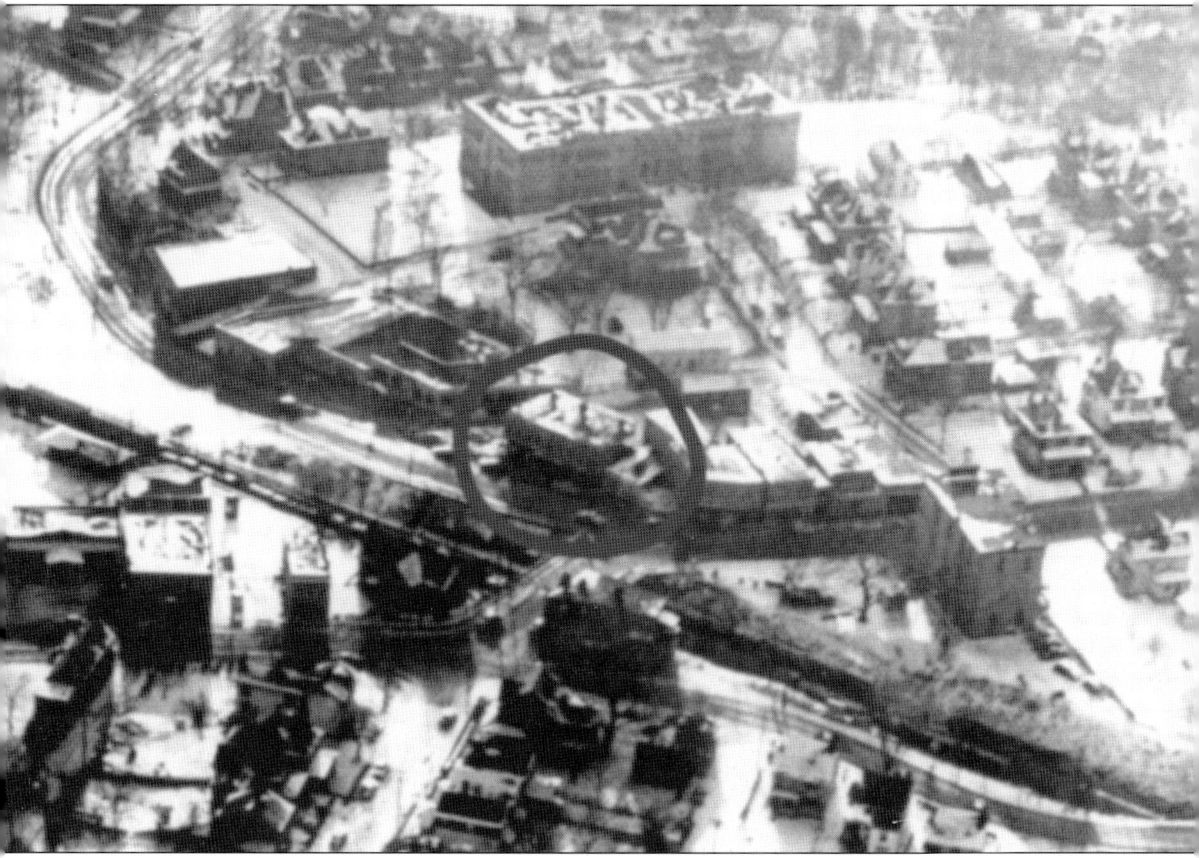

This aerial view, which was taken in the winter of 1955, shows the heart of Ingram's business district. Little changed over the years until the afternoon of January 30, 1968, when a natural gas explosion leveled the building circled. Eight people lost their lives, 18 others were injured, and surrounding buildings suffered severe damage. The explosion was compared to an atomic bomb with flames shooting 75 feet into the air. Debris rained down on automobiles stopped at the traffic light on Ingram and West Prospect Avenues. (Courtesy of John Sacco.)

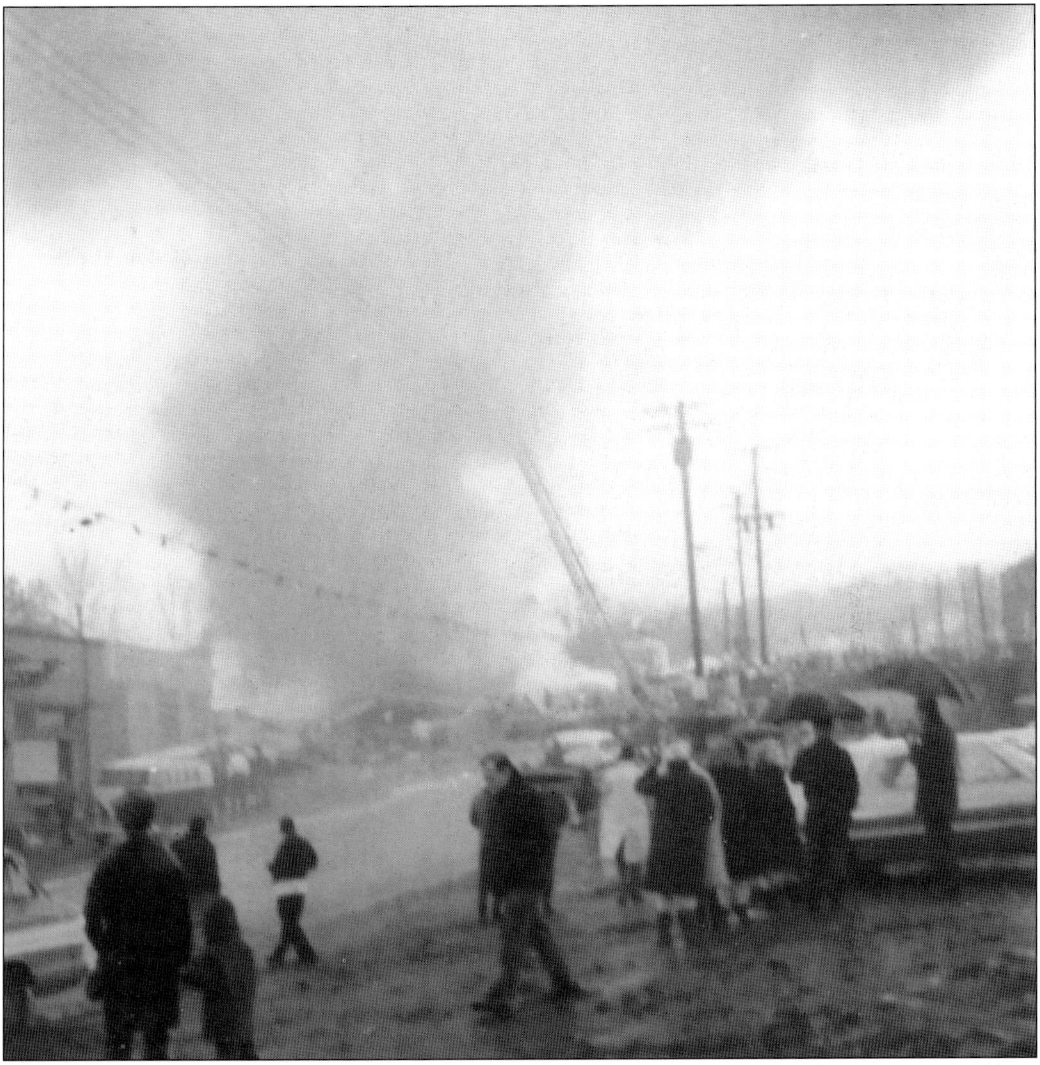

Looking up Ingram Avenue, flames continue to burn where a commercial/apartment building stood only moments earlier. At 10:30 a.m., gas company workers arrived at 8 Ingram Avenue to investigate a possible gas leak. The gas was shut off to the building as workers prepared to dig for a 4-inch low-pressure main line. Almost immediately after the jack hammering began at 1:30 p.m., the building exploded. Workers were blown across the railroad tracks and buried under rubble. (Courtesy of John Sacco.)

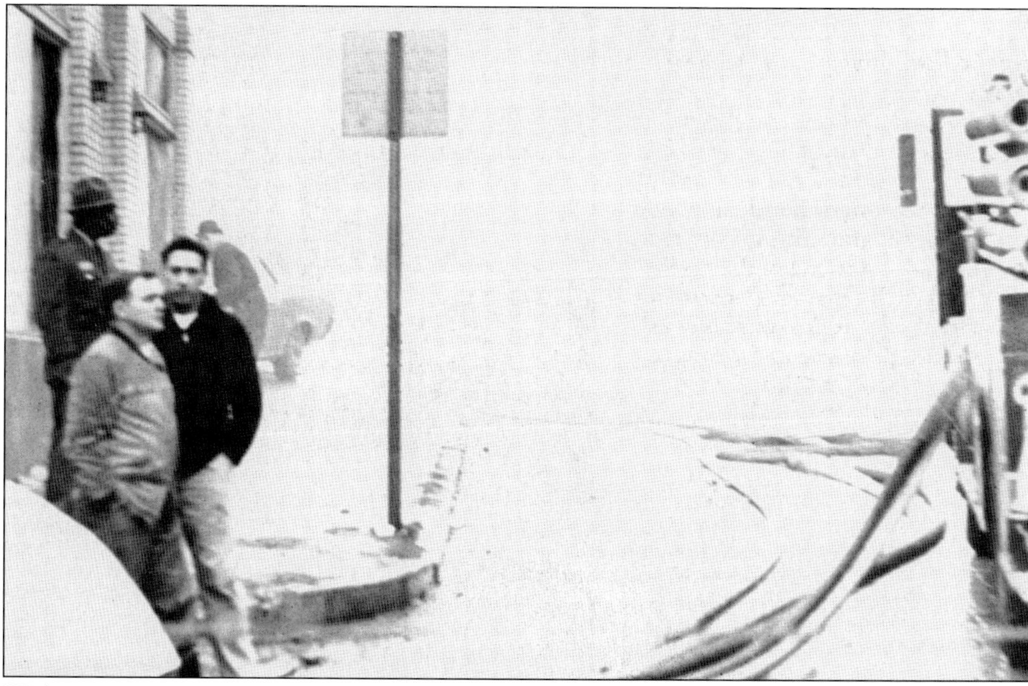

Within minutes after the blast, firefighters and rescue workers began arriving on the scene. This photograph, looking east on Ingram Avenue, shows the dense smoke and dust that blanketed the area. (Courtesy of L. Lomack.)

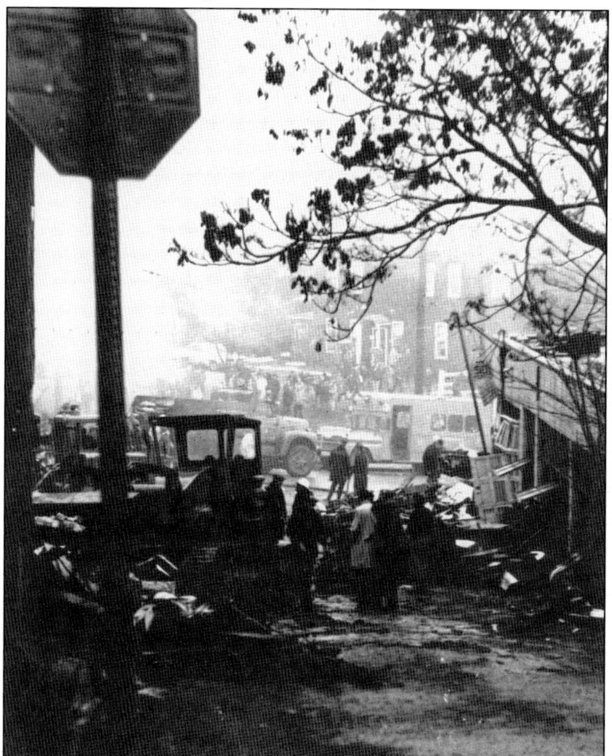

This photograph shows the devastation from Craig Way. The back of the building leveled by the blast stood on the far left. The observers behind the two trucks are standing at the foot of Hodgson Avenue, across the railroad tracks. (Courtesy of L. Lomack.)

This view shows the heavily damaged Ingram Laundromat near the heart of the blast. As rescue workers looked for survivors, a temporary morgue was set up in the building. The Greentree Borough Volunteer Fire Department was one of the many local companies who assisted Ingram throughout the day. Also shown is one of the trucks belonging to the Ingram Department of Public Works, which was also very involved in the rescue and cleanup. (Courtesy of L. Lomack.)

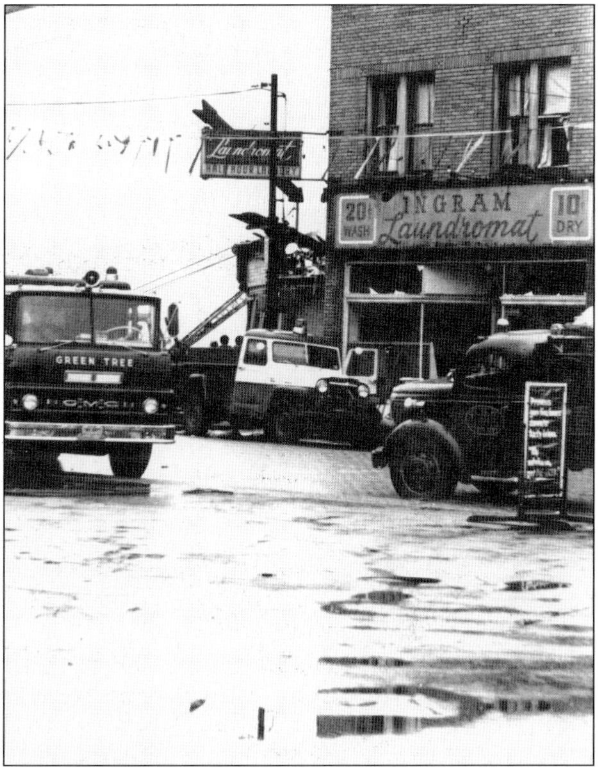

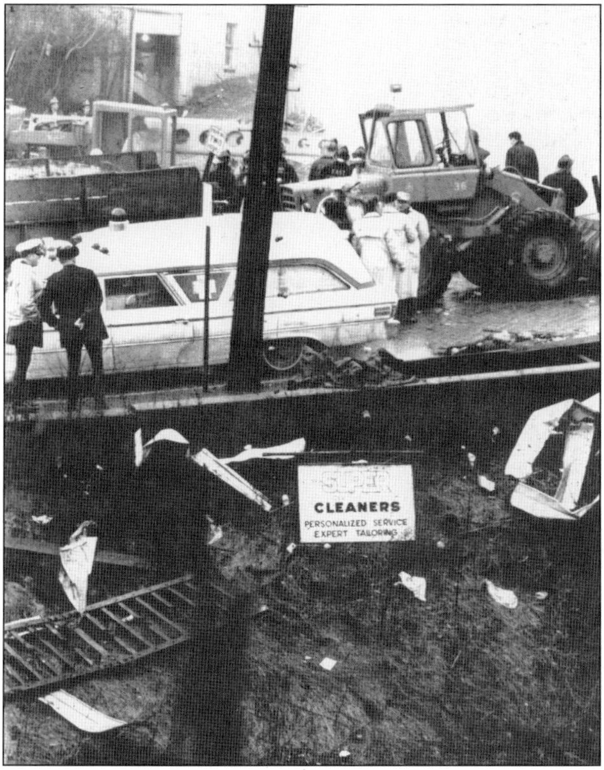

This sign for Super Cleaners is all that survived from the two-story commercial/apartment building that exploded on Ingram Avenue. Eyewitness accounts said that the blast occurred immediately after the gas company crew started their jackhammer. Others believe that a light switch in the gas-filled building triggered the explosion. The actual cause was never fully determined. (Courtesy of L. Lomack.)

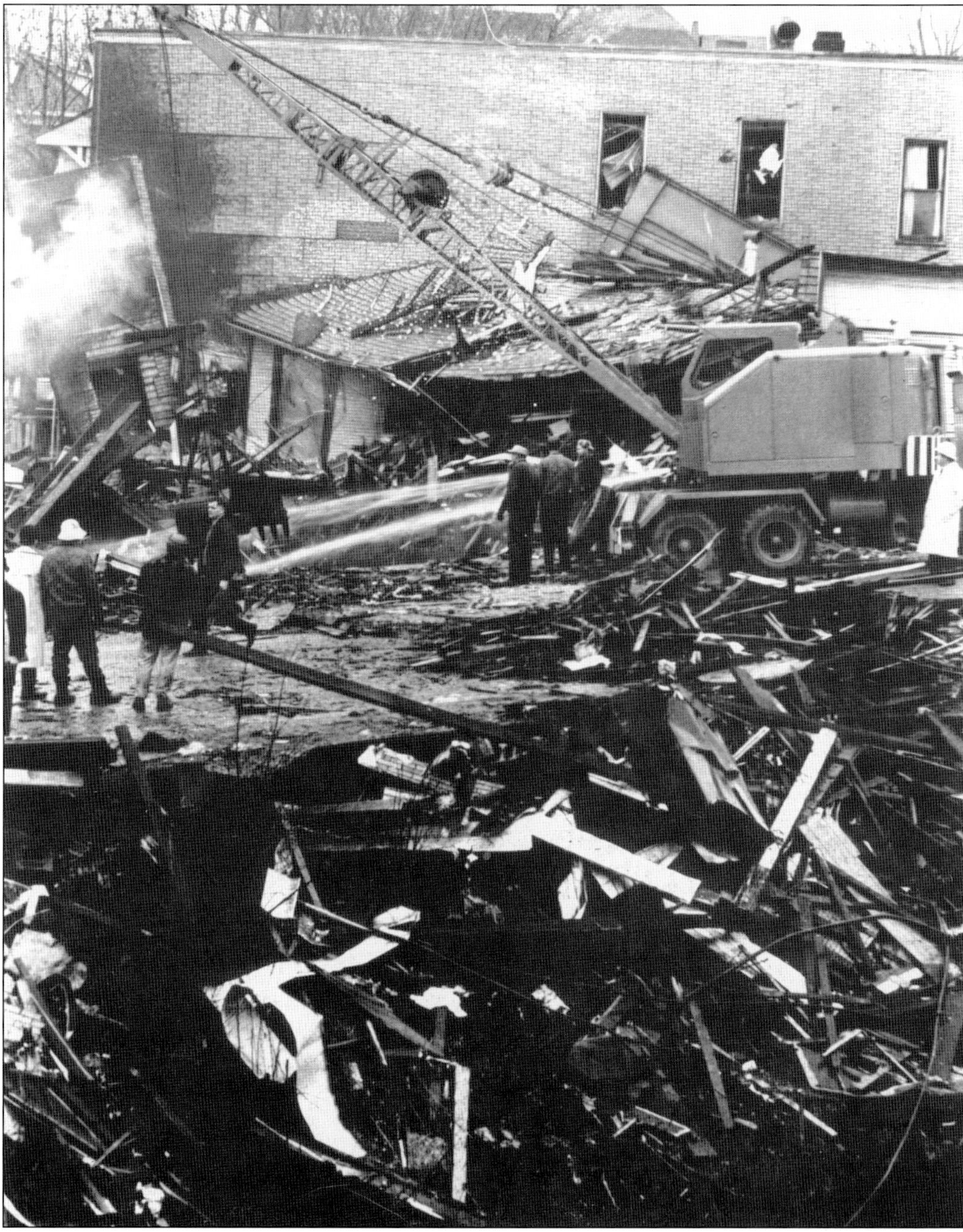

This scene captures the massive cleanup effort near the intersection of Ingram and West Prospect Avenues. Seen here is a crane from the Allegheny County Public Works Department and workers sifting through the rubble, looking for bodies and smoldering hot spots. (Courtesy of L. Lomack.)

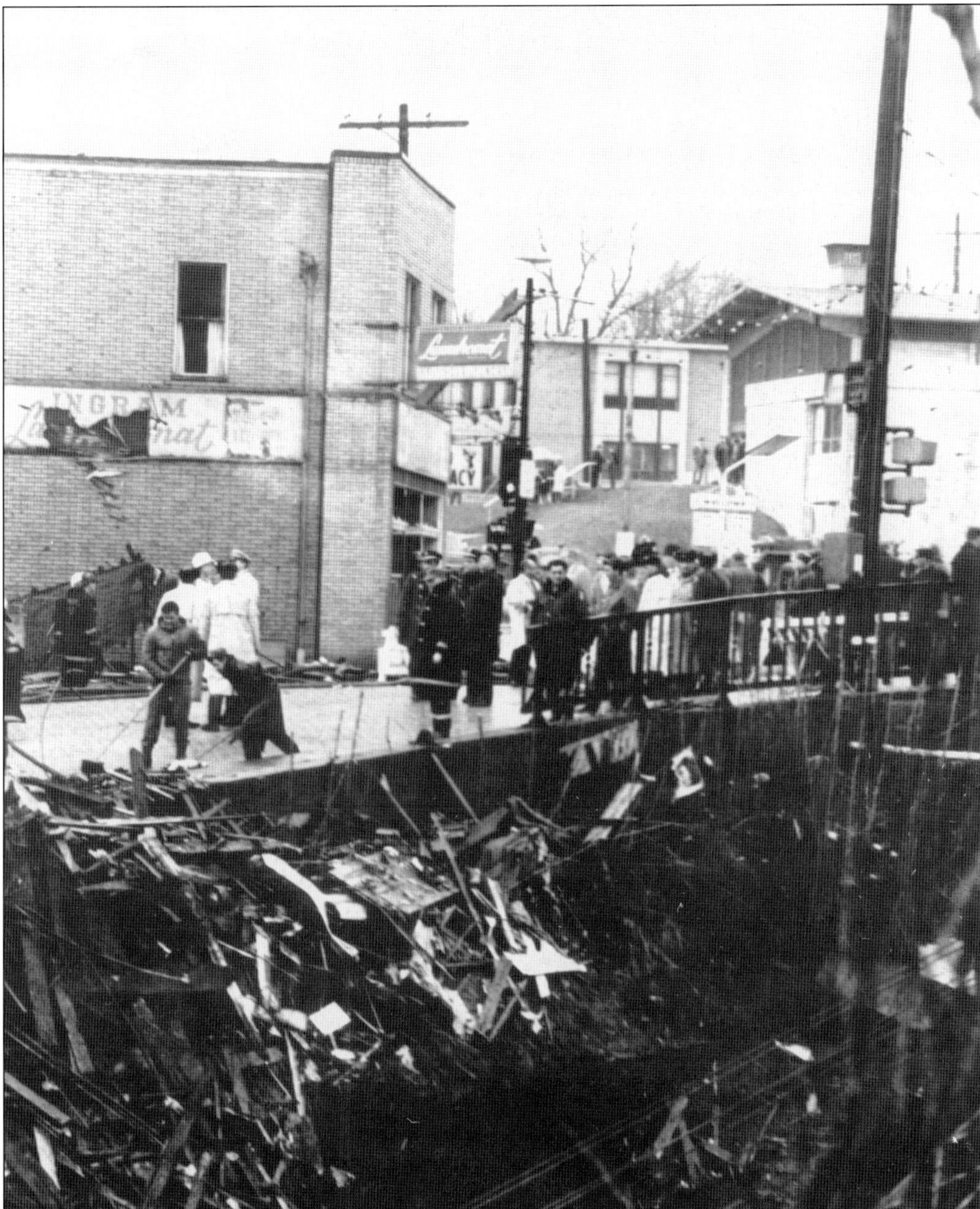

Originally there were six known dead and two missing following the blast. Sadly, the two missing persons were confirmed dead after being discovered under debris. Eighteen others, including rescue workers, were injured but survived the catastrophe. The outpouring of help from concerned residents was tremendous. The tragic event brought the entire borough together. (Courtesy of L. Lomack.)

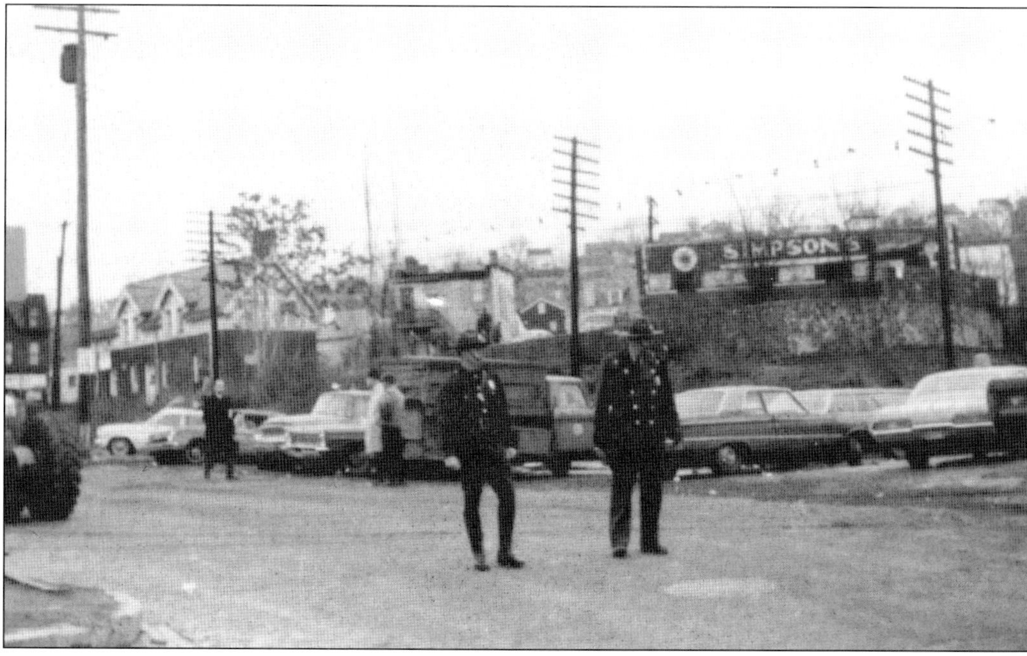

Immediately after the explosion, children were evacuated from the nearby Ingram Elementary School. Windows were shattered throughout the business district and police sealed off the area. (Courtesy of John Sacco.)

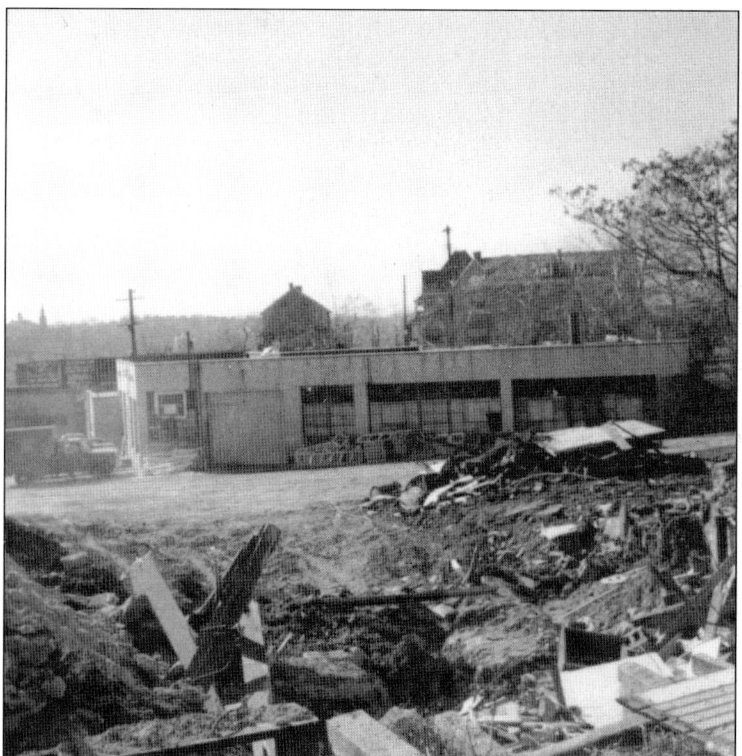

After extinguishing the fires and accounting for victims, the first order of business was to board up damaged buildings. This photograph was actually taken from the foundation of the leveled building. (Courtesy of John Sacco.)

The Pennsylvania Railroad wasted little time in clearing the tracks of their main line. This crane is busy removing rubble from the cut, directly below Ingram Avenue where the blast occurred. During the cleanup effort, trains were detoured over the Scully Branch between Esplen and Wagner Tower. (Courtesy of L. Lomack.)

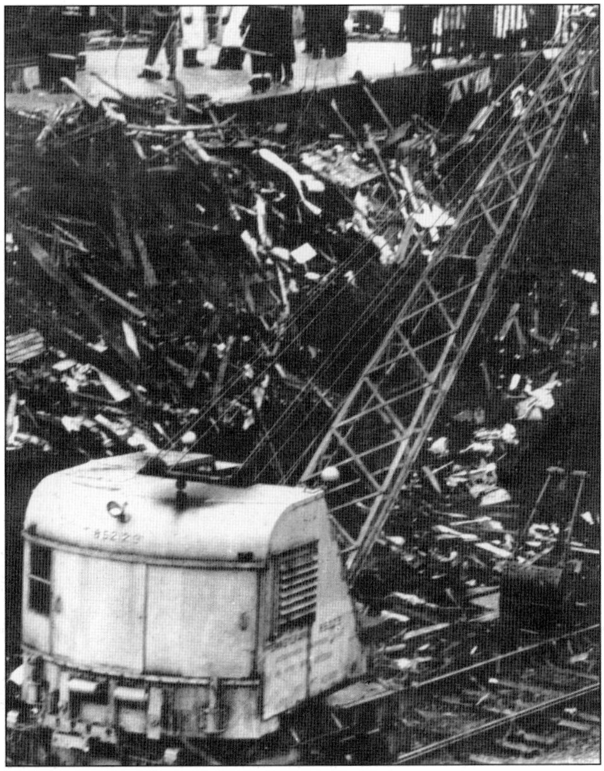

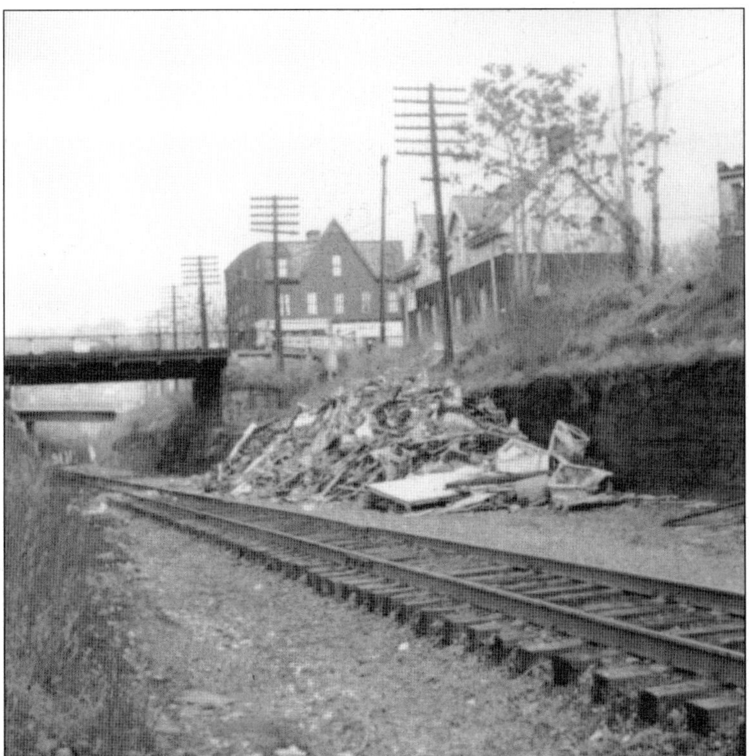

Looking east along the Pennsylvania Railroad main line, a mound of debris remains from the blast. The Tudor-style building atop the hillside is the Ingram Railroad Station. Train service resumed within a few days of the explosion. (Courtesy of John Sacco.)

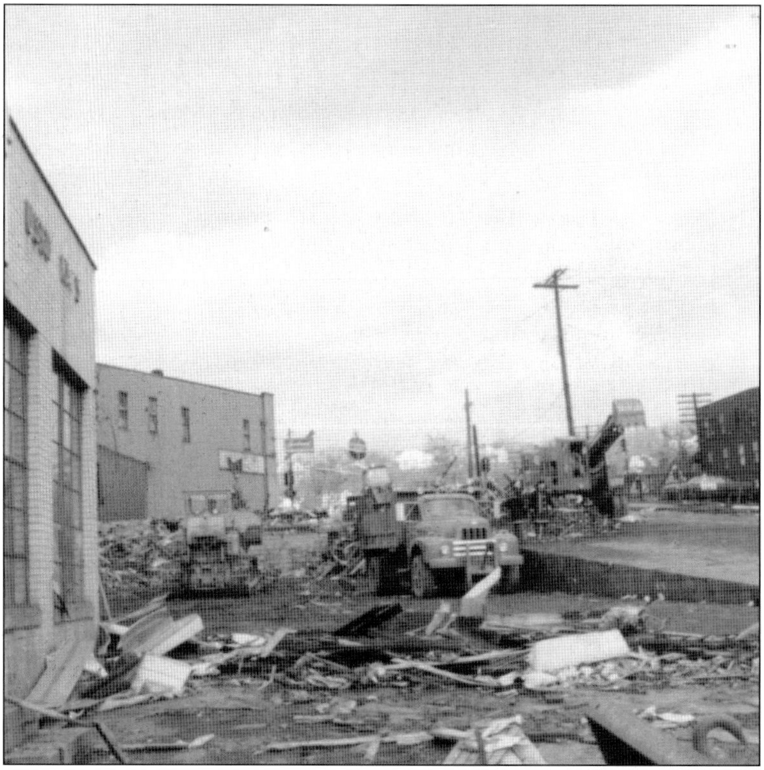

Workers continue the cleanup effort from inside the foundation of the exploded building. Several days passed before the area was reopened to traffic. (Courtesy of John Sacco.)

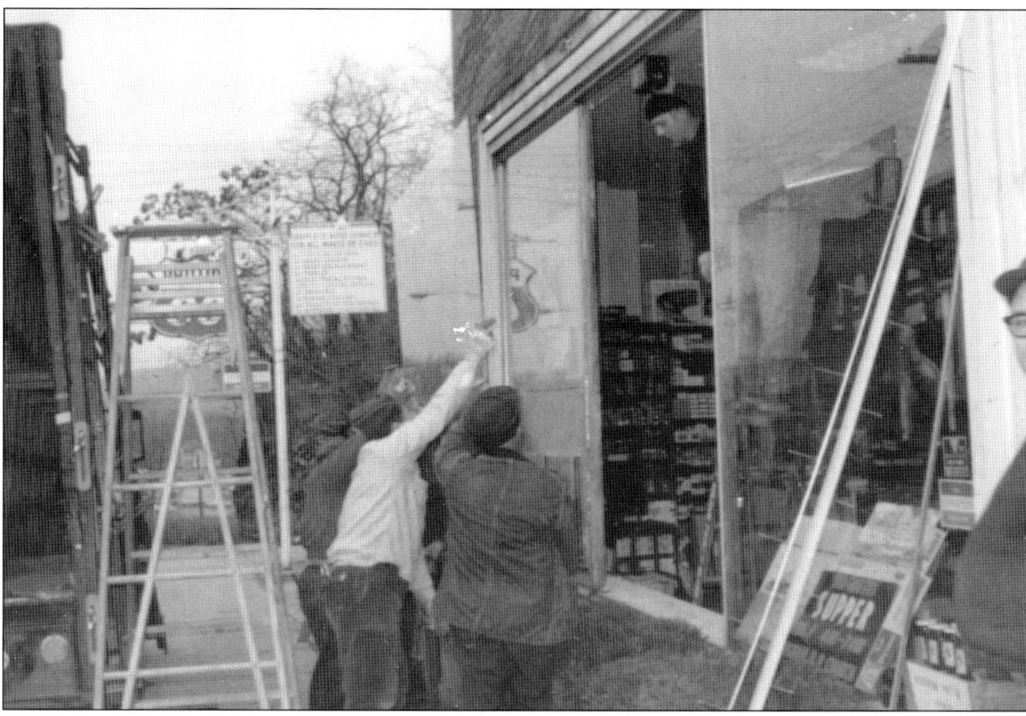

For several weeks after the explosion, merchants were replacing windows. This photograph shows the work underway at Sacco's Hobby Shop. (Courtesy of John Sacco.)

After the cleanup process concluded, gas company workers returned to install a new line along Ingram Avenue. This shows the trench that was dug under the sidewalk. (Courtesy of John Sacco.)

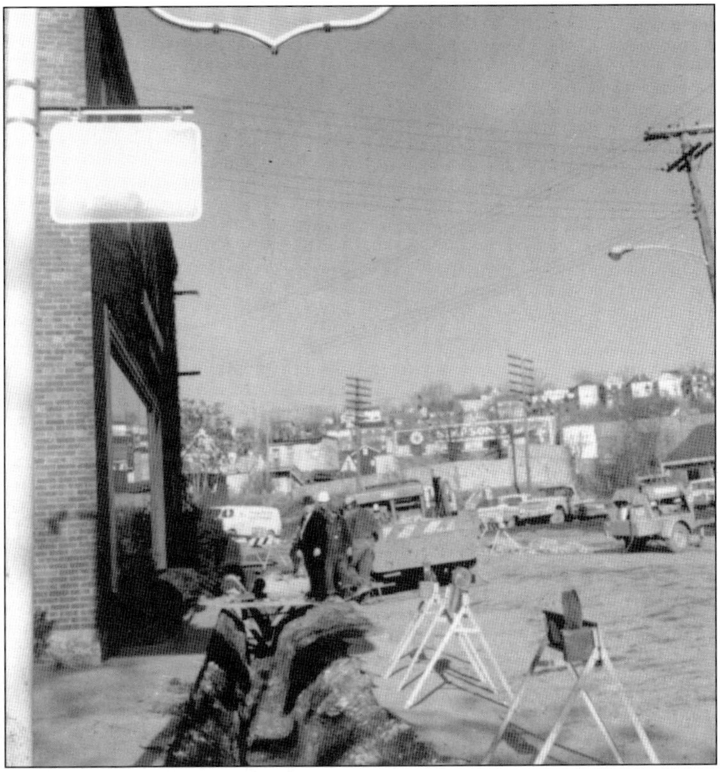

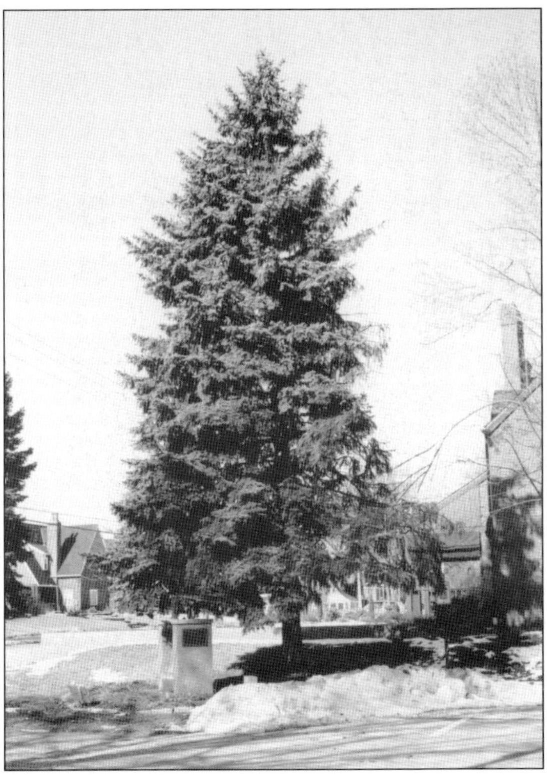

This pine tree, known as Loretta's Tree, was originally planted by the Girl Scouts in a small grassy park area between the doctor's office and the building lost in the explosion. It was planted in memory of Loretta Knudson, an Ingram junior high school girl who died of leukemia in the late 1950s. Somehow the young tree survived and was later replanted by the public works crew, behind the school bell memorial at the borough building. During the holidays, the pine tree is decorated with lights and the community gathers around to sing and enjoy the Christmas season.

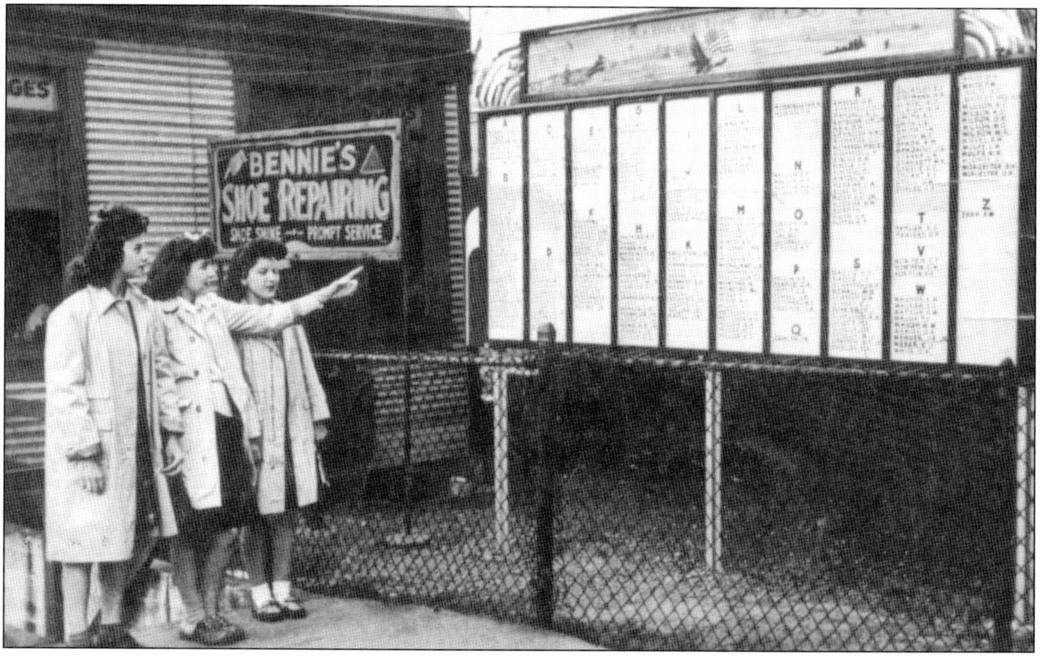

Mary Jane Sims and her friends are observing the names of borough residents serving in World War II. This original memorial stood near the intersection of West Prospect and Ingram Avenues where the explosion occurred. Today two honor roll plaques are displayed in the borough building lobby. Benny Cherchiaro (owner of Bennie's Shoe Repair) had two sons serving in the war.

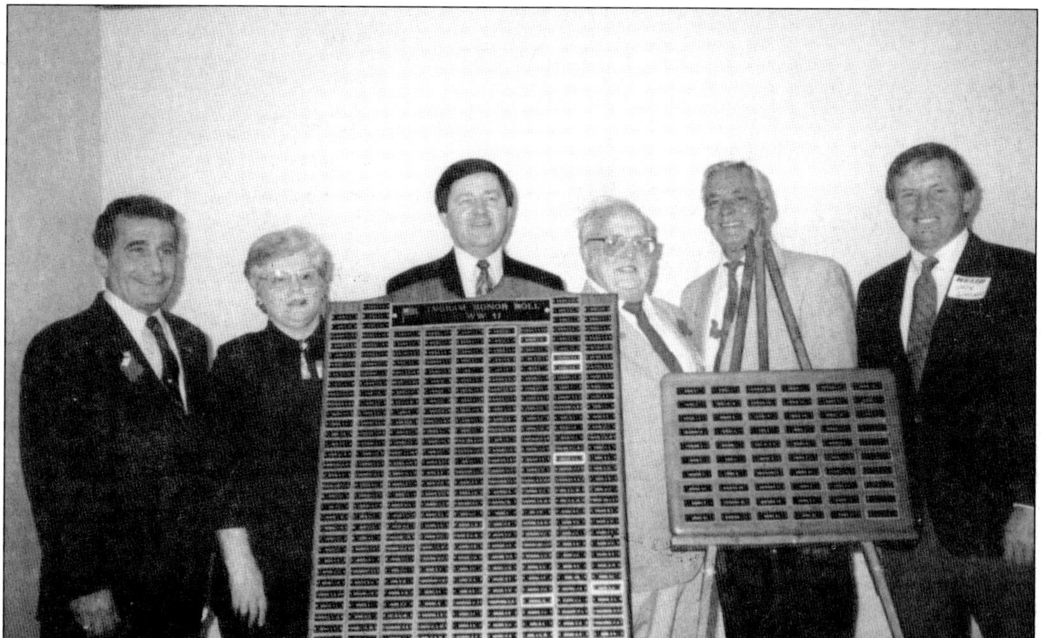

These plaques were the work of Gerald Rabolo. They were dedicated May 30, 1994, in memory of the men who served in World War II. Pictured here are, from left to right, Rep. Tom Petrone; Ingram Council members Mary Parrish, Dave Harris, and Frank Petrell; Ingram mayor Chuck Mitsch; and state senator Mike Wagnor.

Seven

Borough Government

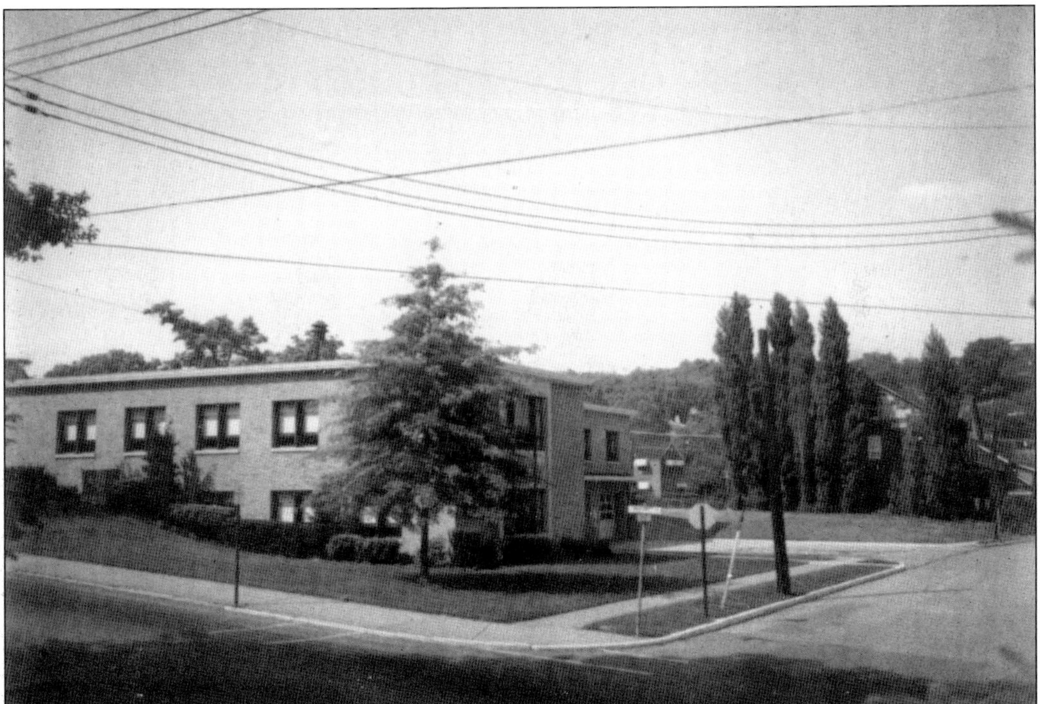

Seen here is the Ingram Municipal Building from the corner of West Prospect Avenue and Thorndale Street. The borough building and fire station were built in 1957. Today, aside from the daily borough business, the Ingram Council meets here regularly. The building is also used for various club meetings, which include the Boy Scouts, Girl Scouts, the Ingram Civic Club, and the Ingram Historical Society.

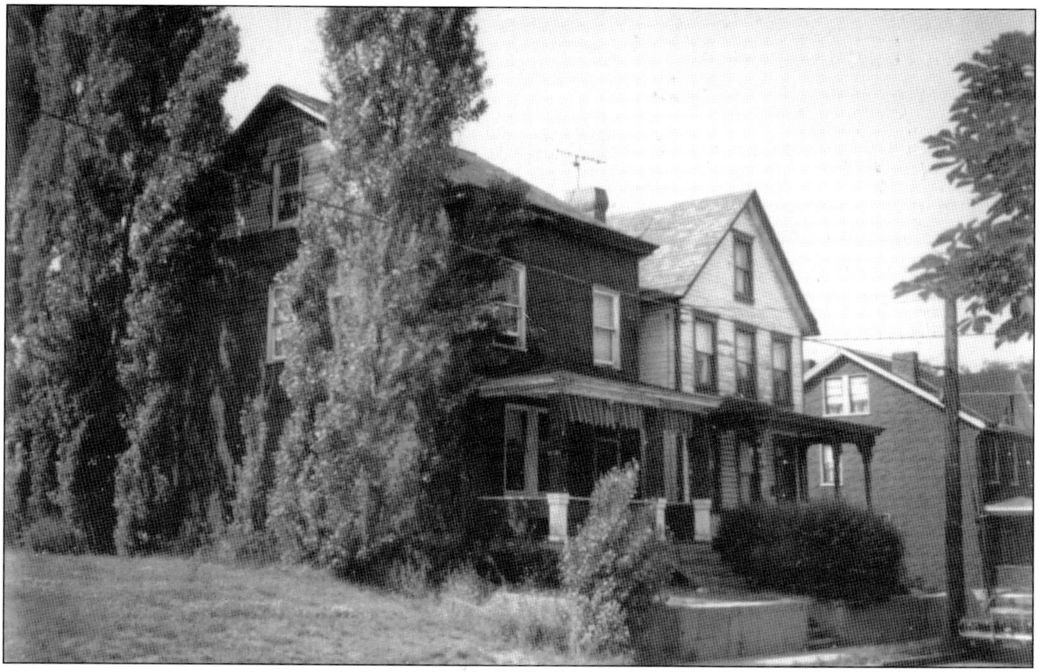

These two homes were located behind the present-day municipal building on Thorndale Street. They were later purchased by the borough and removed to build a "tot lot" playground for small children. This scene was captured in the early 1970s.

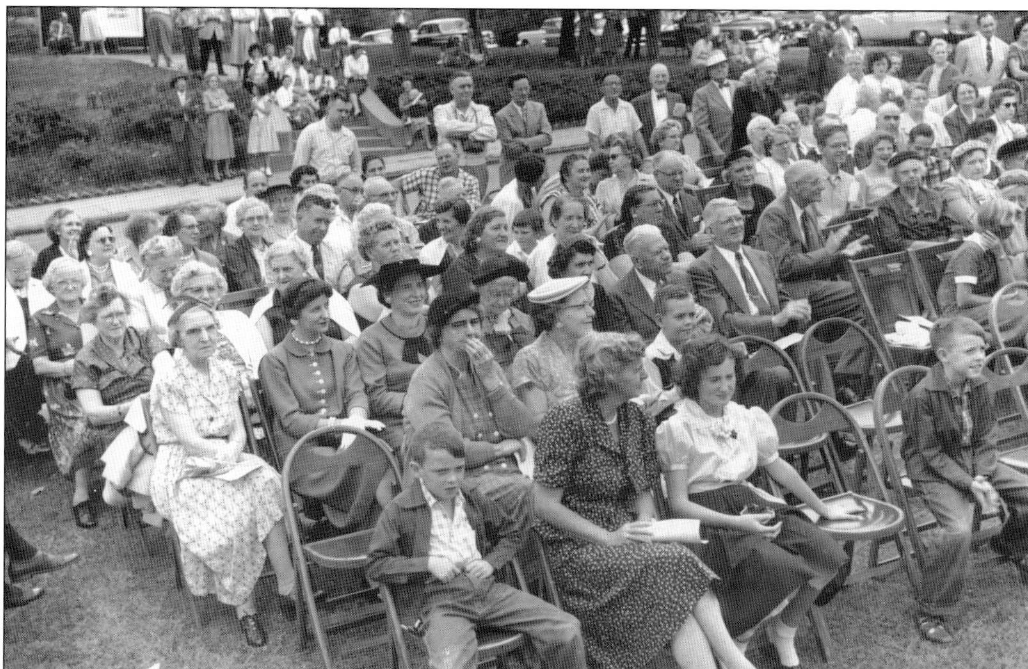

The dedication of the new borough building brought out many from the community, most dressed in their Sunday best. These residents await the flag raising ceremony performed by the Frank R. Kirk American Legion Post No. 145. (Courtesy of John Sacco.)

On Saturday, September 7, 1957, Ingram's new municipal and community building was opened and dedicated. Congressman James Fulton gave the main address. Several ministers and councilmen were part of the program. Flag raising, laying of the cornerstone, and unveiling of the plaque in honor of veterans were the highlights of the day. An open house with refreshments was enjoyed, followed by a social. The evening concluded with music and dancing. (Courtesy of John Sacco.)

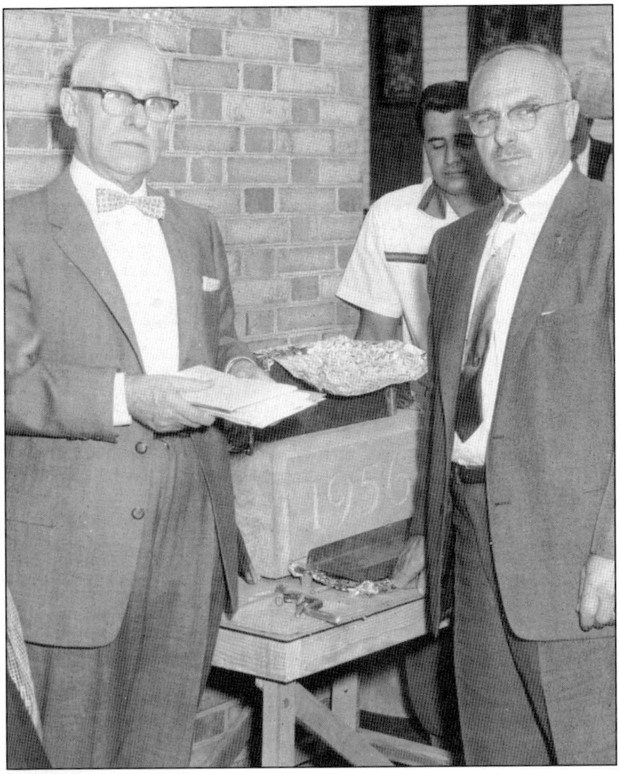

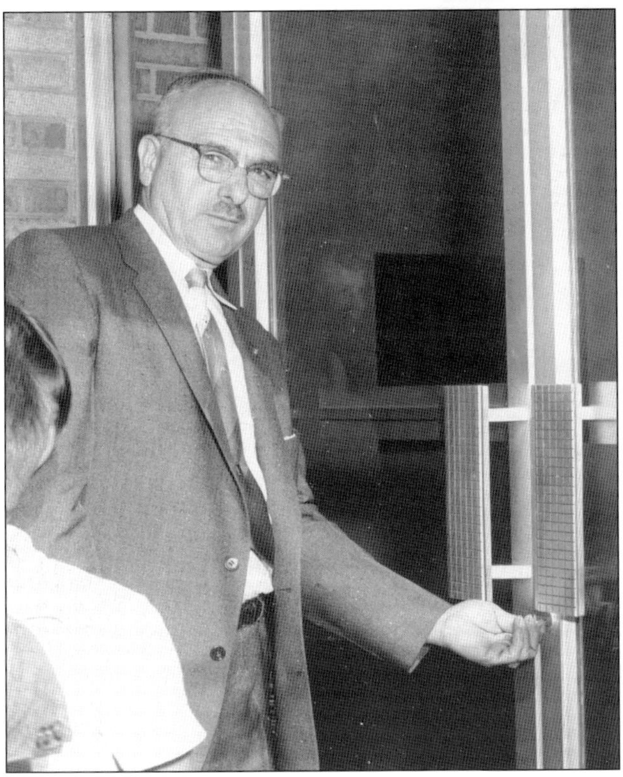

Councilman and building inspector John A. Sacco unlocks the doors to the new Ingram Municipal and Community Building on September 7, 1957. Sacco served as chairman of the building committee. Ground was broken in 1956. (Courtesy of John Sacco.)

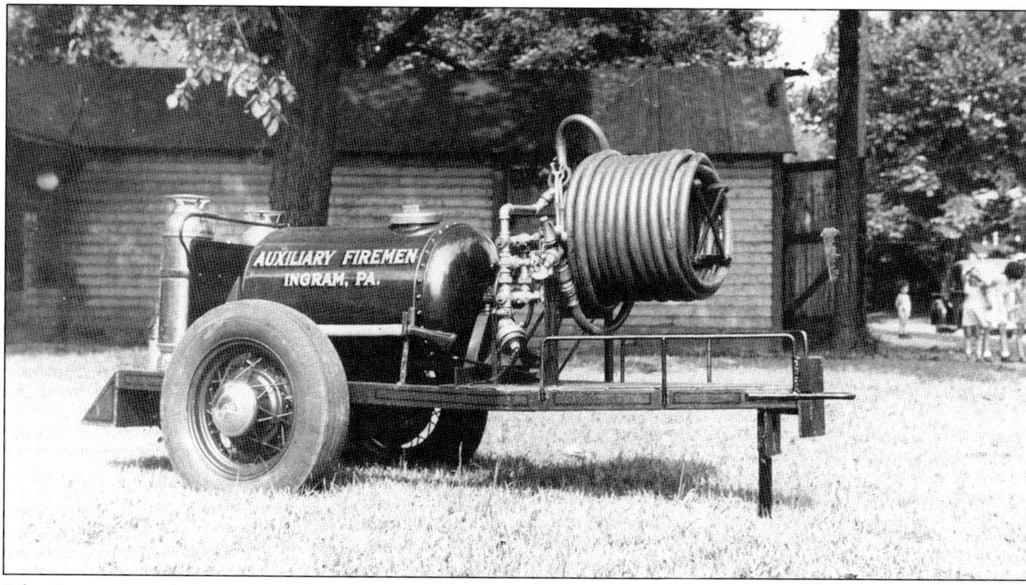

The Ingram Volunteer Fire Department was authorized by the Ingram Council on October 16, 1906. The council elected F. E. Miller as the first fire chief. The complete roster of the first firemen included 32 charter members. Ira Gibben was elected the first president and by-laws were instituted. Original equipment included two hand-drawn hose reels and 1,500 feet of fire hose used on 11 fire hydrants rented from the Chartiers Valley Water Company. Fire extinguishers were placed at five different locations and the schoolhouse bell was used for fire alarms. The all volunteer organization has grown strong over the years. Today there are three fire company stations in the borough. The large ladder truck and ambulance services are located in the municipal building.

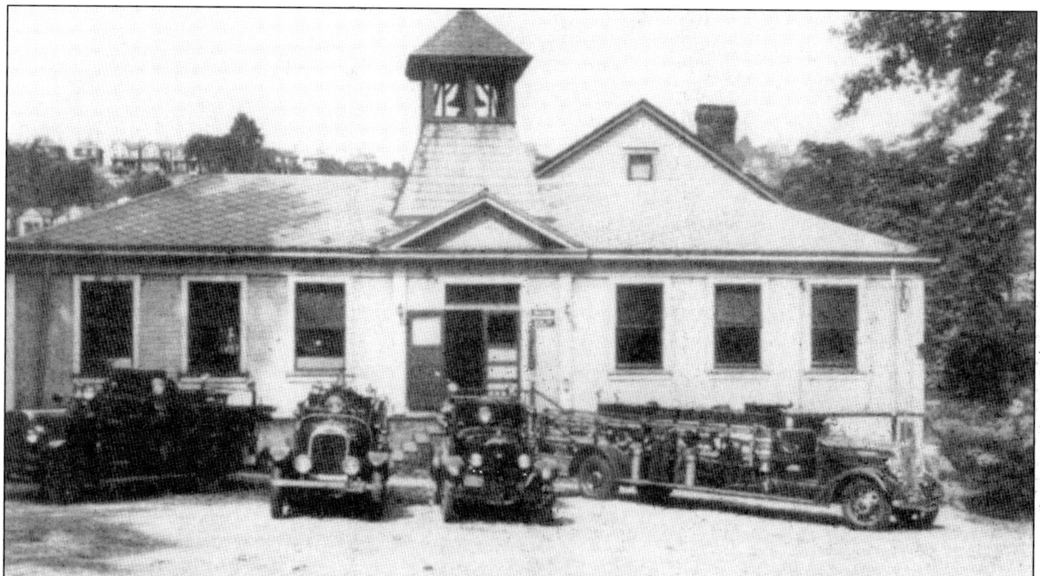

The original firehouse and borough building was located behind the present municipal building on Center Street until 1957. The bell on the building was used for both fire alerts and special occasions.

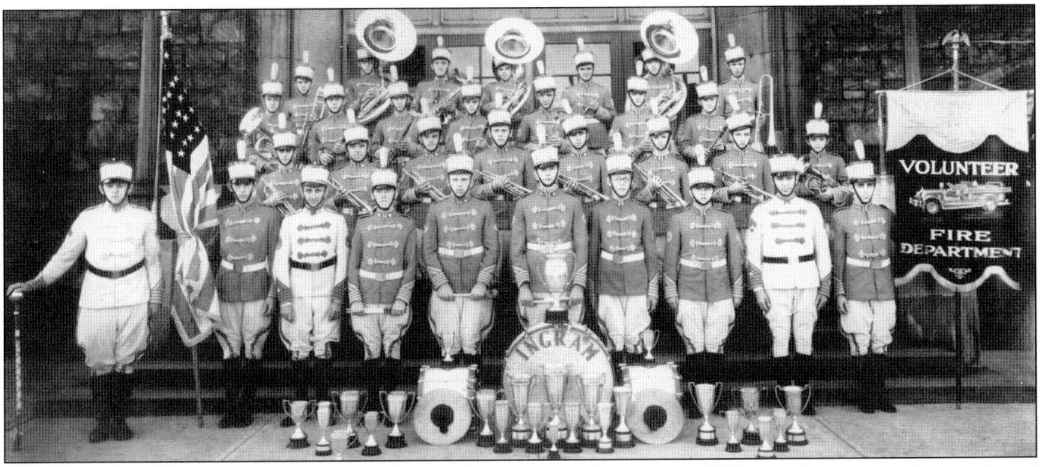

The Ingram Fire Association Band was formed in the early 1900s and consisted greatly of active Ingram volunteer firemen. The band marched at many festivities around town, and the surrounding area. Although the band has long since disbanded, their music is still being played. The Ringold Band, formed by Col. John Ringold in 1898, continues to play their music. At one time it was not uncommon for many of the musicians to play in both bands as they shared close ties with each other. (Courtesy of the Ingram Fire Department.)

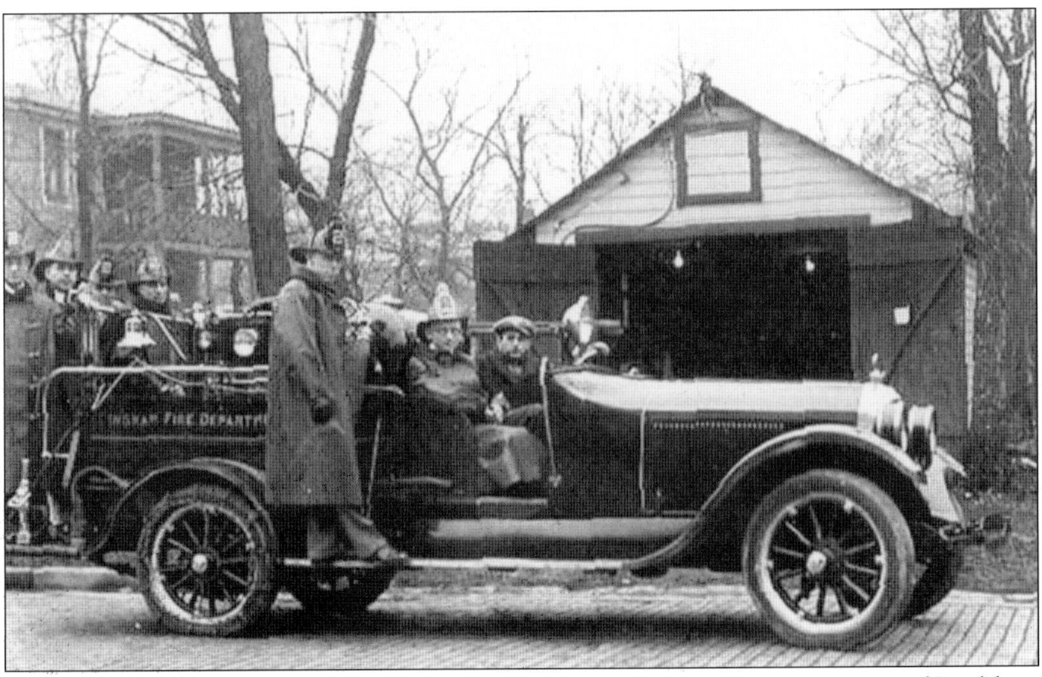

Company No. 2 operated the fire station on Greenwood Avenue between Sampson and Lindshaw Avenues. This picture of the fire station, taken in the 1930s, shows a vintage 1929 fire engine. (Courtesy of the Ingram Fire Department.)

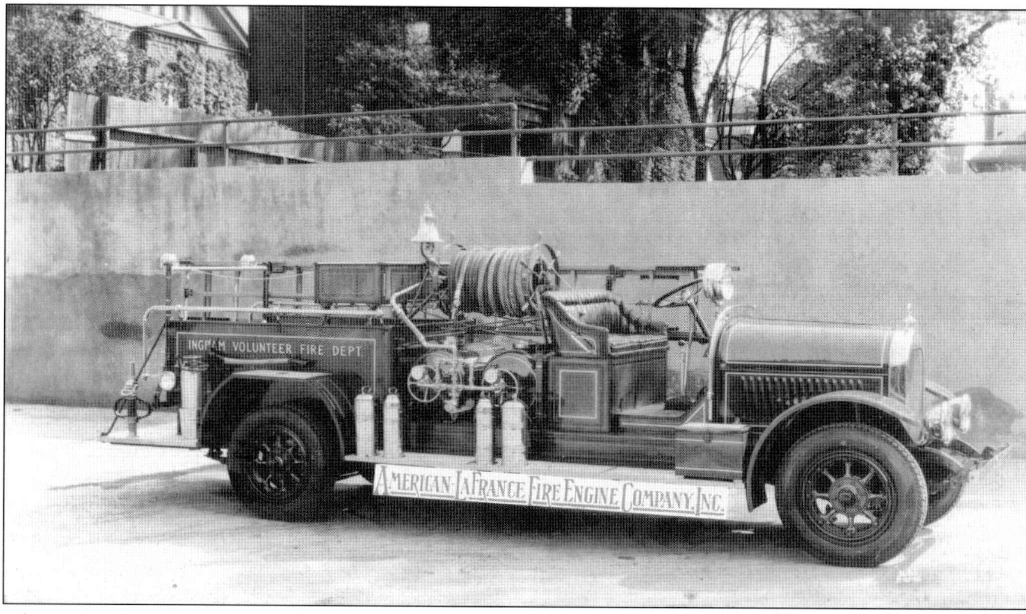

This American La France, 85-foot fire engine was in use for many years at Ingram's Company No. 1 Fire Station. This picture shows the fire truck leaving the assembly line of La France Fire Engine Company of Beloit, Wisconsin, in 1926. At one time, this was the only company that manufactured these vehicles.

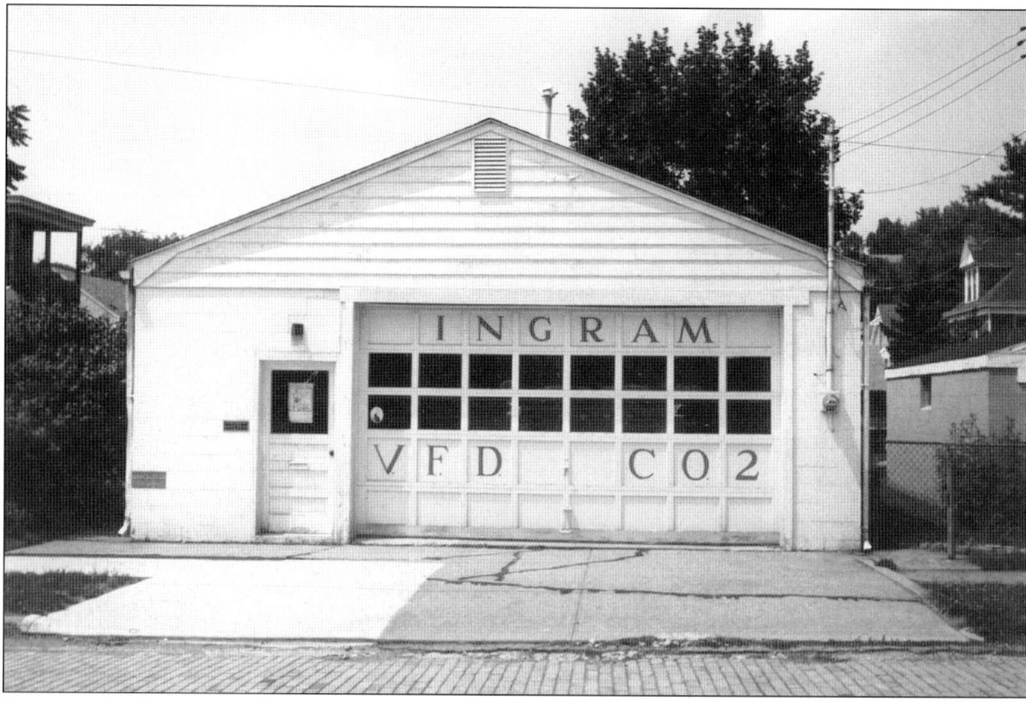

Station No. 2 was rebuilt in the 1960s. In the 1980s, it was remodeled to house a 1986 Ford with an American fire apparatus, 750-gallon-per-minute pump, and a 1947 Dodge truck with a 600-gallon-per-minute pump. The truck was also used as a utility truck for hauling generators, portable pumps, and miscellaneous equipment.

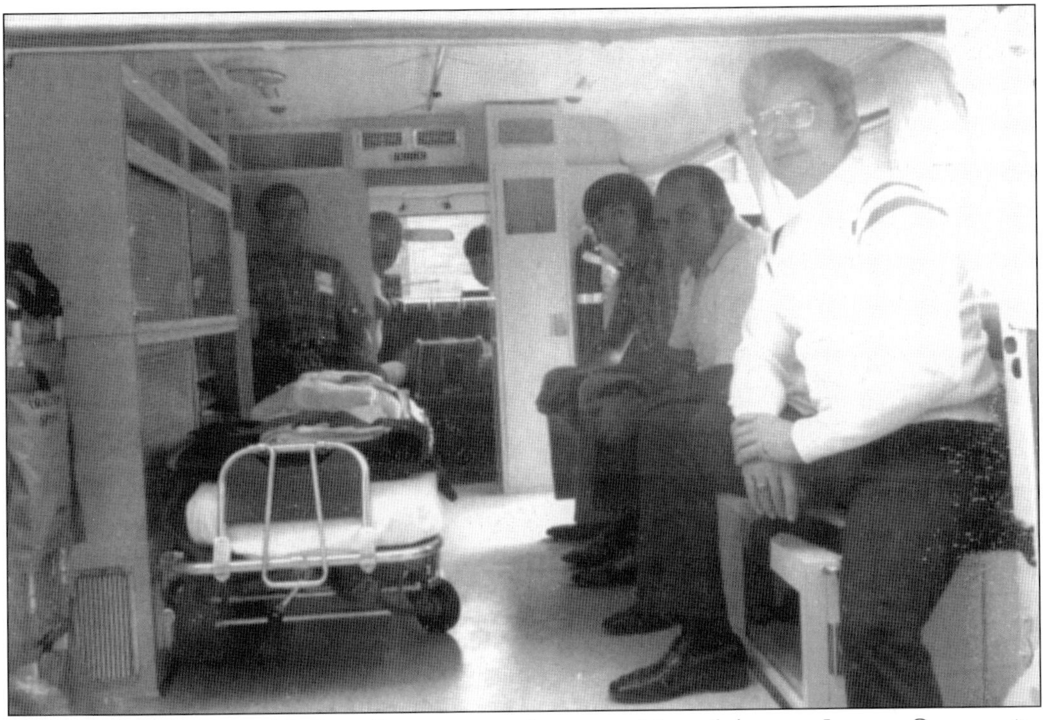

Mayor Jim Hellman and Robert Depp prepare for a test drive of the new Ingram Community Emergency Ambulance Service in 1973. Hellman is also treasurer for the organization. The new vehicle cost $13,000, part of which was donated by local families. At one time, Ingram was one of the few communities to have all their police force trained as emergency medical technicians (EMT). To be an EMT requires an 80-hour training course and the willingness to get out of bed to answer a call 24 hours a day, seven days a week. (Courtesy of Ingram Emergency Medical Services.)

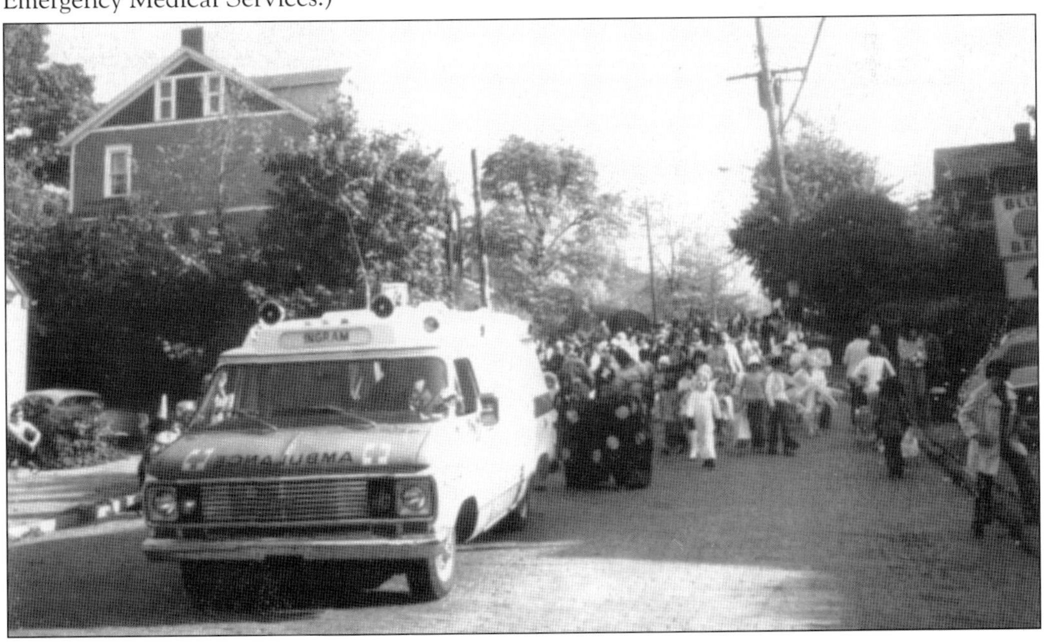

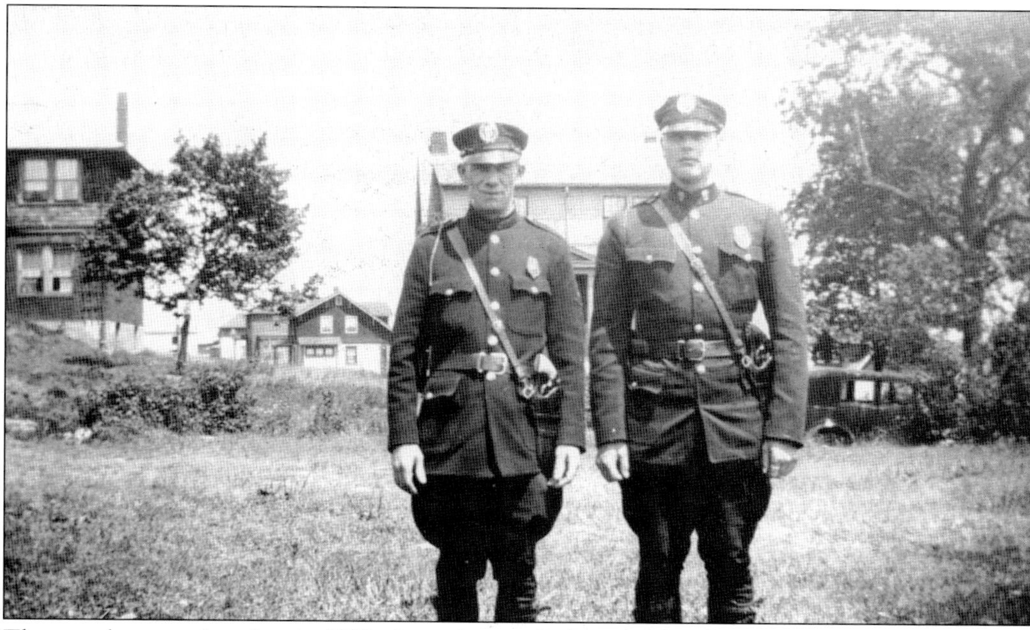

The top photograph, taken in 1929, shows Ingram Police chief William Shaffer (left) and Lt. Len Unger in full uniform. Shaffer served a total of 32 years on the force, 28 of those as police chief. His first four years were spent as a motorcycle patrolman. During his time on the force, he investigated 21 suicides, one murder, and hundreds of robberies. In the bottom photograph, dated August 1943, Shaffer poses in front of the original police station/borough building.

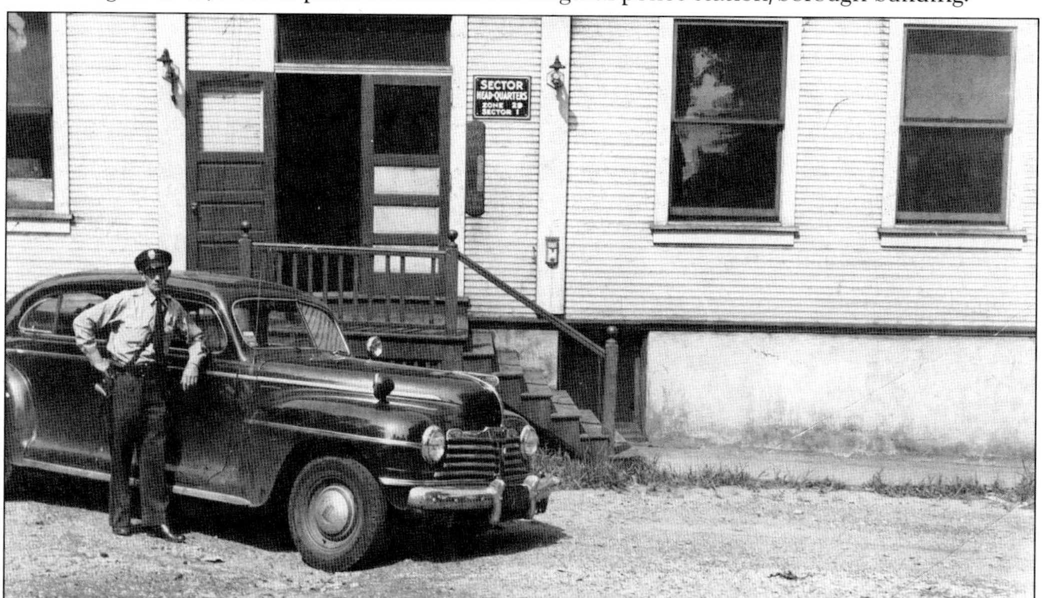

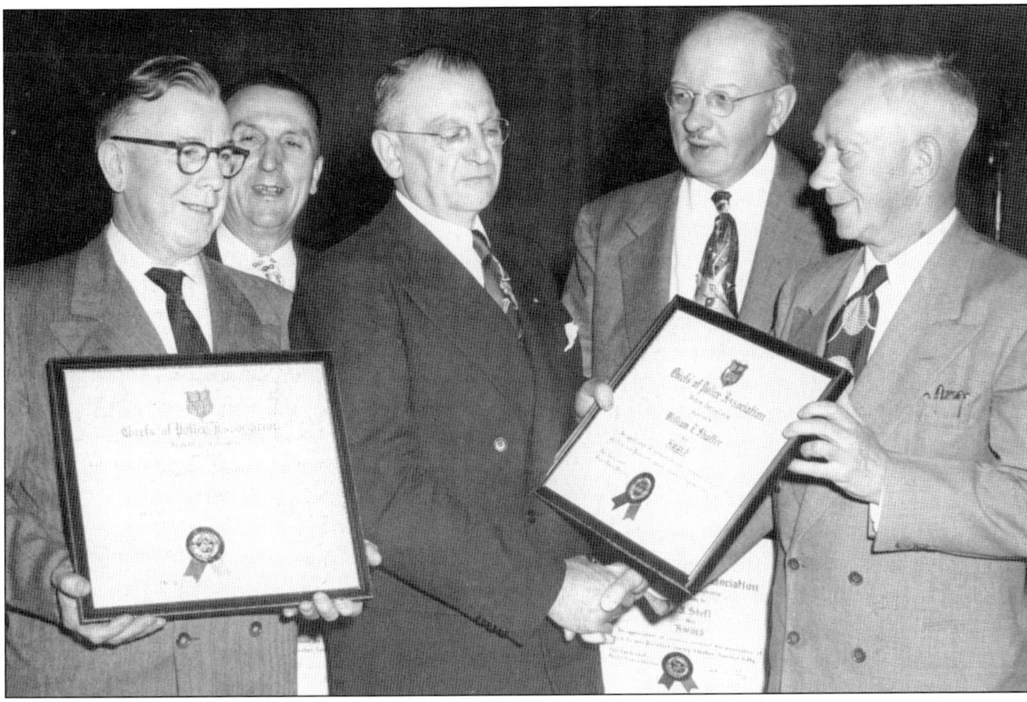

An award was given to Shaffer by the Chiefs of Police Association of Western Pennsylvania in appreciation of his work as president of the association in 1949.

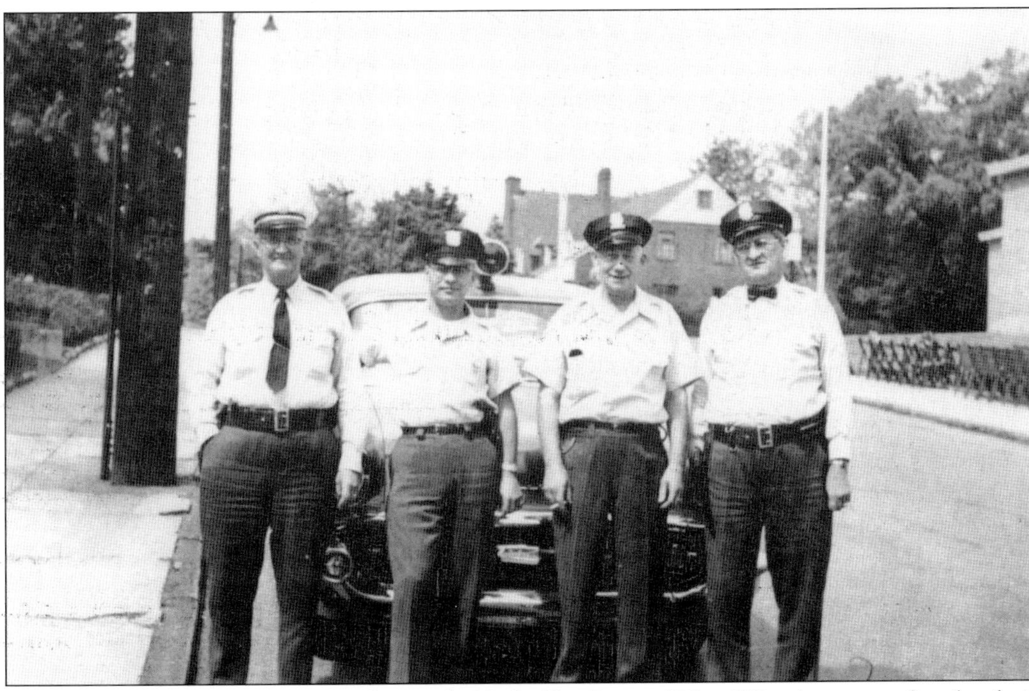

From left to right, Lt. Mickey Walker, Bob Clark, Shaffer, and Tom Waugh are standing by their squad car in front of the present borough building. This picture is looking up West Prospect Avenue during the borough building dedication. (Courtesy of John Sacco.)

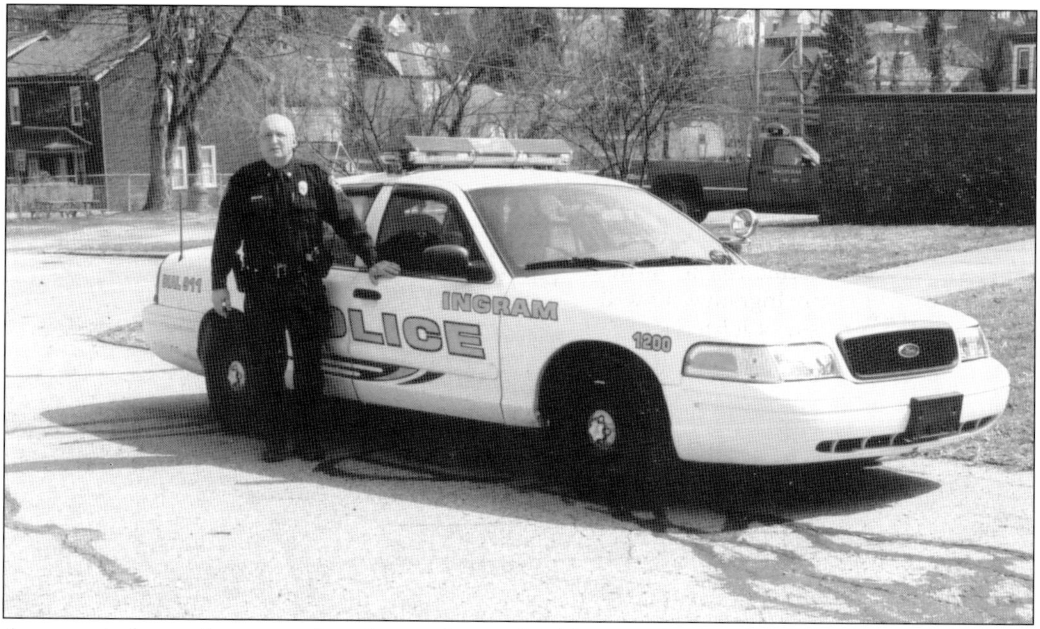

A career in law enforcement has changed considerably since Ingram hired its first police officer, G. F. Dale, in 1902. Today the borough is well adapted to meet the challenges of the 21st century. Police chief John Doherty (shown here) oversees a force of well-trained officers. Each year, police are required to attend classes to be certified by the state. These include firearms, first aid, and CPR training.

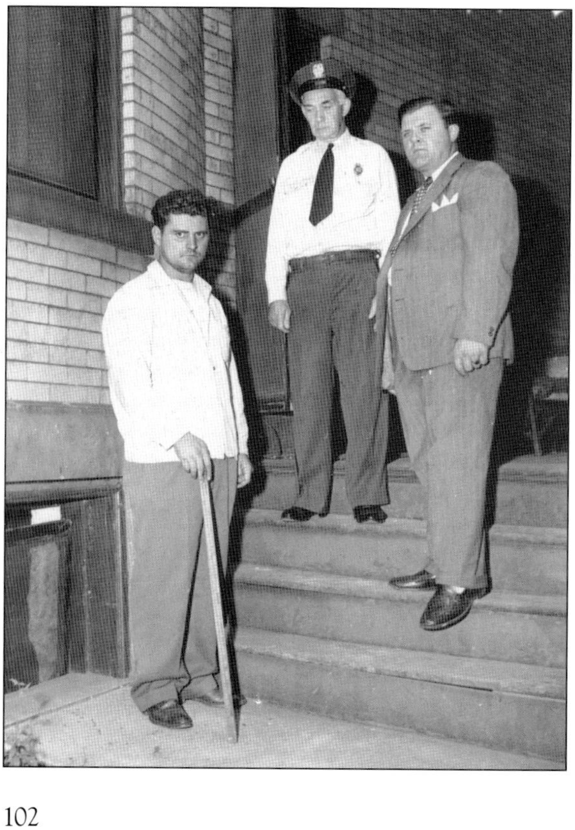

The Ingram police received a call on August 17, 1949, to investigate the murder of Mary Clancy. Neighbors were shocked by the brutal murder, but fortunately the perpetrator, Mary's son John, was quickly apprehended. Those in charge of the investigation are shown here in front of the Clancy's house.

Everyone at the Ingram Borough Building dedication probably had a story to tell about the town. One of the more interesting stories might come from the gentleman pictured here. Felix Sacco was not only the first public works foreman, but the first crew as well, since many times he was without help. With pick, shovel, and wheelbarrow he made sure the roads in early Ingram were well maintained. (Courtesy of John Sacco.)

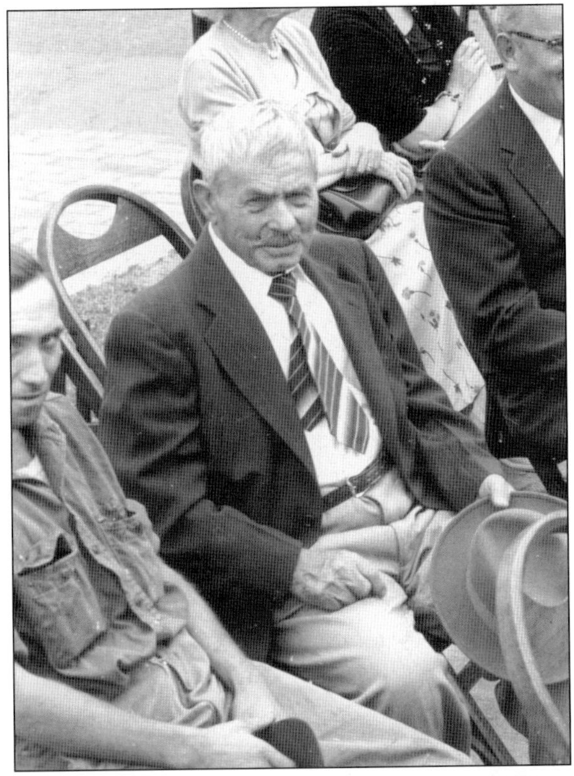

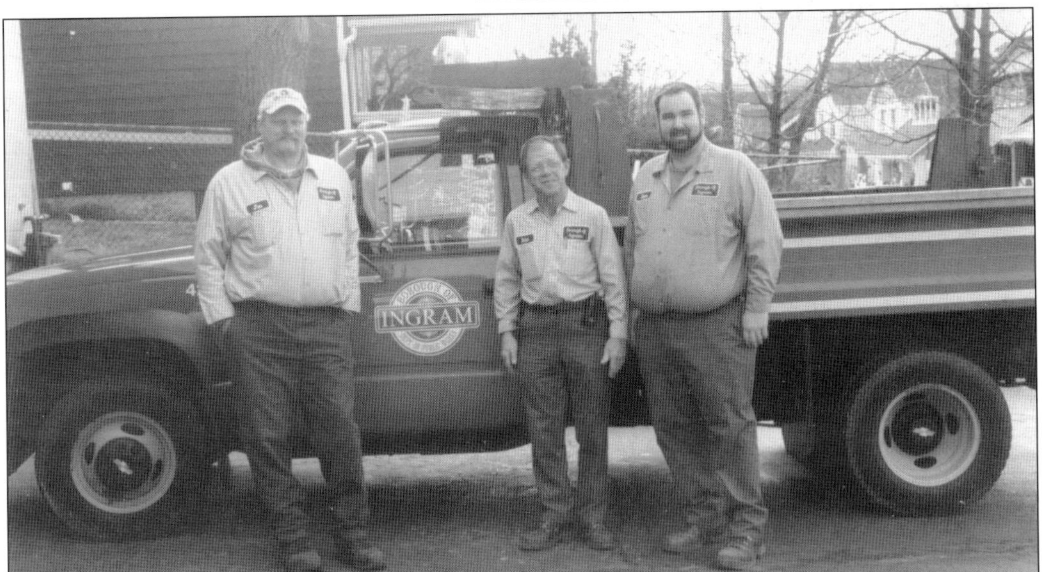

Behind the scenes, the Ingram Department of Public Works is a hardworking, dedicated three-man force. Their duties include street and sewer repair, park maintenance, and many other jobs that increase the safety and pleasure of the community. Their wages thankfully are much better than their 1902 counterparts' pay of $1.65 a day. Pictured in front of truck No. 4202 of the borough's four-truck fleet are, from left to right, Jonathan Hahka, Paul "Butch" Gorchack, and foreman Steven Palmer.

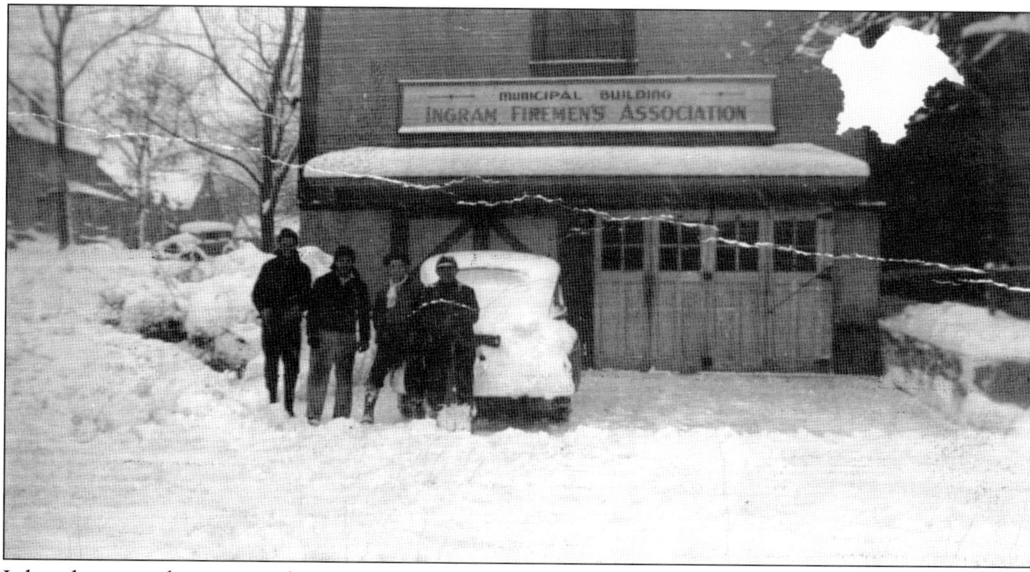

Like their predecessors who tackled the 21-inch snowstorm of February 14, 1940, Ingram's efficient road crew stands ready to clear the mighty Thanksgiving storm of 1950. A total of 30.5 inches of snow covered the borough.

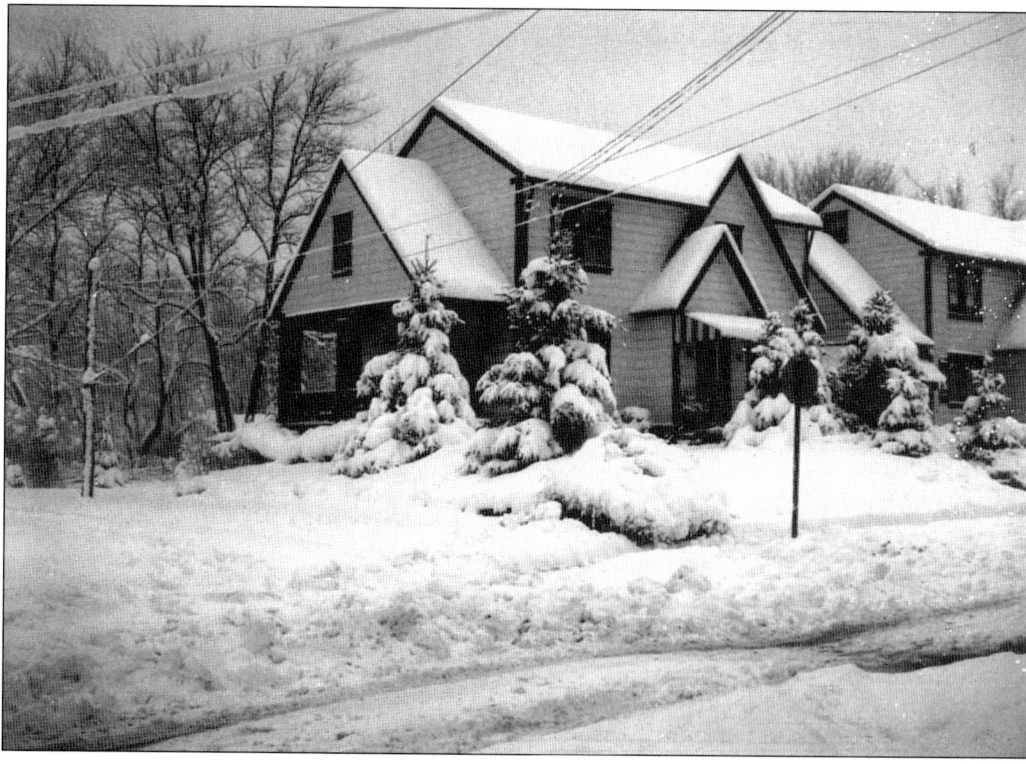

Eight

COMMUNITY LIFE

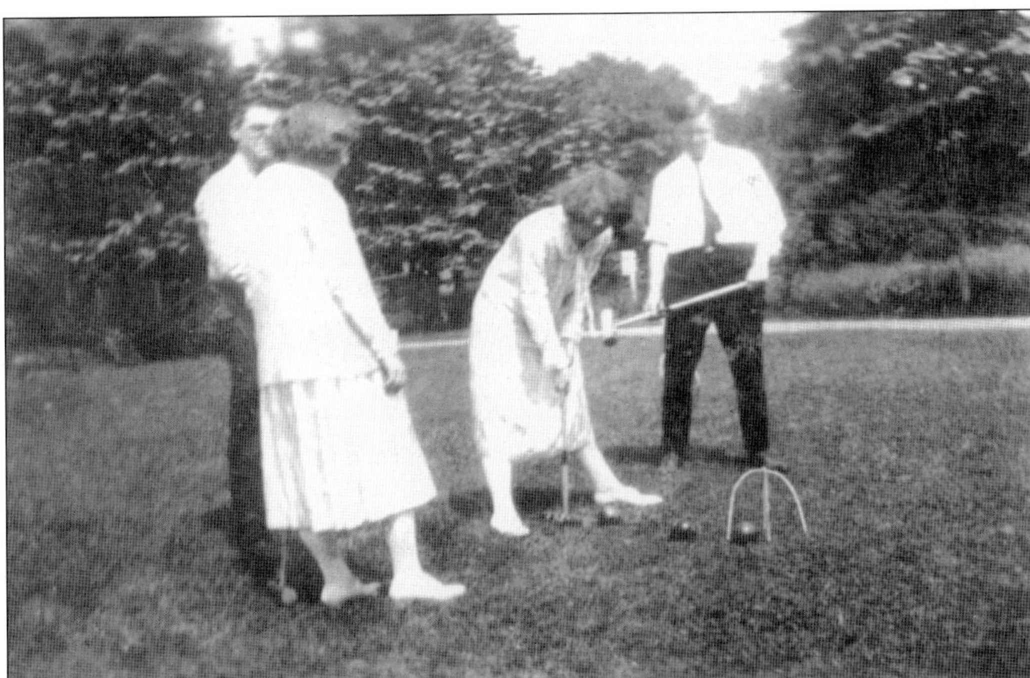

Ingram shared many pastimes with other towns across the country. One fashionable pastime in Ingram was croquet. Croquet flourished and became one of the primary social and recreational activities in the late 1800s and early 1900s. The popular outdoor game is played on a lawn with long handled mallets with which the players hit balls through a series of wickets or hoops.

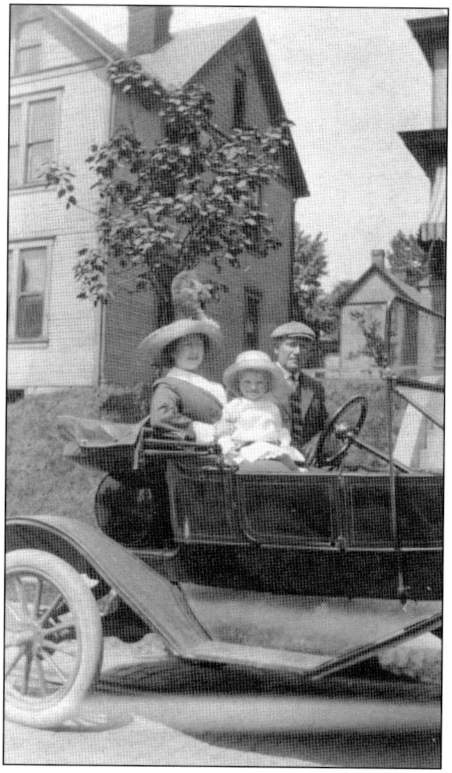

Sunday drives were popular in a time when there were no businesses open or television to watch. After church the family would simply go for a drive in the country. Florence (left), Mary Jane, and Frank Rex take a relaxing Sunday drive down the streets of Ingram around 1917. (Courtesy of Claire Rex.)

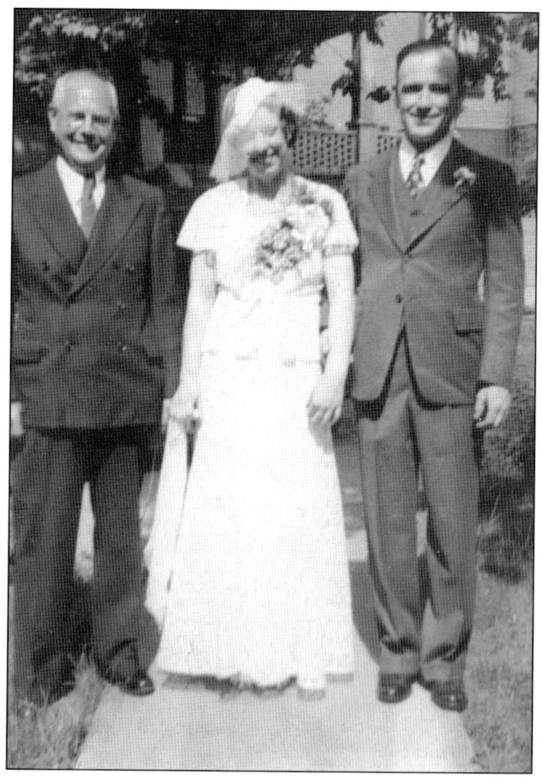

In earlier days, middle-class family weddings were normally held in the home rather than the church. This is the wedding photograph of Ruby Marton and Donald Jessep. The Jesseps were married on June 16, 1936, in Ruby's parents Richard and Catherine Marton's home. The picture was taken in front of the house at 255 Danvers Avenue. When Richard and Catherine acquired their home, in 1924, the street was called Dallas Avenue. Reverend Horter came to the home to perform the ceremony. (Courtesy of Judy Jessep.)

The long anticipation of waiting for Santa to arrive is over, and Christmas is once again celebrated at the Rex home. The family has gathered under the large, decorated tree to open their presents. Many toys, including baby dolls, toy horses, and wagons, will be enjoyed by the children this Christmas and memories will be stored for years to come. (Courtesy of Claire Rex.)

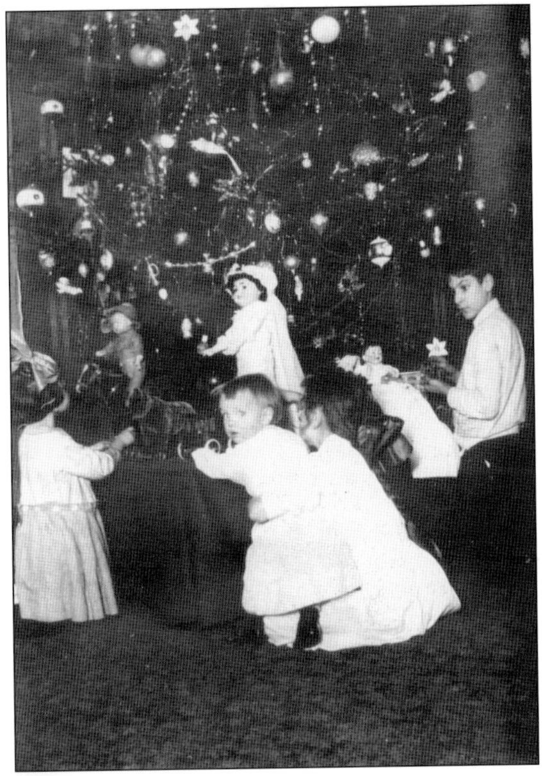

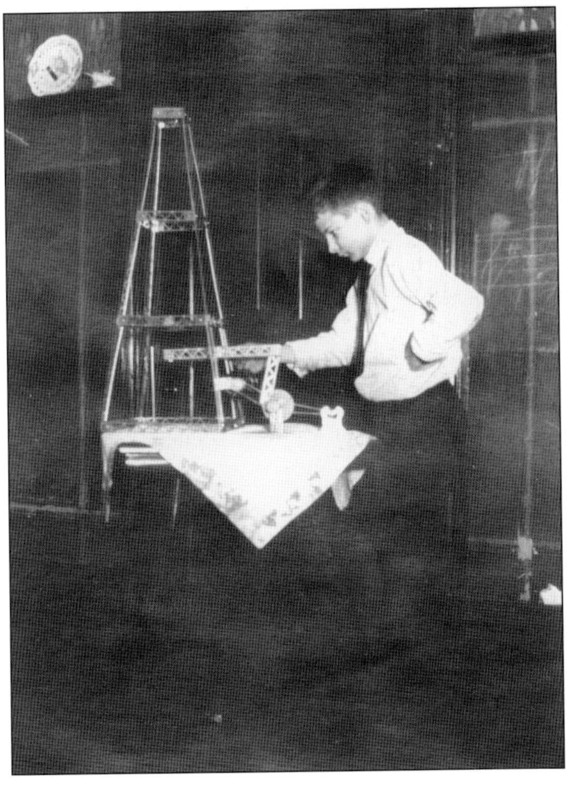

Few people realize that the erector set has been a popular children's toy for over 90 years. It was invented by A. C. Gilbert in 1913. Generations have learned, expanded their imagination, and enjoyed playing with the realistic building components in erector sets. Pictured here, Ford Rex, a young Ingram resident, is using his imagination and having fun. (Courtesy of Claire Rex.)

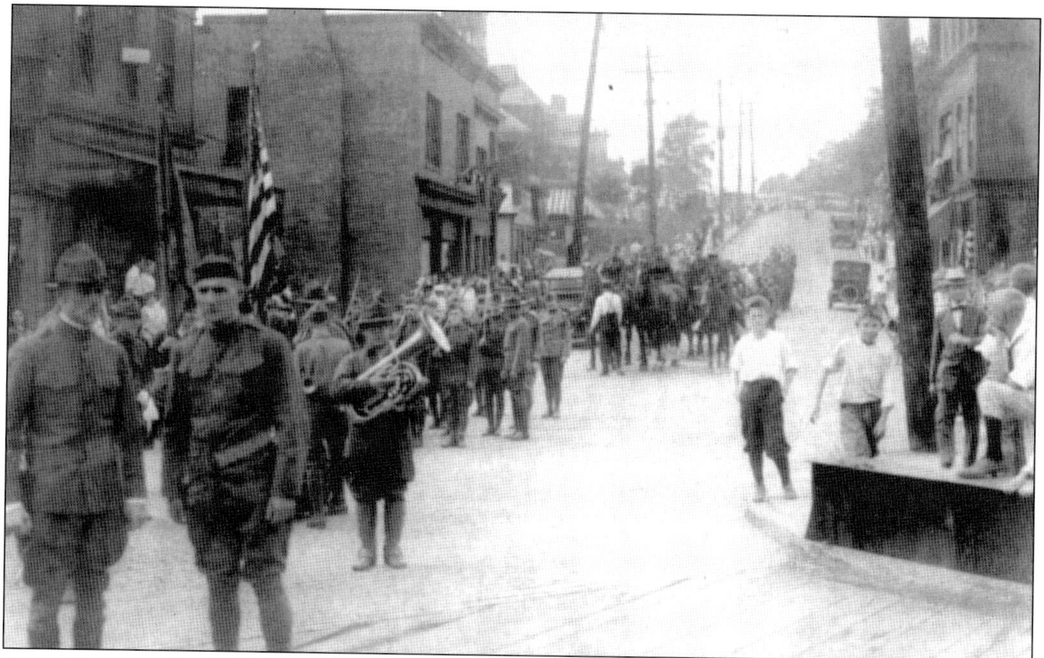

A somber mood was felt throughout Ingram as the funeral procession for Lt. Frank R. Kirk Jr. passed through town. Kirk was killed in action on November 4, 1918, one week before Armistice Day. Residents of Ingram lined both sides of West Prospect Avenue to honor their fallen hero, who gave his life for his country.

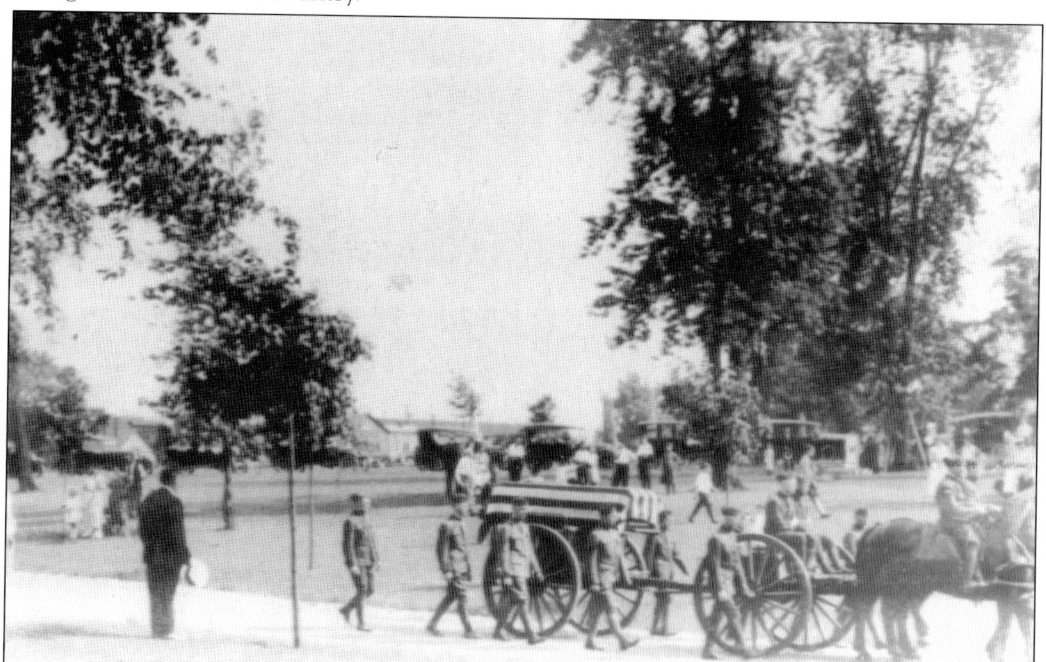

The body of Kirk arrives at its final resting place. Few believe that any other conflict would ever equal the magnitude of World War I. Years later, neighboring Crafton Borough would dedicate the Frank R. Kirk Jr. American Legion Post No. 145 to his memory.

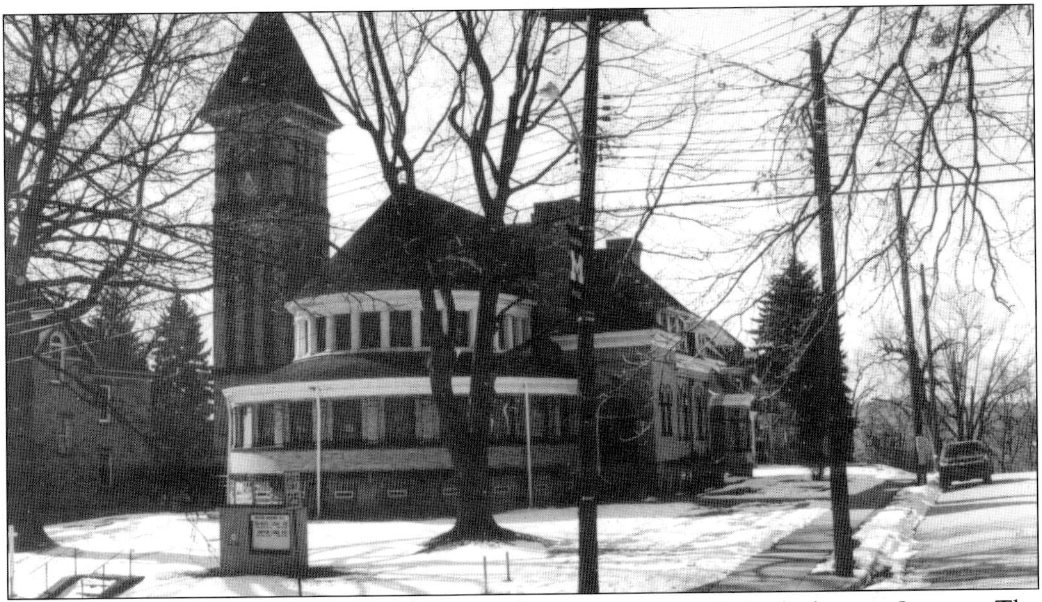

Freemasonry, the world's oldest and largest fraternity, came relatively late to Ingram. The borough's Masonic hall actually began in 1899 as the First Presbyterian Church of Ingram. The congregation, which was later named the Prospect Presbyterian Church, played a vital role in the community until 1970 when it merged with the Ingram United Presbyterian Church. Shortly thereafter, the building was purchased by Guyasuta Lodge No. 513 Free and Accepted Masons. (Courtesy of the Ingram Historical Society.)

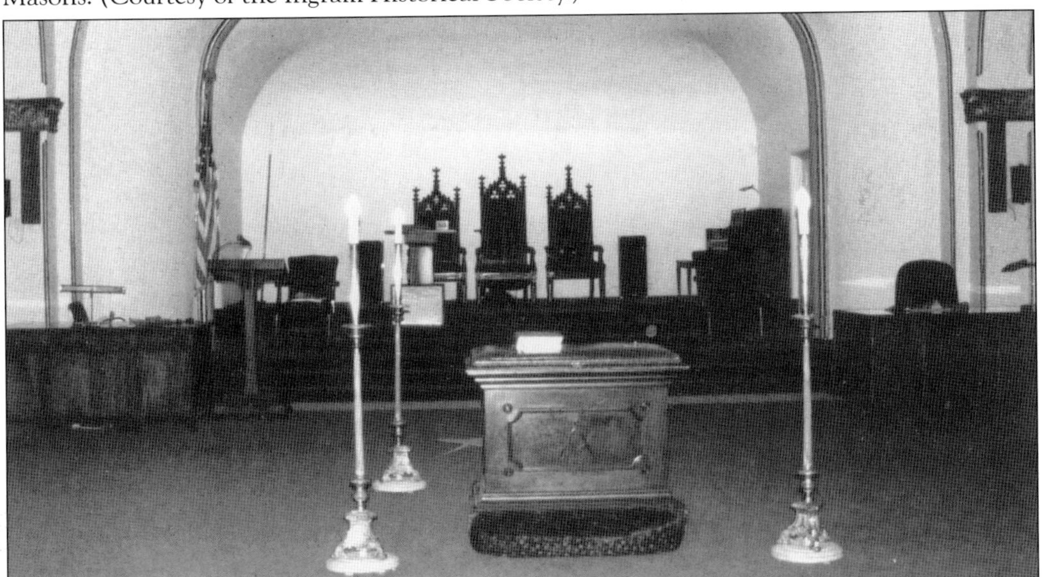

After purchasing the building, Guyasuta Lodge began renovating the interior. On July 15, 1976, the first stated meeting was held in the Ingram hall. Prior to this date, Guyasuta had been meeting in the Crafton Masonic Hall on Nobel Avenue. As fate would have it, Crafton hall was destroyed by a devastating fire on March 5, 1986. Today Ingram Masonic Hall is home to Guyasuta Lodge No. 513, Crafton Lodge No. 653, and Crafton Royal Arch Chapter No. 312. (Courtesy of the Ingram Historical Society.)

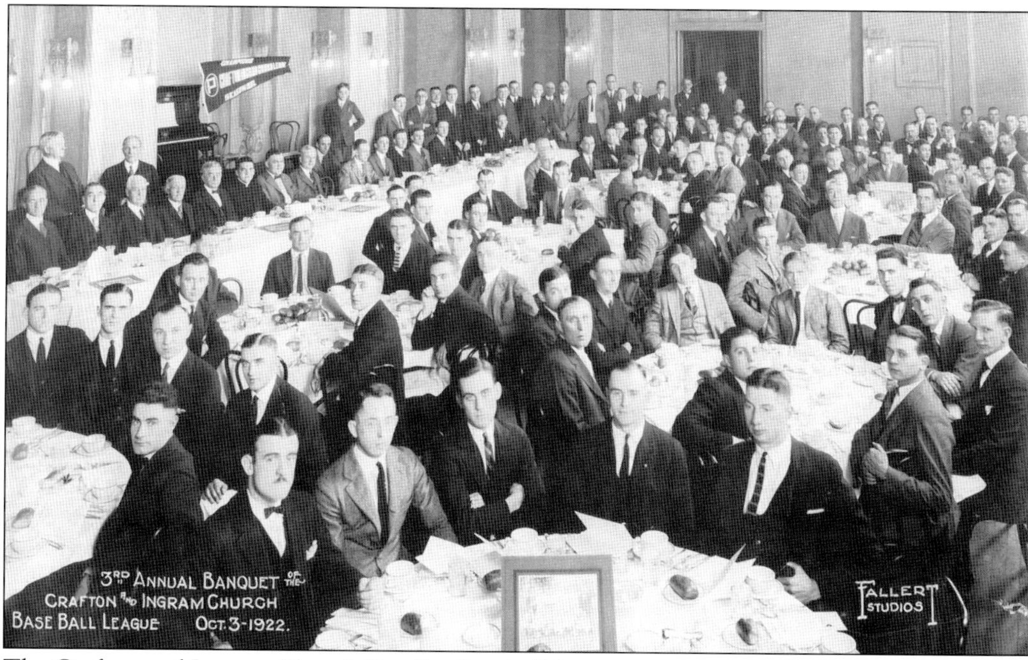

The Crafton and Ingram Church Sandlot Baseball League was comprised of teams representing each church in the area. Besides playing each other, the league hosted visiting teams at the Crafton Athletic Field. The league drew crowds of 2,000 to 5,000 fans at their games. They were rewarded in 1922 with a banquet at the end of the season.

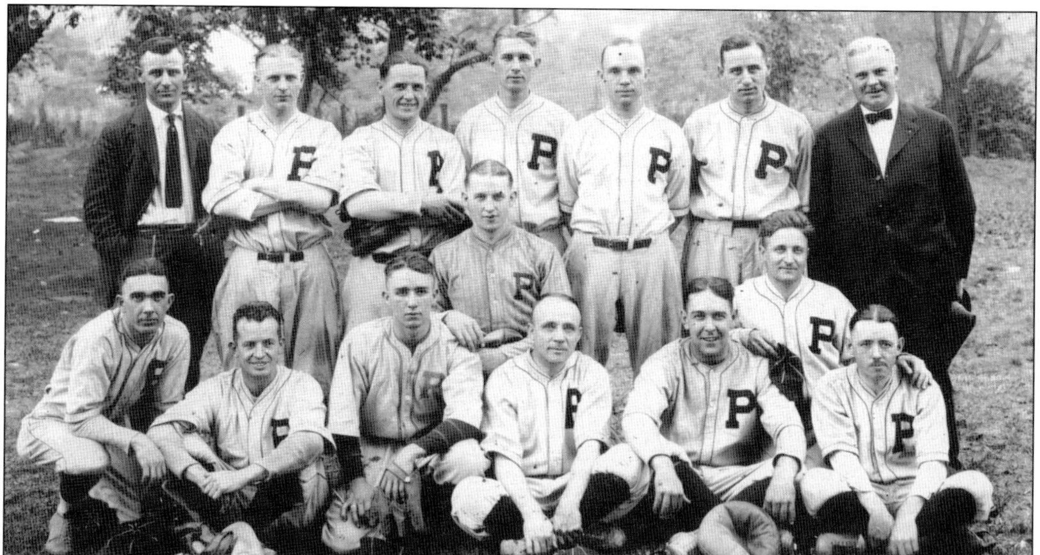

Many community activities centered around local churches. The beginning of the 20th century saw an unprecedented rise in the popularity of baseball. Not everyone could afford to go to a professional game and where there were no professional teams, there were semi-pro, company clubs, and amateur men's leagues. In the days before television, if one wanted to see a game, they had to go to the game. Many members of this Crafton-Ingram baseball team belonged to the Hurst-Miller families.

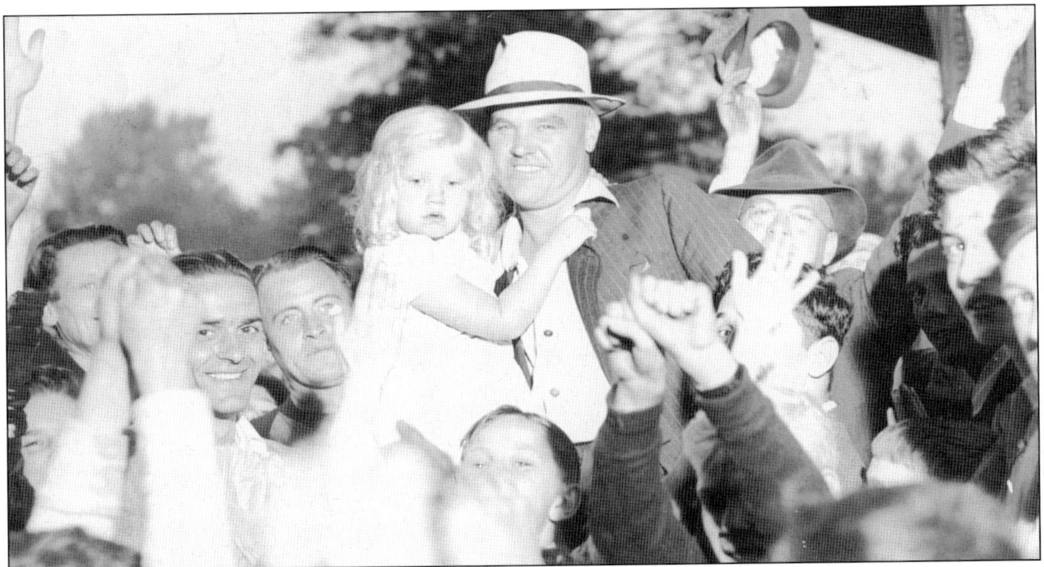

The year was 1940 and the big concern for the country was the turmoil in Europe. On a happier note, many Ingram residents focused on Birmingham, Alabama, where the Crafton-Ingram All Stars were shinning as the Cinderella team from the north. The teams played in extreme temperatures of 100 degrees during the day and 45 degrees at night. Crafton-Ingram took five straight games and won the championship. The all-stars received a runner-up plaque in the World Series of Amateur Baseball. Seen here is the team coming home to a rousing welcome. In the center is manager-player Herb Hurst holding daughter Carolyn, now a member of the Ingram Historical Society.

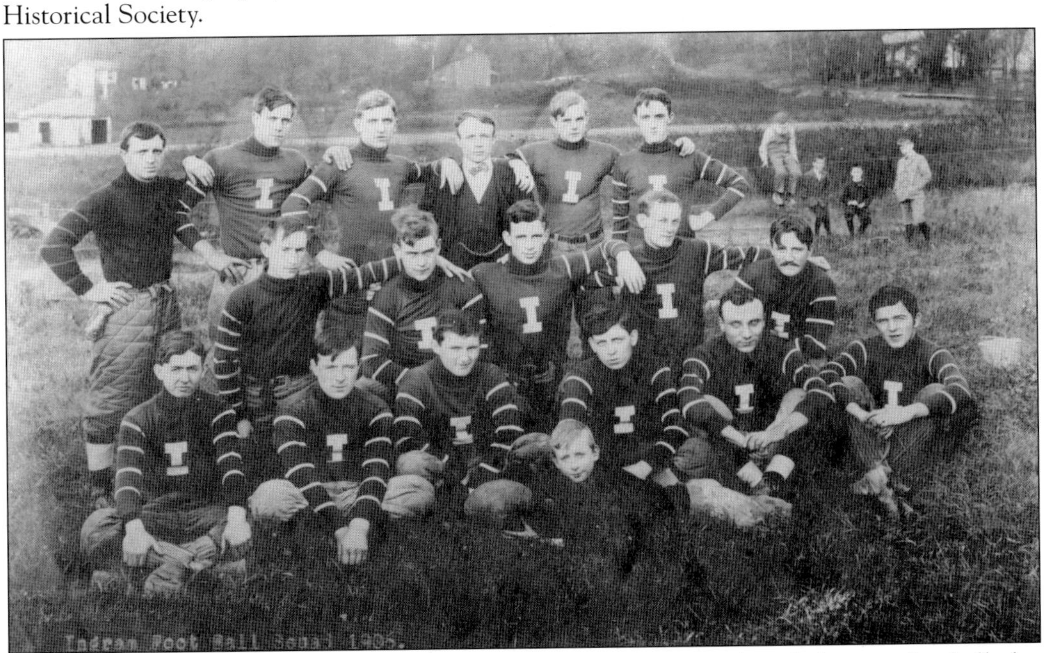

Although baseball was the most popular of team sports in Ingram's early history, football also held an attraction. Teams at this time lacked the safety equipment and padding that current players possess. Unlike the manicured football fields of today, this team played on natural fields. (Courtesy of Claire Rex.)

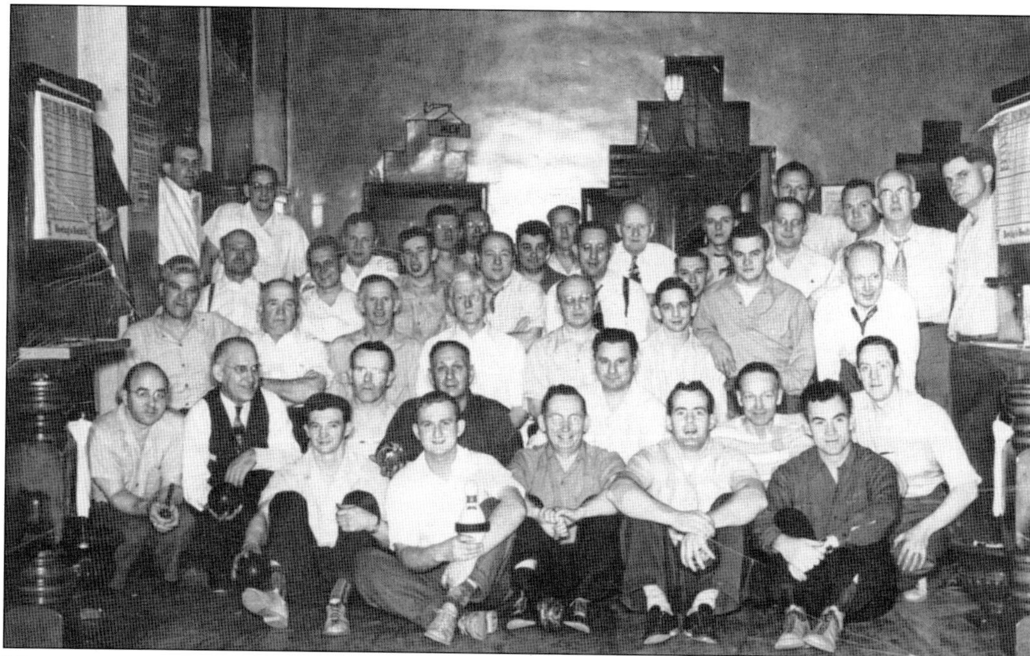

Many community activities centered around the local churches. Duckpin bowling was one of these activities. Originally a summer sport, duckpin bowling became so popular that winter leagues were organized. This group of bowlers belonged to the Ingram United Presbyterian Church during the 1940s. Notice the size of the bowling ball and pins held by the men.

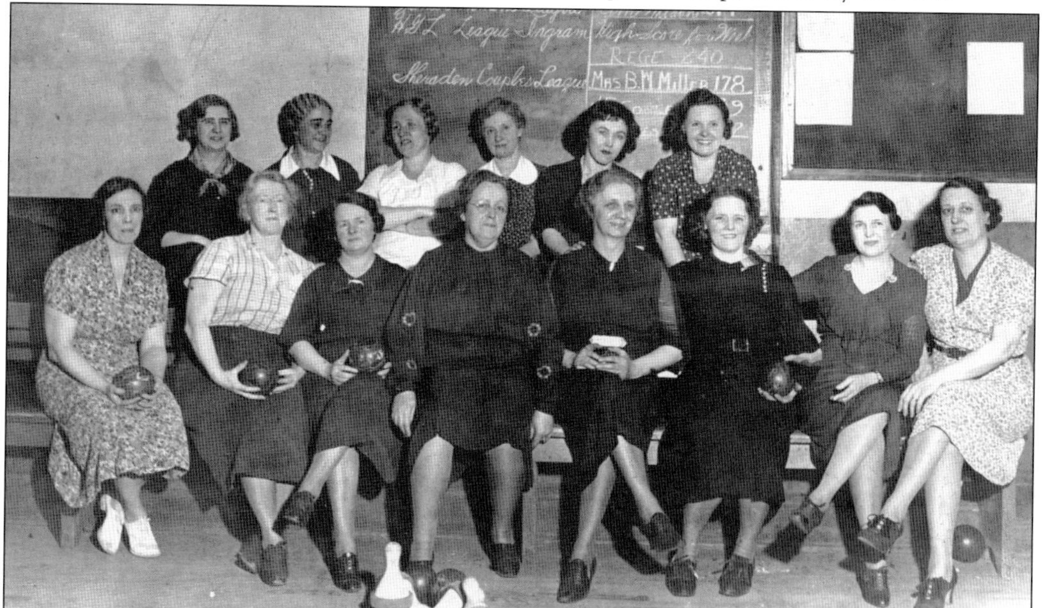

Bowling has been a popular sport for both men and women. The members of the H.G.L. League of Ingram included Margaret Rex, Margaret Johnson, Bess Baer, Fran Polen Hazel McClelland, Mary Lew, Margaret Minister, Esther McNelis, Helen Cole, Ruth Brimmer, Grace Brimmer, Jean Wallace, Cora Larson, Ella Stuart, Grace Phillips, Bets Howard, Emiline Kennedy, Jess Wilson, Nell Rex, Pauline Magill, and Lida Murdock.

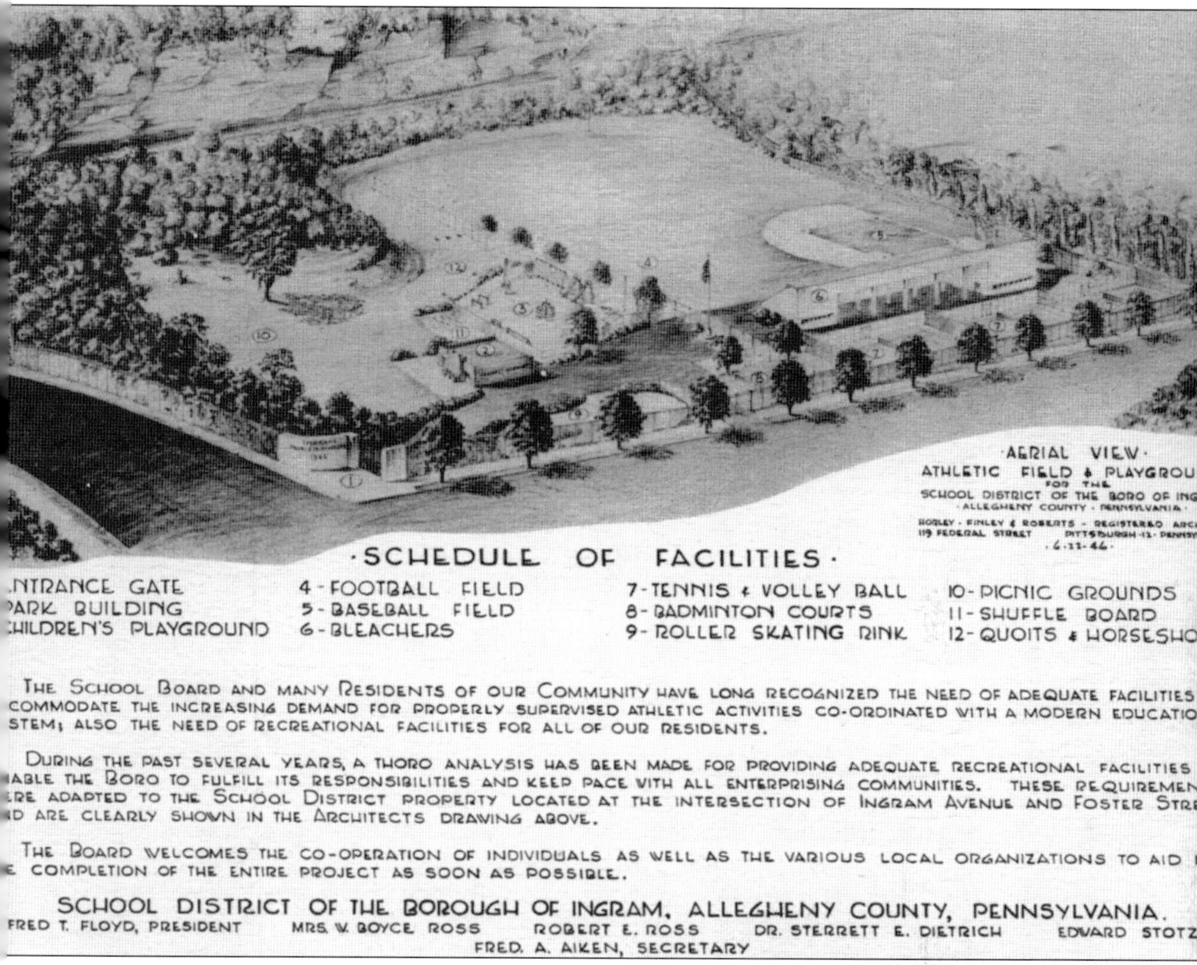

Designed in June 1946, Ingram Park is the center of outdoor life in the borough. The original design was created by the school board of the Borough of Ingram to provide recreational facilities for borough residents, as well as accommodate the demand for supervised athletic activities to support the educational system. This original 1946 design included a football field, badminton court, and even a roller-skating rink. This particular plan was never adopted.

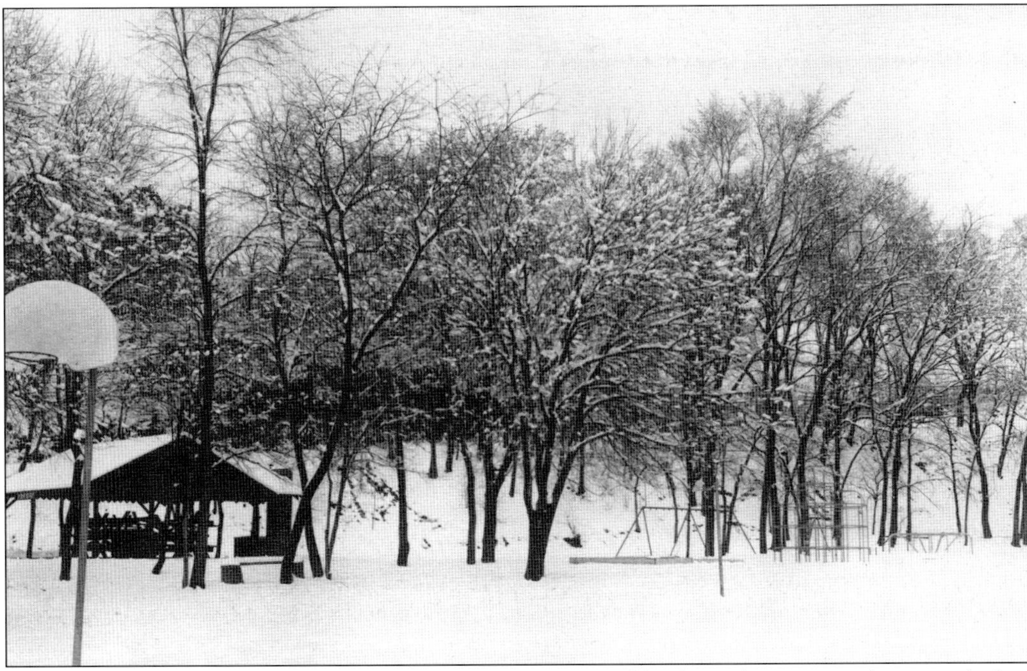

Winter comes to Ingram Park as a light dusting of snow blankets the trees and picnic shelter. The basketball hoop and swings will sit idle until spring.

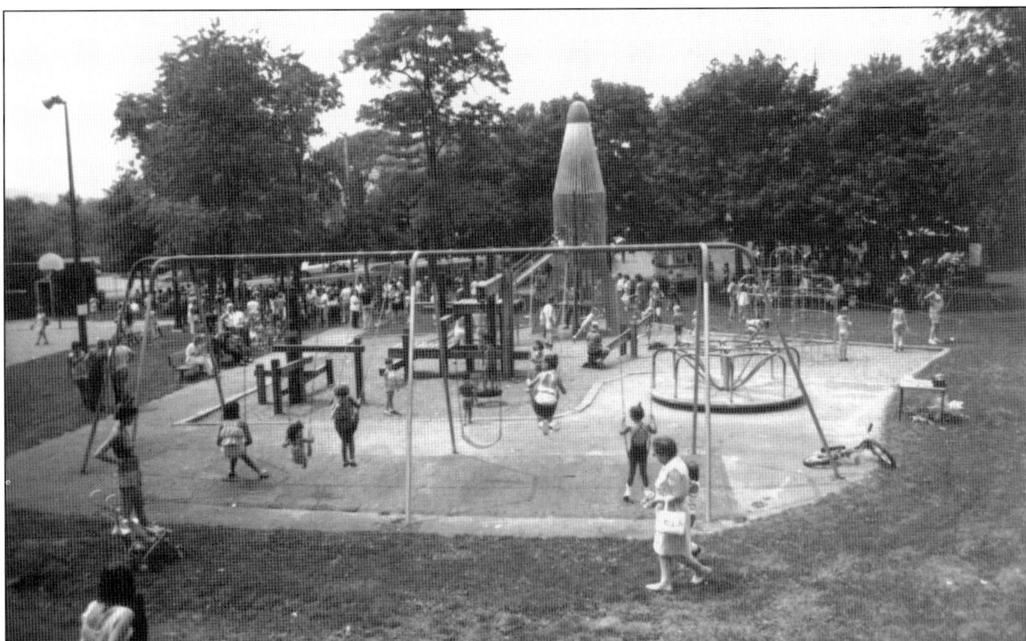

Ingram Park was a busy place in the early 1970s. The climbing rocket slide was the main attraction for borough children. An open-framed iron structure built in 1968, the two-story rocket permitted a great view from the interior nose platform and a long slide from its middle section. Do to safety violations the rocket slide was dismantled in the late 1990s when the park underwent remodeling.

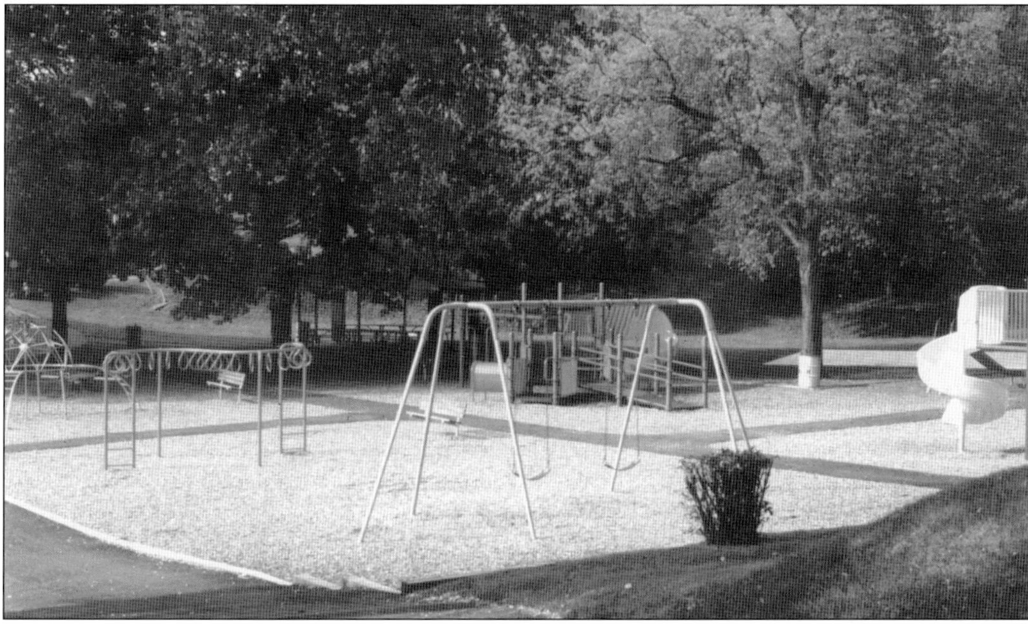

Today's park, which includes bright colors and child-friendly apparatus, was remodeled in 1999. A summer day at the park includes Little League baseball games, Ingram girl's softball games, tennis players, bocce tournaments, and family picnics. A sand volleyball court is always in use on summer evenings. A handicapped accessible walking track circles the park, allowing exercise and a great view of the days activities.

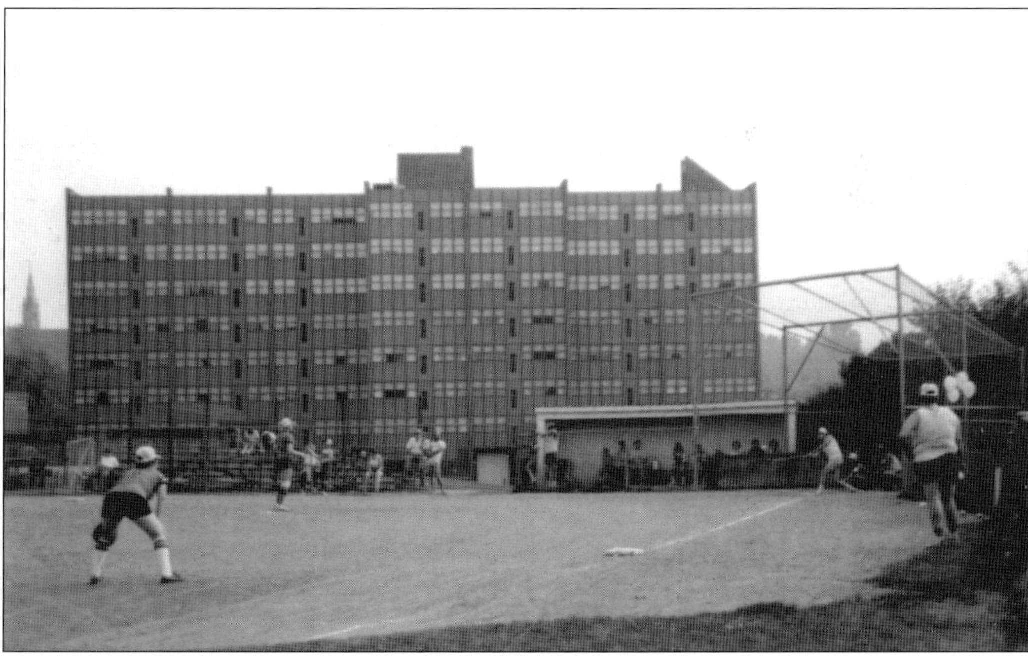

In 1951, the Crafton-Ingram-Thornburg (CIT) Baseball Association was born. Originally it consisted of only four Little League teams. In 1953, the pony league was added. Ingram girls softball started in 1970 when Joan Clark and Jackie Whitaker approached Ingram council for permission to use the fields in the morning. In the background is Crafton towers.

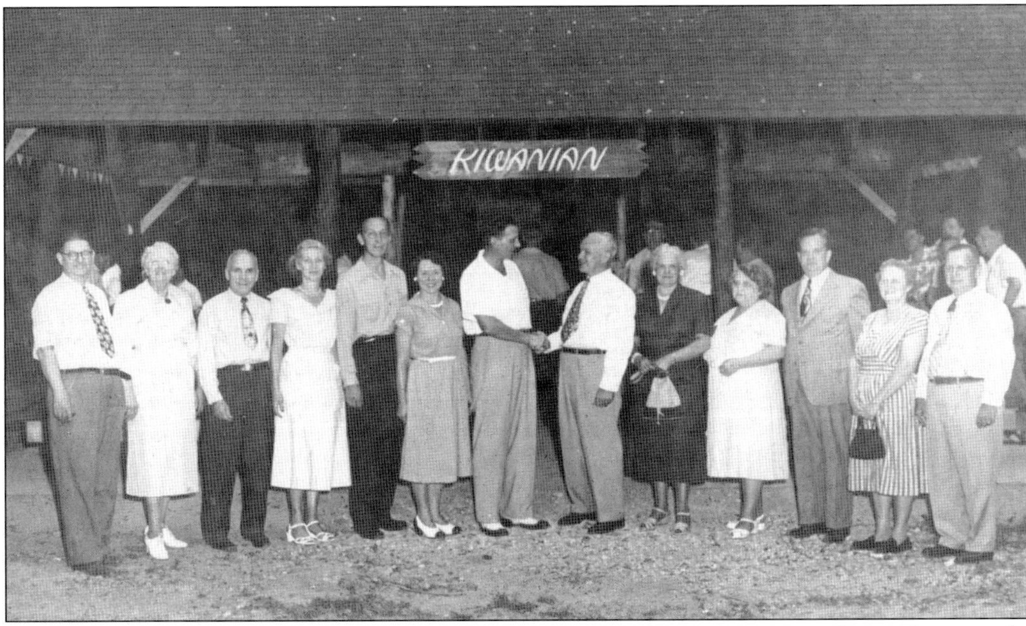

In 1955, the members of the Chartiers Kiwanis Club and their wives enjoyed a cookout in the shelter that their members designed and constructed. This pavilion is a popular area for family picnics, reunions and community celebrations.

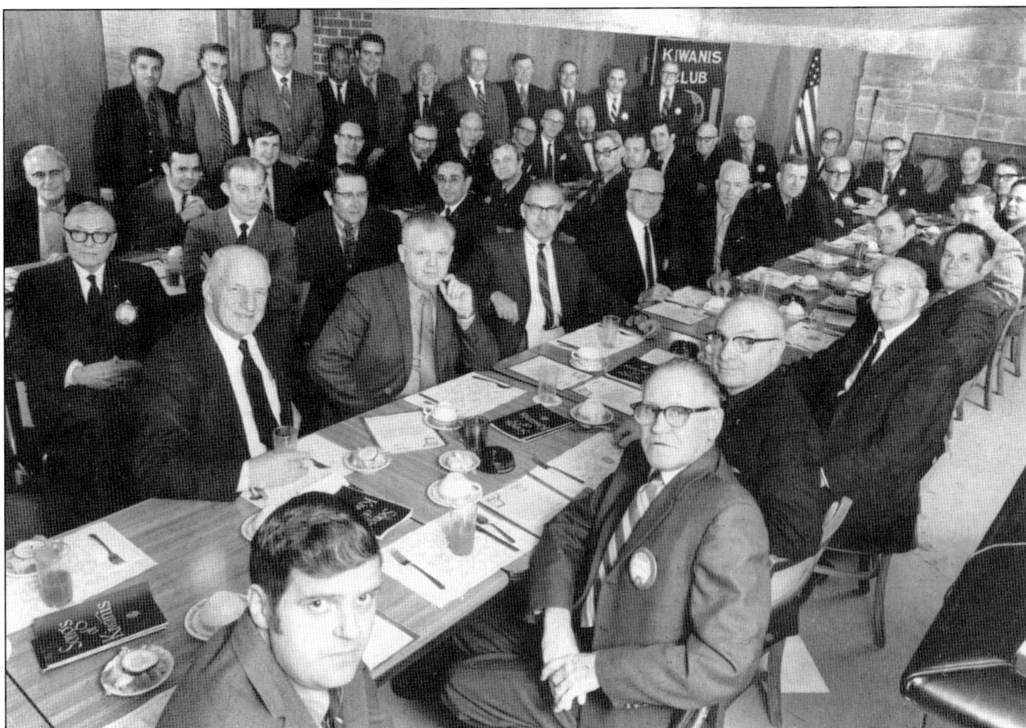

This photograph shows a dinner gathering of the Chartiers Kiwanis Club in the 1960s. Hard work, support, and service have been the mission of this dedicated group since their inception.

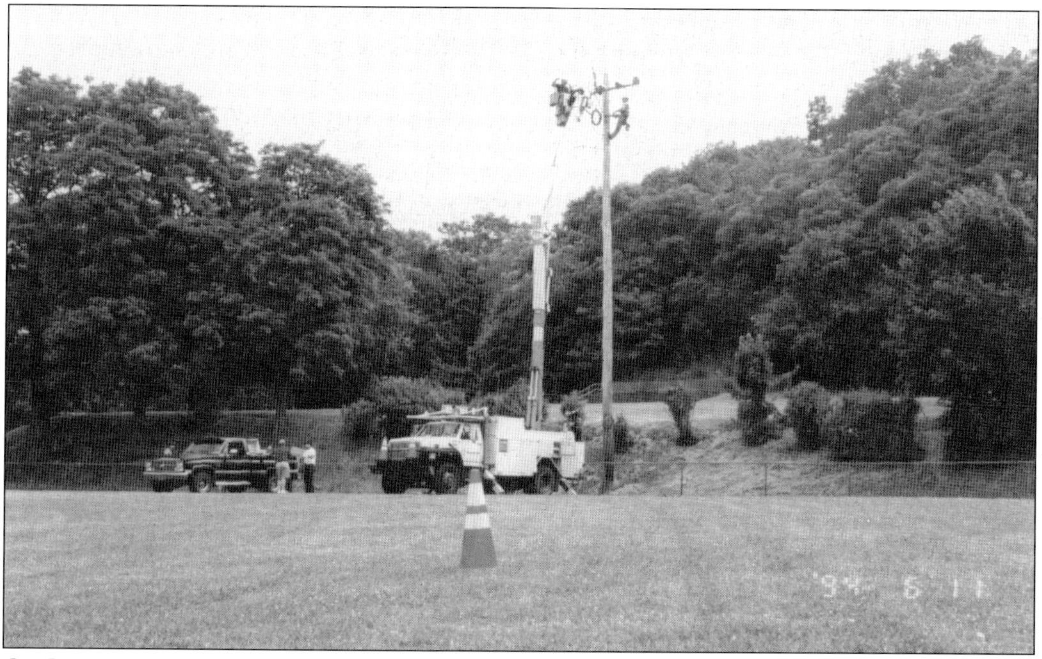

On June 29, 1994, after a concerted effort and cooperation between the CIT Baseball/Softball Association and Ingram Borough, the lights at Ingram field were dedicated. The three foot trenches were dug between the poles, the electrical cable placed and covered all in one day by local volunteers, Duquesne Light Electric Company, and the Ingram Department of Public Works.

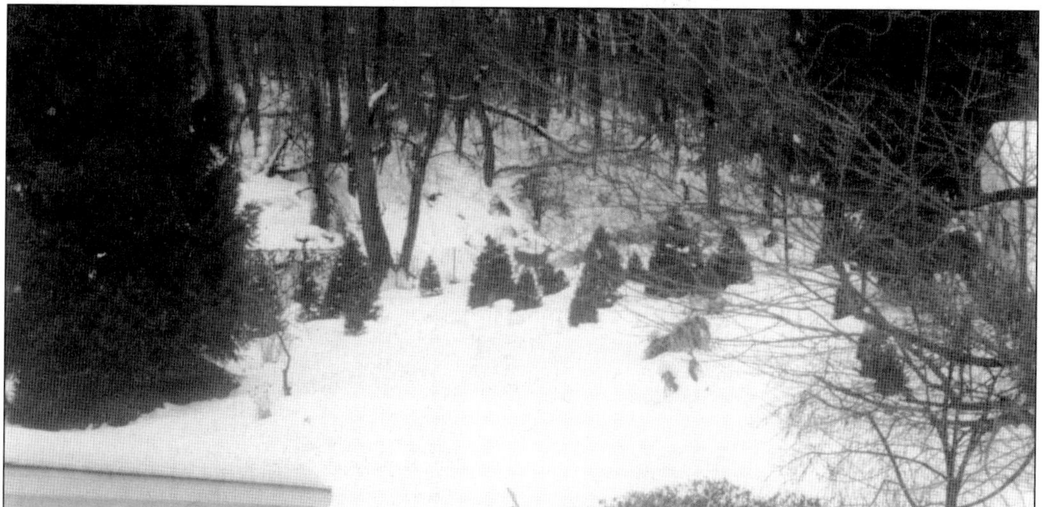

A new park and playground was proposed in the 1960s. The location was to be four acres on the northwestern line of Ingram between the ends of Greenwood and Valois Avenue. Although some work was started, the park never materialized. The land remains a wooded area home to a multitude of wildlife. The Chartiers Nature Conservancy, formed in 1992, now owns part of it and with support from both the local Boy Scout troop and neighbors, is maintaining its beauty for all of Ingram. A new park was constructed on the other side of Ingram, however, on land donated to the borough. This park became known as Grandma's Park and had a lot of activity until it was removed due to safety concerns in 2004.

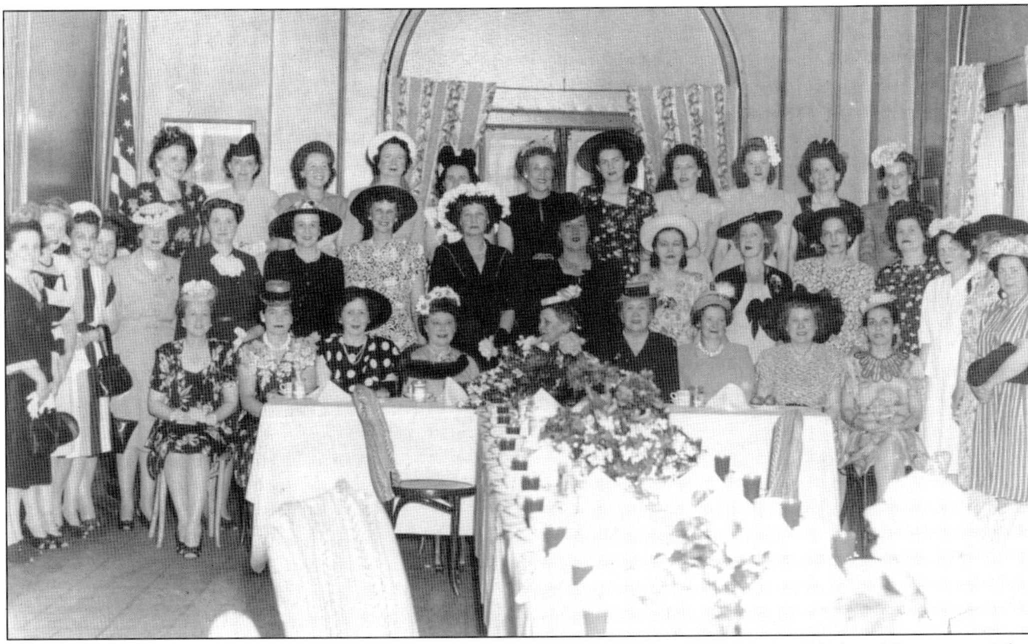

In October 1929, a group of young women formed the Junior Women's Club of Ingram. This organization later became the Ingram Civic Club. Each administration added a special chapter to the proud record. During the 50 years of the club's existence, its members served and enriched the community. A formal tea for Ingram Civic Club members was held each year at a local church.

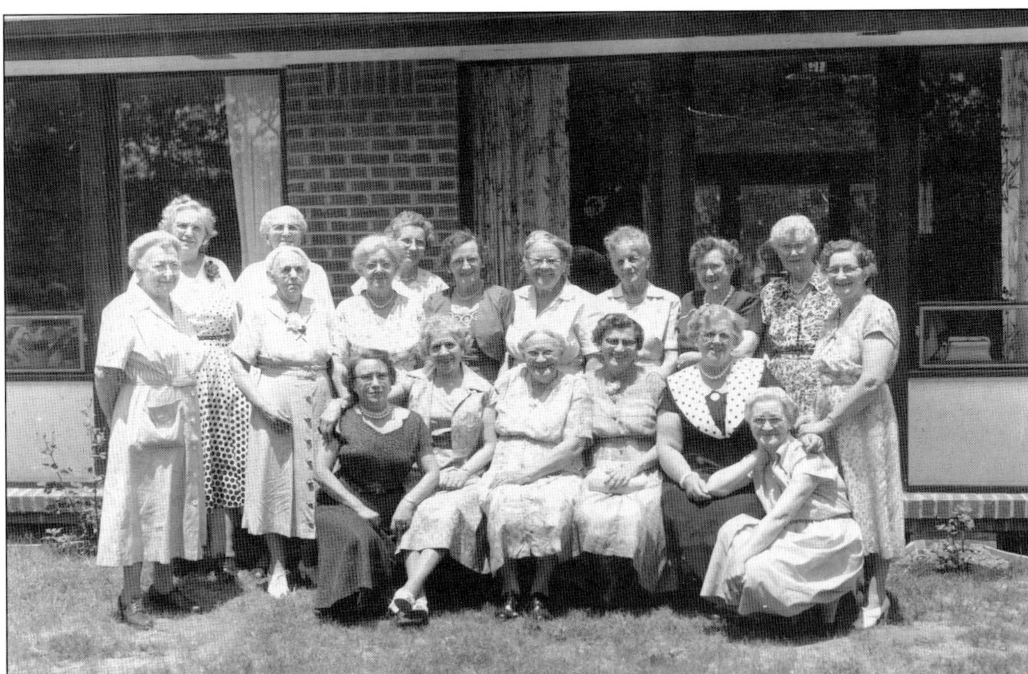

During the war years, the Ingram Civic Club helped the war effort by selling defense stamps, collecting grease, and flattening tin cans. The Ingram Civic Club became federated in 1950. In 1957, the first meeting was held in the new borough building.

In the 1950s, a yearly event around the area was when the photographer and his horse visited. Parents had their children's pictures taken, complete with western costumes. Here, at the Ingram Public School path, are Bimmy and Mary Pat Lucas posing for one of those pictures in 1950.

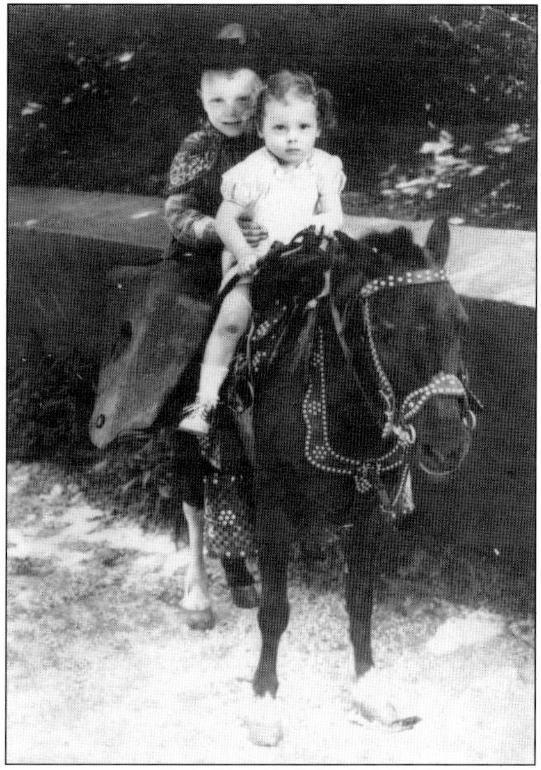

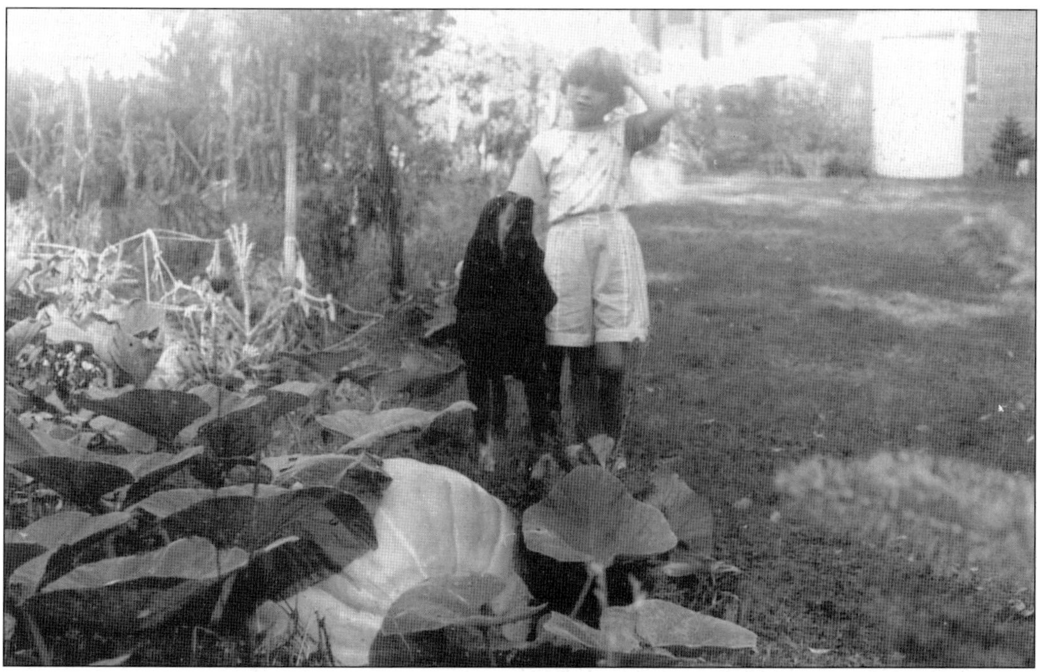

Many of Ingram's residents enjoy spacious back yards. Hard work, dedication and green thumbs have produced some beautiful picturesque gardens. The large pumpkin in this photograph is headed for a ribbon at the annual Ingram Civic Club garden show.

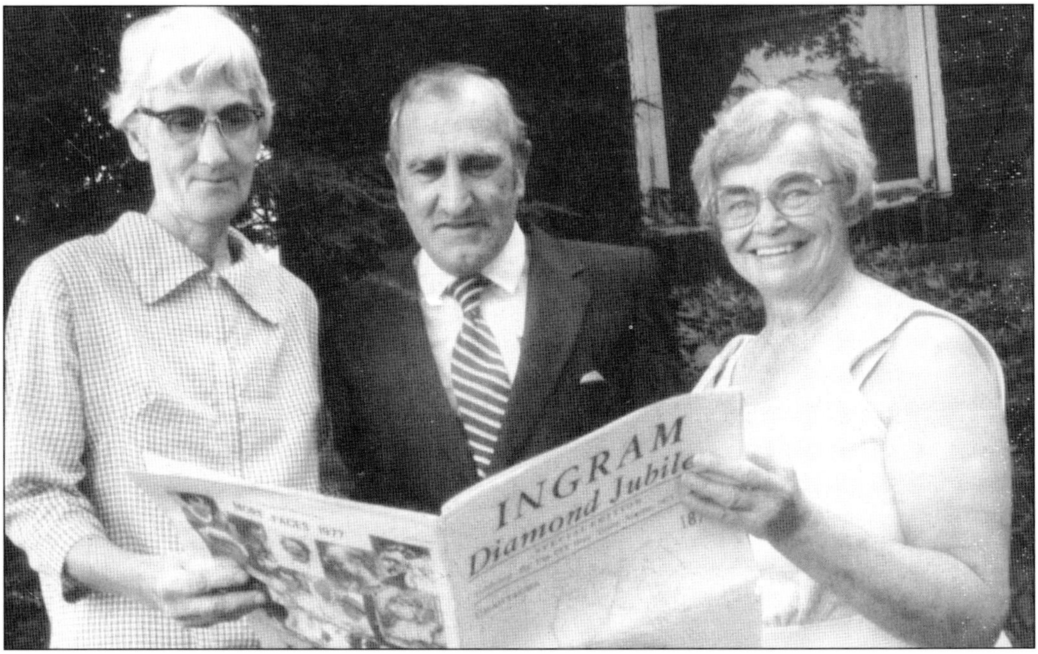

The first Ingram Days celebration was held for Ingram's Diamond Jubilee in 1977. Since then it has grown into a weekend celebration held each summer. A parade starts the activities. Antique cars are always a favorite, with local bands and community groups marching alongside Shriner's cars and clowns. Ingram organizations have booths to sell food and crafts, plus a variety of carnival games. Fireworks top off the weekend activities.

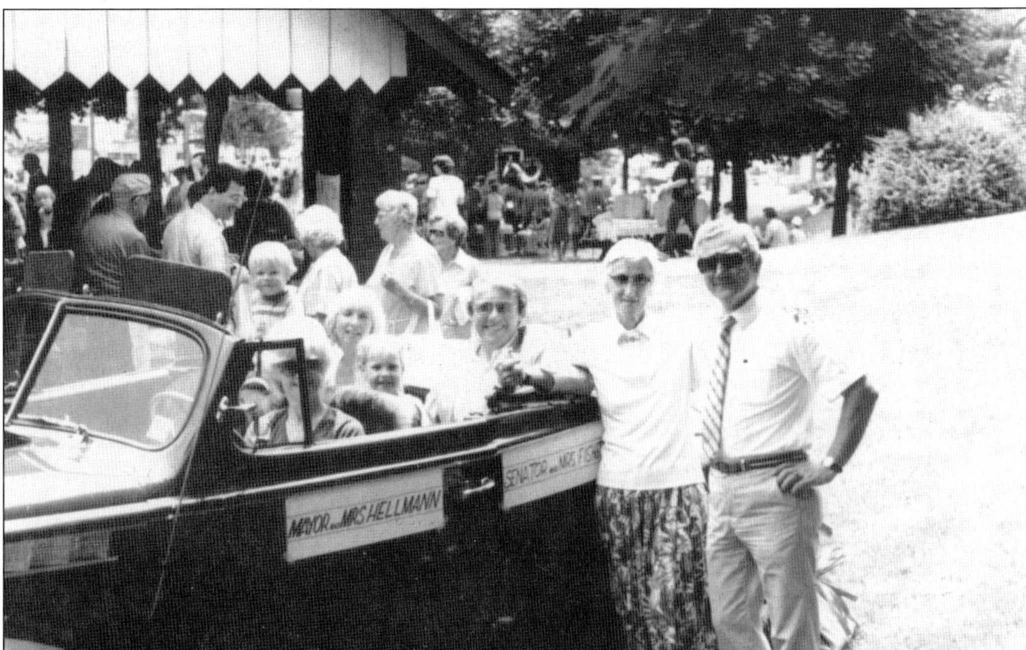

Ingram Days has become a popular annual event. An early Ingram Days celebration featured Mayor Jim Hellmann's antique automobile. Notice the Ringold Band at the shelter in the background.

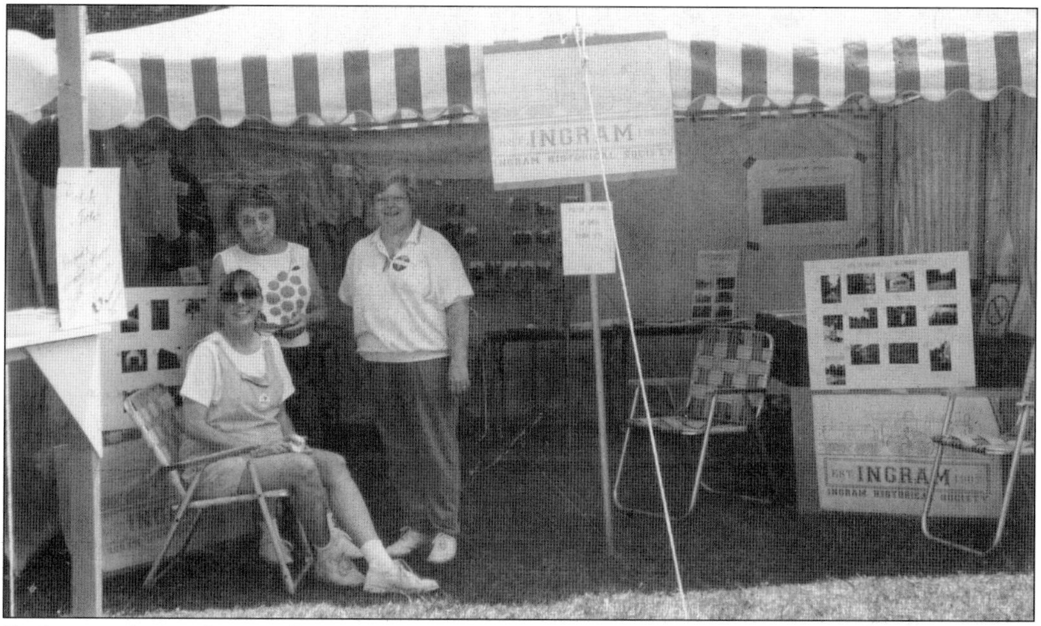

Each year, during Ingram Days, various Ingram clubs and organizations set up tents or booths for food, games, and displays to raise money for their groups. During the celebration, the Ingram Historical Society participates with a tent full of interesting historical artifacts, gift items, and prizes. A different historical theme is presented each year for the education and enjoyment of the public.

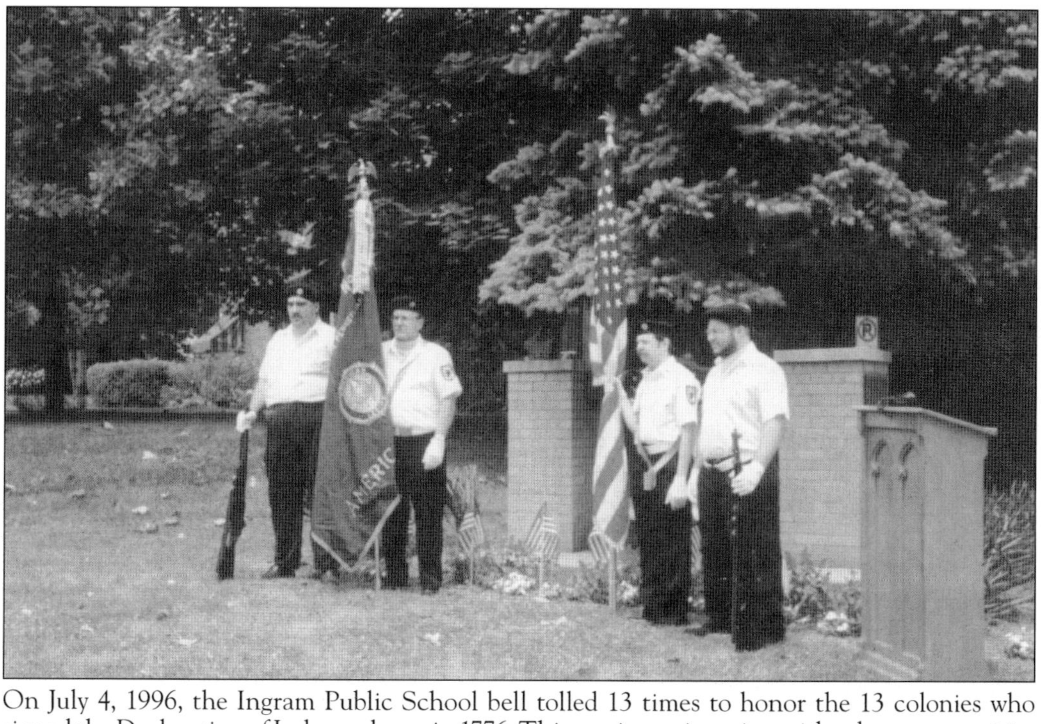

On July 4, 1996, the Ingram Public School bell tolled 13 times to honor the 13 colonies who signed the Declaration of Independence in 1776. This was in conjunction with other communities across the United States of America.

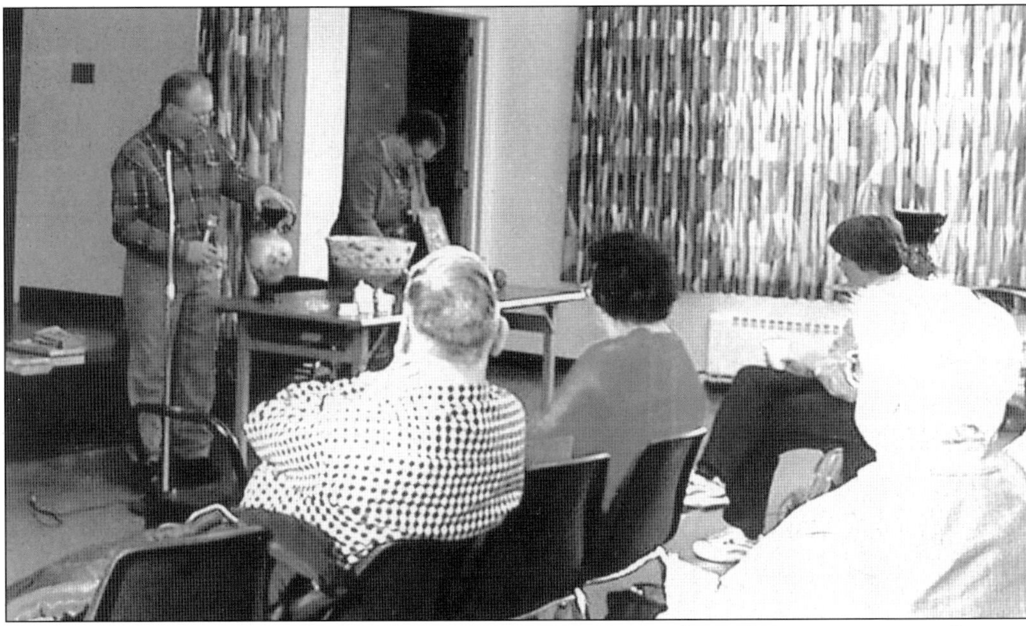

For Ingram's centennial celebration in 2002, a committee was formed to organize special events to commemorate the occasion. The committee decided to arrange for a special event to be held each month of the centennial year. The first event was the antique appraisal held January 20, 2002, by Fox Auctioneers. In an adjoining room was a display of artistic craft items by Ingram residents, past and present.

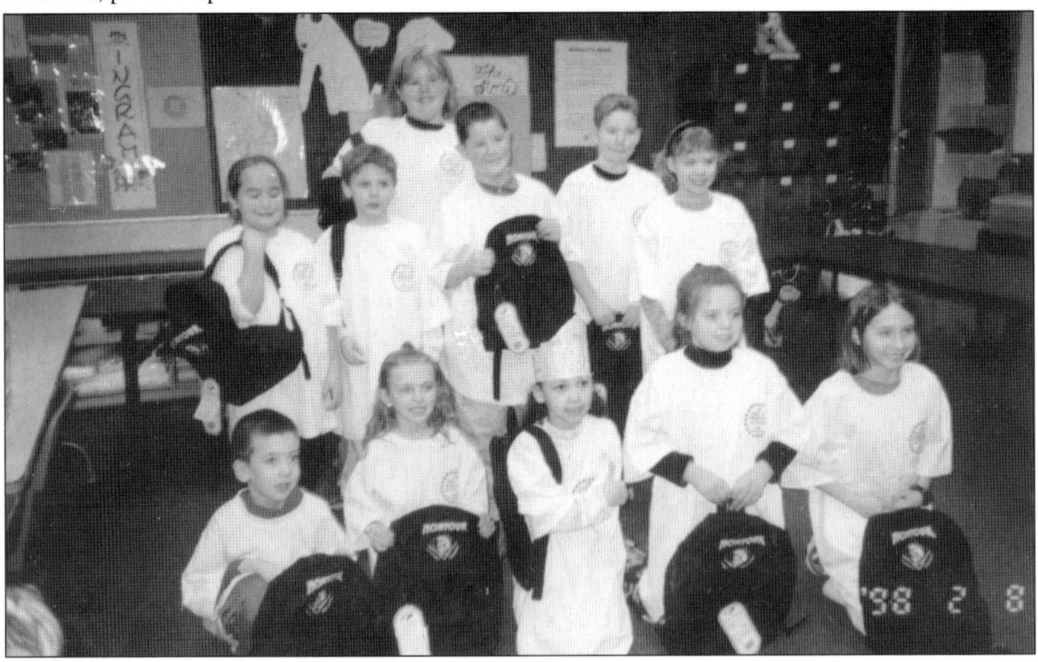

On February 6, 2002, the centennial committee donated special prizes for the Reading is Fundamental program at Ingram School. The committee also sponsored essay contests. The subject was "What was it like to be a child in Ingram in 1902." There were two winners from each class and each received a special medallion engraved with "I am Part of Ingram's History."

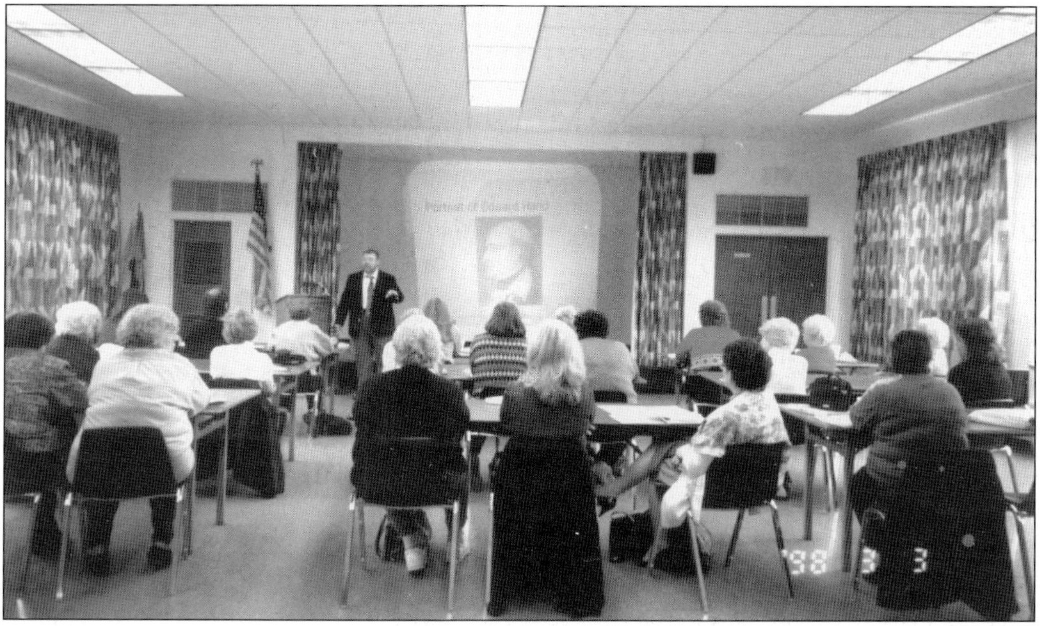

On March 2, the Ingram Historical Society sponsored a genealogy workshop. The program began with a historic talk given by John Farley. Sharen Williams followed with a lecture on "Beginning Genealogy." Elissa Powell, C.G.R.S., and Louanne Eisler from the Butler Library were also speakers.

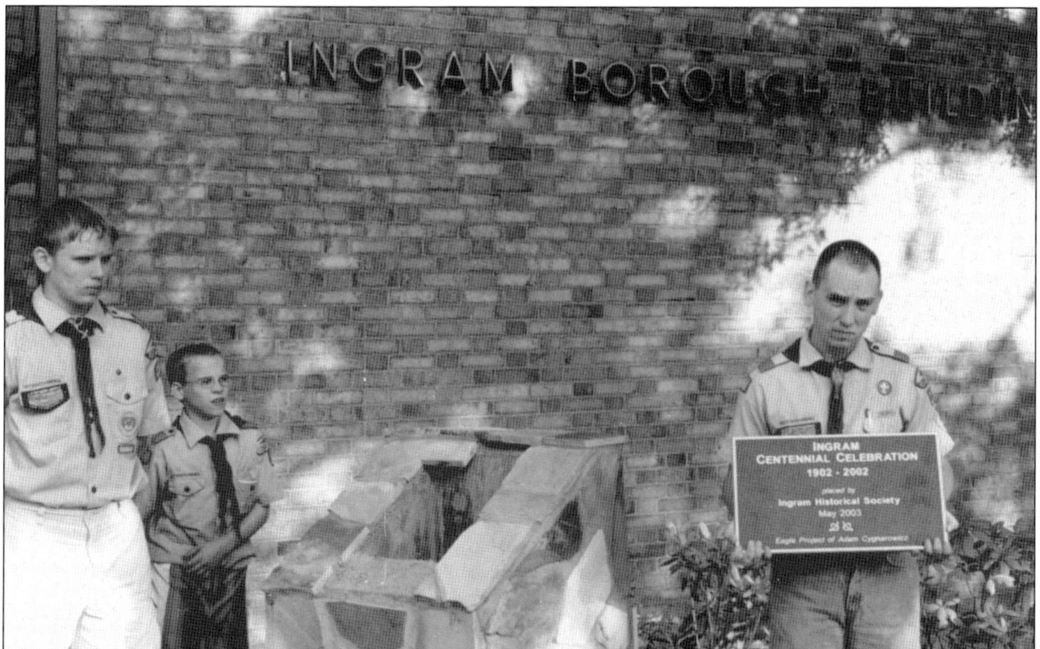

The dedication ceremony of the Ingram Historical Society's centennial time capsule, occurred in May 2003. The time capsule memorial was the Eagle Scout project of Adam Cygnarowitz. The ground-breaking ceremony was held the year before during the centennial celebrations.

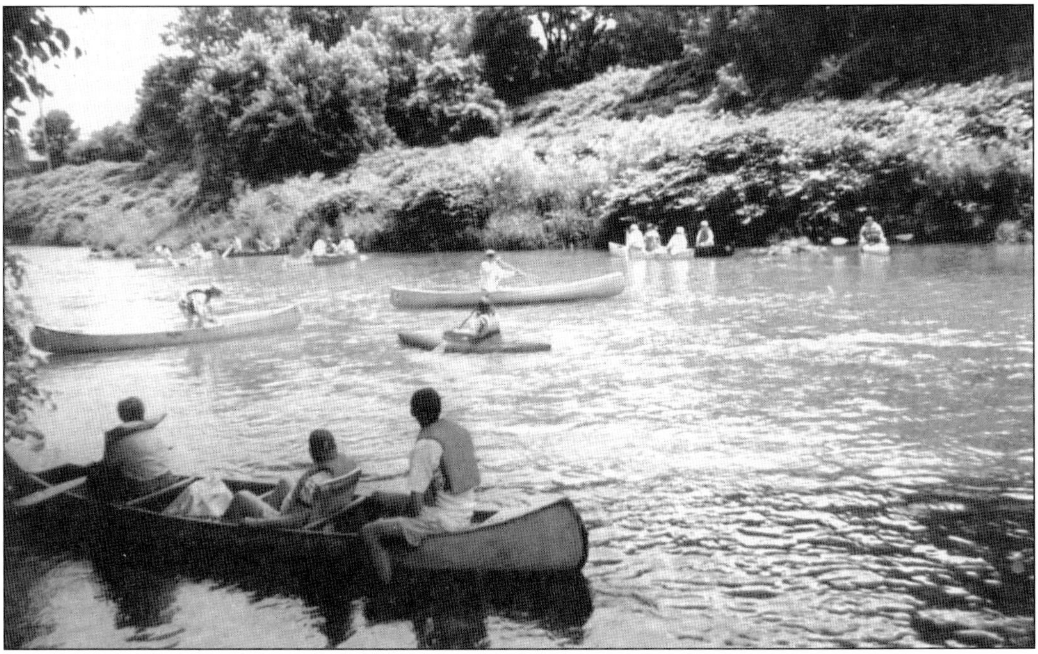

One of the most popular events of the centennial was a canoe trip down the Chartiers Creek held on June 22. The event began with a luncheon at the Sharp Edge Restaurant. After lunch the canoes were launched with a crowd of well wishers cheering them on. The event was sponsored by the Chartiers Nature Conservancy.

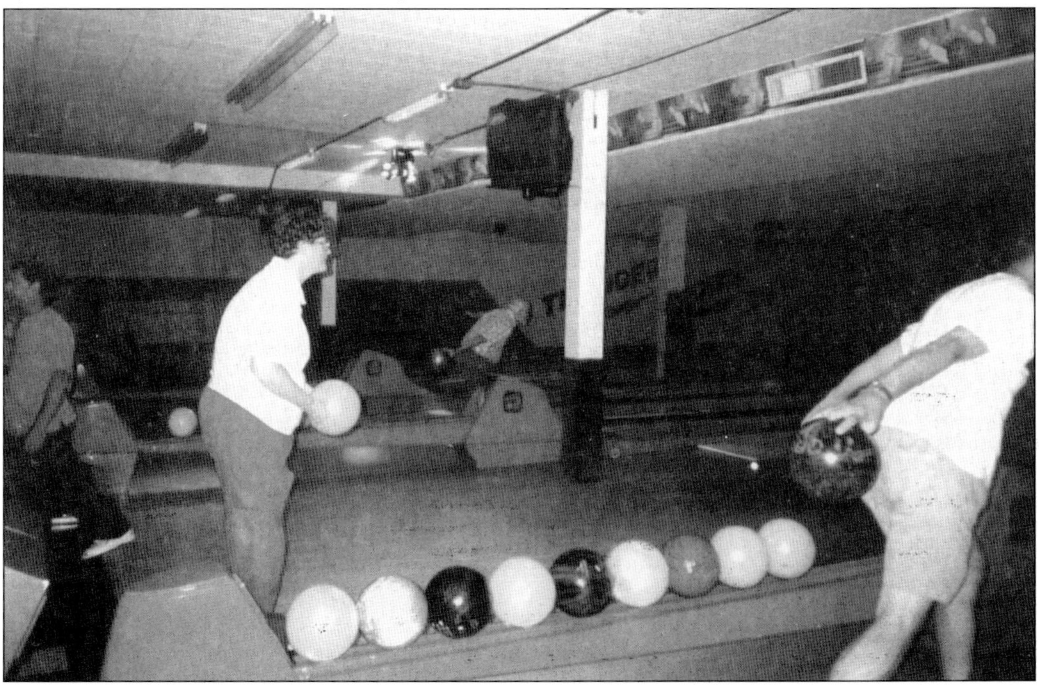

On August 2, 2002, the actual anniversary date of Ingram's incorporation, the centennial committee held a family cosmic bowling night. All in attendance enjoyed the evening together and were treated to pizza, soda, and a special centennial cake.

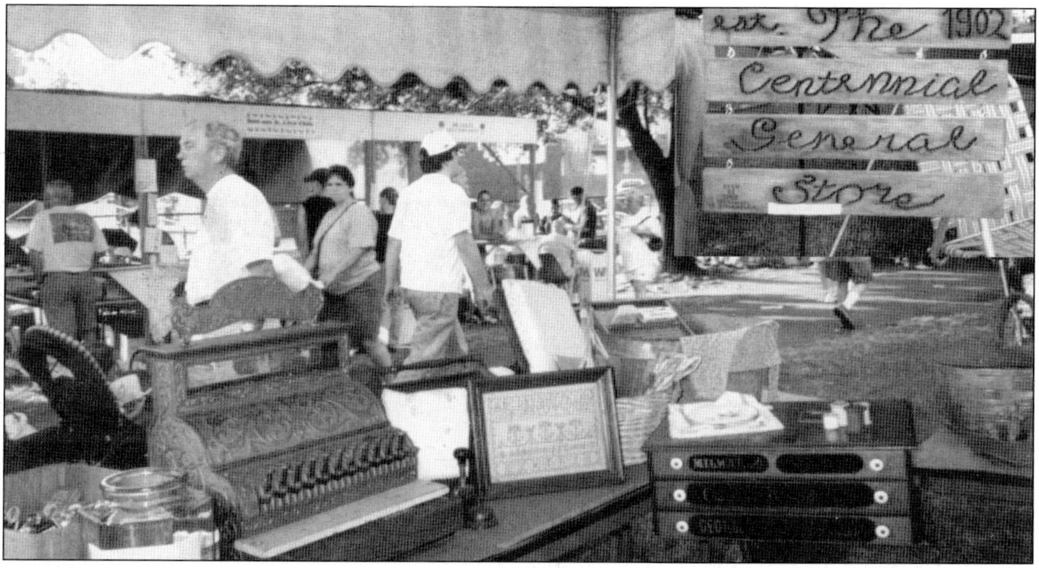

For 2002, the Ingram Historical Society booth featured an old fashioned country store called the "Centennial Store." In the early days of Ingram, one could find almost anything in the general store, from food to hardware. The historical society also featured old fashioned games for the Ingram children on the park ball field. Temperatures soared into the 90s during Ingram Days, but the children were real troopers, sticking it out under the hot sun to compete for the prizes. Because of their stellar efforts, all the children who participated were rewarded with prizes and a medal for their efforts.

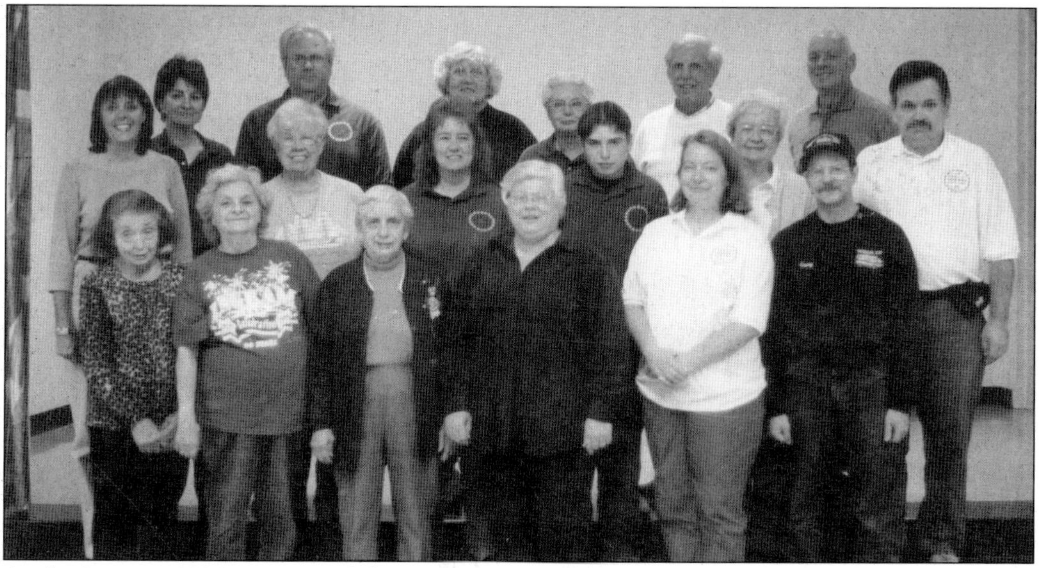
At the January 1994 meeting of the Ingram Borough Council, Mary Parish presented the idea of starting the Ingram Historical Society. The mayor and seven council members unanimously voted to support the historical society and offered the group free use of the borough building for their monthly meetings. The first meeting of the society was held at the Ingram Borough Building on January 31, 1994. The purpose of the group is to gather, research, and share information regarding the history of the borough of Ingram. This photograph was taken in 2002 during Ingram's Centennial Celebration.

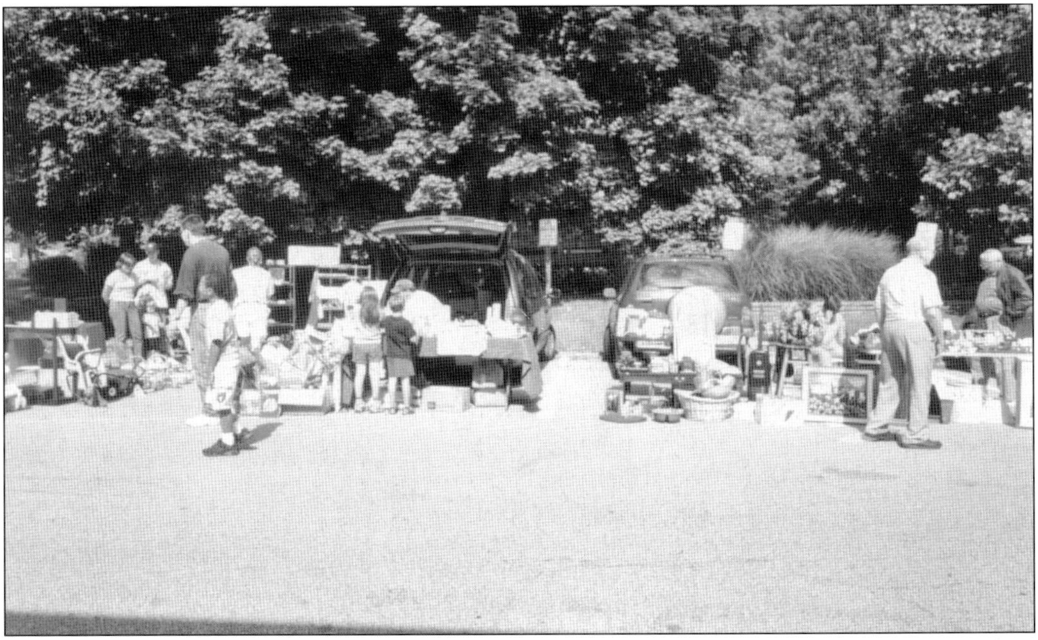

In September 2002, the Ingram Historical Society held their second annual flea market, following the 2001 event that raised money for the groups centennial celebration. The first was such a success the Ingram Historical Society decided to make it an annual event. Each year the borough building parking lot and social hall are filled with vendors and crafters.

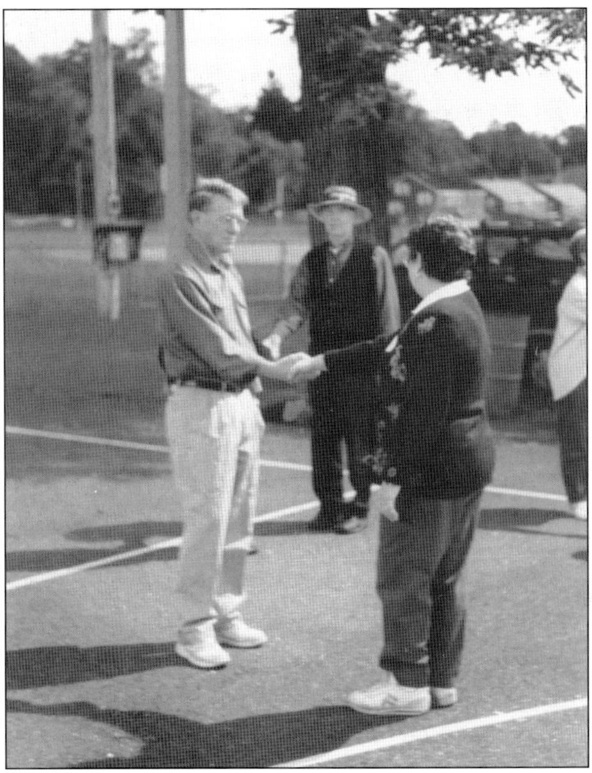

October 5, 2002, brought another family event, a square dance in Ingram Park. The event was free for all who wanted to participate. Hot dogs were cooked and drinks served by the members of the emergency medical group. The kids bobbed for apples as in olden days.

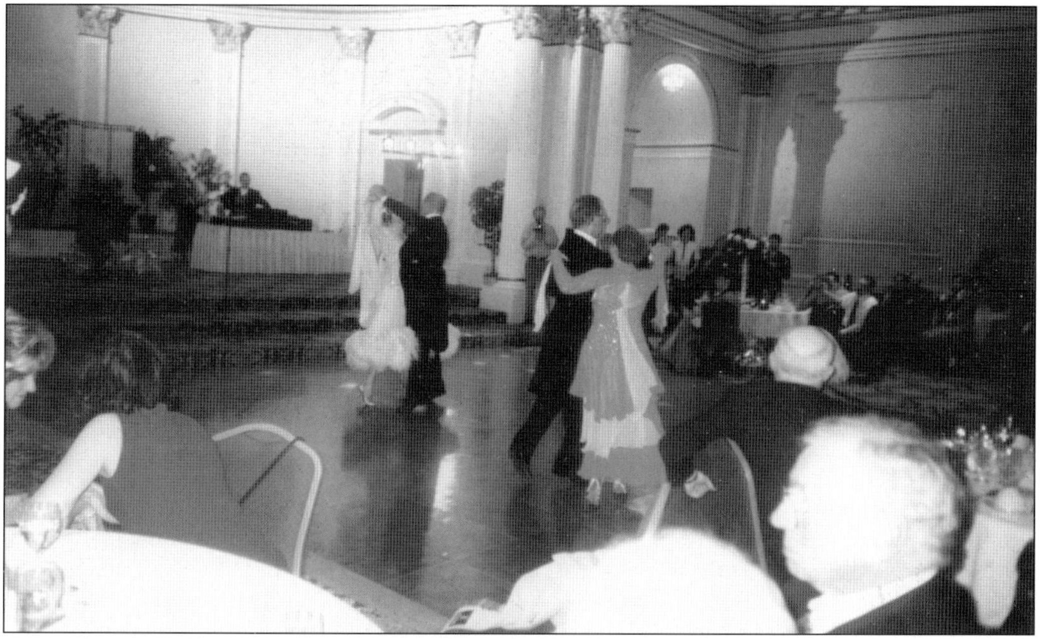

The crowing event of Ingram's 100-year celebration was the Cotillion held at Cathedral Hall in McKees Rocks on November 16, 2002. A dance exhibition was given by Dryden Dance Studio and Ingram was honored with a special presentation by Pennsylvania state representative Tom Petrone.

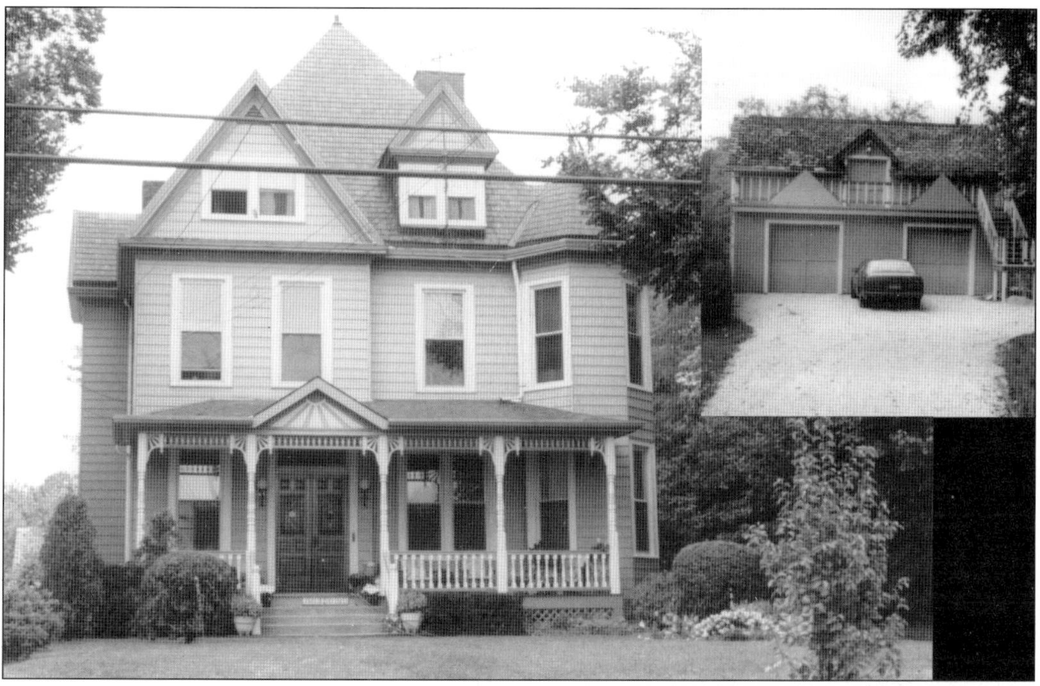

The year 2002 ended with a historic house tour on December 7. Featured in the tour were the homes of Don Bauman, Jerald and Carolyn Croushore, Michael and Darlene Kaliman, and Ascension Church (the former trolley carbarn). Tours and transportation were hosted by Ingram Historical Society volunteers.